Queers in Court

QUEERS IN COURT
Gay Rights Law and Public Policy

Susan Gluck Mezey

ROWMAN & LITTLEFIELD PUBLISHERS, INC.
Lanham • Boulder • New York • Toronto • Plymouth, UK

ROWMAN & LITTLEFIELD PUBLISHERS, INC.

Published in the United States of America
by Rowman & Littlefield Publishers, Inc.
A wholly owned subsidiary of The Rowman & Littlefield Publishing Group, Inc.
4501 Forbes Boulevard, Suite 200, Lanham, Maryland 20706
www.rowmanlittlefield.com

Estover Road
Plymouth PL6 7PY
United Kingdom

British Library Cataloguing in Publication Information Available

Library of Congress Cataloging-in-Publication Data

Mezey, Susan Gluck, 1944-
   Queers in court : gay rights law and public policy / Susan Gluck Mezey.
      p. cm.
   ISBN-13: 978-0-7425-4931-9 (cloth : alk. paper)
    ISBN-10: 0-7425-4931-3 (cloth : alk. paper)
   ISBN-13: 978-0-7425-4932-6 (pbk. : alk. paper)
   ISBN-10: 0-7425-4932-1 (pbk. : alk. paper)
    1. Gay rights—United States. 2. Gays—Legal status, laws, etc.—United States.
3. Homosexuality—Law and legislation—United States. I. Title.
KF4754.5.Z9M49 2007
346.7301'3—dc22   2006034321

Printed in the United States of America

∞ ™ The paper used in this publication meets the minimum requirements of
American National Standard for Information Sciences—Permanence of Paper for
Printed Library Materials, ANSI/NISO Z39.48-1992.

I dedicate this book to Rebecca and Norah
in the hope that when they grow up,
the world will be more tolerant of diversity.

～ Contents

⧼⧽ Acknowledgments

IN fleshing out the plan of the book in its initial stages, I benefited from conversations as well as lengthy e-mail exchanges with Jay Barth. Jay also graciously agreed to read and comment on the entire draft of the manuscript, and I appreciate his suggestions, which helped to improve the book. In the research and writing of an earlier version of chapter 3, which was initially presented as a paper at the 2005 American Political Science Association, I was ably assisted by Loyola University graduate students Nathaniel Gest and Mary Hakken-Phillips; they also helped in tracking down cases, congressional materials and other government documents, law review articles, and polling data for the other chapters. To the extent this analysis sheds light on the complex political, social, and legal issues involved here, I thank them for the role they played. Of course, no one other than myself is responsible for any errors.

I want to thank Loyola University for giving me the time and resources to complete the book by granting me a leave of absence and supplying me with research funds. Within Loyola, law school librarian Julia Wentz helped immeasurably by facilitating access to the legal databases that are necessary to an analysis of litigation. Nora Englund was extremely accommodating in forwarding documents to me during my leave and providing lots of assistance throughout. And Chris Anzalone at Rowman & Littlefield has been great to work with from the time we first spoke at the Law & Society meeting in Chicago; I appreciate his support and encouragement throughout this project. Lynn Weber and the staff at Rowman & Littlefield have also been helpful to me.

On a personal note, I am grateful as always to Michael Mezey, my husband and best friend, whose love and support helped make it possible for me to accomplish my writing during this leave of absence as well as every other time. The book would likely have been written anyway, but he played a crucial role in helping it get done on time and, hopefully, done well.

My children, Jennifer Mezey and Jonathan Levy—proud parents of the lovely and irrepressible Rebecca—and Jason Mezey and Deirdre McMahon—equally proud parents of the delightful and adorable Norah—have made my life more fulfilling than I can begin to describe. They keep my focus on what is truly important, and my life would be incomplete without them.

This book is dedicated to our youngest generation in the hope that many of the battles discussed in it will be resolved in favor of equal rights and dignity by the time they reach political and social consciousness.

~ Table of Cases

ᴥ Introduction

THIS book examines the gay community's efforts to achieve social and legal reform in the United States over the last fifty years within the "rights-based" discourse characteristic of earlier civil rights struggles.

The twentieth century was characterized by individuals seeking social reform through a variety of traditional and nontraditional political activities. Known as identity politics (based on such shared characteristics as race, national origin, sex, and disability), members of minority groups challenged discriminatory laws and social norms that constrained their lives. Not surprisingly, "gay and lesbian legal and political advocates' attempts to chip away at hurtful and debilitating legal precedent, appeals for recognition of the humanity of queers, and efforts toward lobbying and demonstrating, all sound[ed] chords among those familiar with the African-American civil rights movement" (Neal 1996, 683). Indeed, in 1968, the North American Conference of Homophile Organizations, an entity consisting of fifteen gay rights organizations that sought to mobilize gays, disseminate information about discrimination and bias, and support litigation, fashioned the "Gay Is Good" slogan and adapted the "Black Is Beautiful" theme of the Black Power movement (Feldblum 2000, 151).

A relative latecomer to identity politics, the gay rights movement was proclaimed as "the civil rights movement of the 1990s" by the editorial leadership of the *New York Times* (Vaid 1995, 107). Yackle (1993, 79) optimistically characterized the gay and lesbian movement as "another great civil rights movement, this one on behalf of gay, lesbian, and ambisexual citizens, which will lead ineluctably to the elimination of legal burdens on the basis of sexual orientation."

Today, gays and lesbians are the only group to experience the discrimination of being denied the right to choose a marriage partner in almost all states and to serve openly in the military. But although the manifestation of

1

invidious discrimination against gays and lesbians has differed from that against other minority groups—gays and lesbians were not denied the right to vote or to sit at lunch counters, nor was there a common policy of being paid less for doing the same or comparable work—there is a shared experience of discrimination in housing, public accommodations, and employment. Predictably, based on their common experiences of exclusion and oppression, gays and lesbians adopted the rhetoric of equality of rights under the law from other minority groups.

As with other social movements, the gay rights movement is not a monolithic whole, and gay rights activists have advocated different strategies for promoting social change. In particular, some question the wisdom of pursuing a strategy that attempts to work within the system and bring about changes in the legal status of gays and lesbians.[1] Rimmerman (2000, 2), for example, notes that the predominant strategy followed by gay rights advocates is "assimilationism," emphasizing a "rights-based perspective . . . within the broader framework of liberal, pluralist democracy." The competing model, "liberationism," opts for focusing energies outside the system. Rimmerman questions the effectiveness of the assimilationist approach and urges a more broad-based grassroots strategy.

Vaid (1995, 106) is also skeptical of the legal rights approach, maintaining that by pursuing a civil rights strategy, the gay community "consciously chose legal reform, political access, visibility, and legitimation over the long-term goals of cultural acceptance, social transformation, understanding, and liberation." Tom Stoddard, icon of the gay rights movement and veteran of numerous litigation battles, acknowledged the usefulness of legal change, but argued that law reform that results primarily in "rule-shifting" is insufficient to create social change; true reform requires "culture-shifting" as well. He believed the 1964 Civil Rights Act epitomized legal reform as "rule-shifting" as well as "culture-shifting" because it "expressed a new moral standard" and "changed cultural attitudes" (Stoddard 1997, 973–4). In general, he believed that the prevailing cultural norms and attitudes are more likely to be changed through legislative action "since it is much more likely than other forms of lawmaking to engage the attention of the public" and foster "public acceptance" of the change (982; see Feldblum 1997).

In hewing most closely to the civil rights model, lesbians and gays have asserted their claims of legal reform largely through litigation, emulating many of the tactics and long-term strategies of the civil rights groups that came before them. However, unlike most members of other civil rights movements, the consequences of open acknowledgment of their identity are formidable barriers to the mobilization of gay rights activists. Antigay attitudes accompanied by discriminatory practices in employment, housing, criminal justice, public accommodations, and family law make it difficult for members of the gay community to pursue their political agenda, especially at the national level (see Schroedel and Fiber 2000; Smith and Haider-Markel 2002). Additionally, the conflict over values and the nature of the opposition, drawn largely from "religious traditionalism and the Christian Right," intensifies the resistance to the gay rights movement (Green 2000, 121; see Button, Rienzo, and Wald 1997, chap. 1).[2]

Anti–gay rights advocates view the gay community's complaints of discrimination as illusory because, they argue, gays and lesbians have superior economic and political resources. Moreover, they insist that gays do not seek protection from discrimination; rather, they maintain, the goal of gays is to obtain special rights. Confronted with evidence of discrimination against members of the gay community, gay rights opponents contend that because sexual identity is a self-selected behavioral characteristic that can be altered at will—unlike race, ethnicity, sex, and disability—gay men and lesbians are not entitled to the same protection of the antidiscrimination laws that other minority groups enjoy.

The perception that homosexuality stems from individual choice represents a majority view in the nation, although Americans have become more convinced over time to view sexual orientation as an innate characteristic. The implications of these attitudes are crucial for acceptance of gay rights claims because individuals who believe that sexual orientation is predetermined at birth are more likely to be supportive of gay rights than those who believe that homosexuality stems from other sources (Button, Rienzo, and Wald 1997, 61).

A June 1977 Gallup poll found that only 13 percent of the respondents believed that "homosexuality is something one is born with," while 56 percent thought it "due to factors such as upbringing and environment." By 1996, the percentage agreeing that homosexuals were born that way had risen to 31 percent, with 40 percent responding that homosexuality was caused by "upbringing and environment." The belief that homosexuality is an innate characteristic rose to 38 percent in May 2005, with 44 percent now believing homosexuality was a product of upbringing and environment (Gallup 2006b).

Thus, although the number of people who believe that homosexuality is an innate characteristic more than doubled in the almost thirty years since Gallup first asked the question in 1977, most Americans are still evidently reluctant to regard homosexuality as innate, a situation that should cause the gay community some concern. Another source of concern is that public disapproval of homosexual relations persists, as is evident from a Gallup survey conducted from May 8 to 11, 2006. The respondents were read "a list of issues" and told that "regardless of whether or not you think it should be legal, for each one, please tell me whether you personally believe that in general it is morally acceptable or morally wrong"; 51 percent of the respondents thought "homosexual relations" were "morally wrong," while 44 percent believed them "morally acceptable" (PollingReport.com 2006c).

Another force operating against gay and lesbian liberation is the fact that some members of traditional minority groups reject the comparison of their struggle for civil rights with that of gay men and lesbians. Neal (1996, 681–2) writes that there are members of the African American community, for example, who believe that their discriminatory experiences differ in part because members of the gay community are able to conceal their sexual identity. Moreover, she notes, some African Americans also contend that gays—particularly white men—are not confronted with the social, economic, and educational obstacles that they are and should be barred from taking advantage of the antidiscrimination laws that they struggled to achieve.

In discussing relationships between the African American and gay communities, Vaid (1995, 188) notes that polls show that African American respondents are more supportive of gay rights when the survey questions relate to discrimination and equal rights. She cites the result of a 1993 *New York Times/CBS News* poll showing that 53 percent of African American respondents believed in the need for gay rights laws, compared to only 40 percent of white respondents. Similarly, Lewis and Edelson (2000, 203) indicate that minorities are more likely to support gay rights than whites are.

A glance at the website of the Human Rights Campaign (HRC) shows that there is substantial support from African American members of Congress (and persons of color generally) on the organization's scorecard of congressional votes on issues of concern to gays.[3] The website also indicates that representatives of the gay community have joined with other members of the civil rights community to sit on the executive committee of the Leadership Conference on Civil Rights—the leading national civil rights coalition—and work with the Congressional Black Caucus and the National Association for the Advancement of Colored People (NAACP) on issues of mutual interest, including racism in the gay and lesbian community and homophobia in the African American community (see generally www.hrc.org).[4]

Schacter (1994) argues that in an effort to prevent alliances such as these from forming, gay rights opponents have promoted a "discourse of equivalents" in which they question whether lesbians and gay men are sufficiently like existing protected classes—based on race, sex, disability, or national origin—to merit protection under civil rights laws.[5] "Current civil rights laws," she contends, "are held out as the normative baseline against which the gay civil rights claim is tested to determine whether the fit between established and aspiring law is sufficiently close to confer legitimacy" (285). Evidence of this discourse frequently appears in judicial opinions with judges citing it to justify ruling against gay rights claims.

FOCUS ON THE COURTS

The history of social reform movements shows that groups with little political power seek judicial intervention to offset their inability to exercise political clout at the ballot box. Like women and racial minorities, lesbians and gays, believing the courts a more likely arena in which to challenge inequality than representative bodies, turned to the judiciary to vindicate their rights through litigation. Recent works by Andersen (2005) and Pierceson (2005) stress the importance of the courts and litigation in effecting societal change in gay rights cases and marshal convincing evidence to support this view.

Gay rights activists began to pursue litigation as a strategy for social reform in the 1970s; prior to that time, aside from isolated cases challenging censorship of gay reading material and film, there was little attempt at coordinated litigation activity (see Pacelle 1996). With opposing sides battling each other in the courtroom, the language of rights is the most commonly heard rhetoric as gay rights advocates direct their efforts at reforming restrictive laws and policies (Button, Rienzo, and Wald 2000; see Andersen 2005).

The movement was greatly influenced by the planned litigation campaign of the NAACP Legal Defense and Educational Fund (known as the Inc. Fund) and the Women's Rights Project of the American Civil Liberties Union (ACLU), among others (see Cain 2000). In 1972, the Lambda Legal Defense and Education Fund was formed to spearhead the effort to create social change through litigation. Like its predecessors, the Inc. Fund, the National Organization for Women Legal Defense Fund, and the later-formed Disability Rights Education and Defense Fund, Lambda has participated in most of the key gay rights cases before the courts either by sponsoring litigation or signing onto amici curiae briefs. A few years after the formation of Lambda, two other groups, also largely focused on litigation, were launched: the Lesbian

Rights Project, now known as the National Center for Lesbian Rights, established on the West Coast in 1977, and the Gay and Lesbian Advocates and Defenders (GLAD), founded in Boston a year later.

The significance of litigation in gay rights advocacy was further demonstrated in 1980 when another public interest law firm specializing in gay rights litigation, the National Gay Rights Advocates, was organized, lending its name and prestige to litigation, primarily through its involvement in amici curiae briefs. Also in 1980, the HRC, today the single largest gay, lesbian, bisexual, and transgender advocacy group in the nation, was created.[6] Although the HRC is engaged primarily in political action, it indirectly aids the litigation efforts of the other groups through public education and raising awareness of gay rights issues. The ACLU, which played a role in the early First Amendment challenges, was initially reluctant to involve itself in issues of discrimination against gays.[7] Gradually, however, its involvement grew, and in the mid-1980s, it created the ACLU Lesbian and Gay Rights Project, adding its name to the roster of public interest litigation firms advocating for gay and lesbian rights (Brewer, Kaib, and O'Connor 2000). Gay rights advocates devoted much of their early litigation effort in the state and federal courts to challenging laws criminalizing sodomy. The focus soon broadened to contesting discrimination in public accommodations; military service; employment, including sexual harassment; child custody, adoption, and family law issues more generally; and same-sex marriage policies. Comparing litigation with other methods of achieving social and political reform, Lambda's executive director stated some years ago, "The courts have been a relatively successful place for Lesbians and Gay men to go—a more successful place in many ways than political avenues have been for expanding Lesbian and Gay rights" (quoted in Rimmerman 2000, 70).

THE EFFICACY OF LITIGATION?

The central role of the courts in social reform movements gave rise to a long-standing debate in the political science and legal communities over the efficacy of the courts in achieving social change (see Schultz 1998).[8] The inquiry into the question of whether the judiciary is an effective instrument of reform was instigated largely by controversy over the effectiveness of *Brown v. Board of Education* (1954) in desegregating the nation's schools, with several critics arguing that the courts failed to achieve this goal (see Klarman 1996; Cain 2000). This debate appears largely confined to the academy as, for over half a century, whether wisely or not, civil rights groups have viewed the courts as potential allies in their efforts to seek social reform. As Cain (2000, 1) aptly points out, "whether one believes that courts do in fact cause social change, courts are nonetheless crucial in any battle over equal rights."

Cain (2000, 1) believes gay rights groups are wise to pursue litigation, noting that "courts understand and apply the notions of equality much more readily than legislatures or than members of society in general." Lewis and Edelson (2000, 198) go even further by bluntly stating that "when Congress enters the debate and the forum grows more public, gay rights advocates generally lose."

ACTIVIST (COUNTERMAJORITARIAN) COURTS?

The chief assumption behind minority group appeals to the courts is their belief in the judiciary's willingness to oppose the majority will on their behalf. This belief is shared by a good many political scientists and lawyers who perceive the courts as likely to protect minority interests at the expense of majority rule (see, for example, Casper 1976). The extent to which the courts, especially the United States Supreme Court, play such a countermajoritarian role in exercising the function of judicial review has also been subject to extensive debate. Countermajoritarianism, often described in common parlance as judicial activism, largely characterizes rulings in which the courts override the policies of the more political, that is, representative, branches of government or contravene majority public opinion (Canon and Johnson 1999).[9] Chief Justice Harlan Fisk Stone's reference to special judicial protection of "discrete and insular minorities" in his famous footnote 4 in *United States v. Carolene Products* (1938) exemplifies the conventional view of the Court's countermajoritarian role.[10]

From an academic perspective, Bickel (1962) is one of the first analysts of the Court's "countermajoritarian difficulty," warning that the Court must be cautious about "thwart[ing] the will" of the decisions of the other branches of government (17).[11] Many scholars, including one of the earliest and most notable, Dahl (1957), have questioned the accuracy of depicting the Supreme Court as a countermajoritarian institution (see Klarman 1996; 2005; Hutchinson 2005; Friedman 1998; Mishler and Sheehan 1993 as examples of the voluminous literature on the subject).[12] In discussing whether the Court has played what he terms a "heroic countermajoritarian function," Klarman (1996, 2) argues that the reality is more nuanced than most have described. He sides with Dahl in believing that most of the Court's rulings in civil rights and liberties cases reflect "a strong national consensus." In his view, the Supreme Court settles contentious issues in a only small number of rulings, and in those cases, he argues, it reflects the popular view, with about half the nation's support behind the opinions.[13]

Klarman maintains that had the Court struck the Georgia sodomy law in *Bowers v. Hardwick* (1986) instead of upholding it, it still would not have been a trendsetter for, at the time, half the population would have supported such a decision.[14] And later, in assessing the Court's role after it had finally overruled *Bowers* in *Lawrence v. Texas* (2003), Klarman (2005, 445) emphasizes that the Court was certainly not in "the vanguard of a social reform movement," adding that it "rarely if ever plays such an adventurous role." Hutchinson (2005) concurs, contending that *Lawrence* is not a countermajoritarian decision because it reflected the nation's increasingly tolerant understanding of the right of personal privacy in sexual matters in the early twenty-first century.

More recently, *Lawrence* has served much the same role as *Brown*, precipitating a cottage industry of scholarship discussing its effect on the gay community and the role of the Court in sexual privacy cases, and more generally, on gay rights litigation (see, for example, Parshall 2005). *Lawrence* has also been analogized to *Brown* for its role in instilling optimism about the future of gay and lesbian legal rights in the United States (see Leslie 2005). Whatever the interpretation of *Lawrence* and its role in lifting the spirits of the gay community, most agree that it validates the Dahl thesis by reflecting the prevailing view of the public on consensual sodomy. By 2003, a majority of Americans opposed prosecutions for private acts of adult consensual sodomy and, indeed, few states had sodomy laws by this time (Gallup 2003a; see Hutchinson 2005). The consensus, therefore, is that *Lawrence* does not exemplify countermajoritarianism, "heroic" or otherwise (Klarman 2005).

This study goes beyond the concern with *Lawrence* and examines judicial rulings—in the state and federal courts—in a wide array of gay rights cases over the last fifty years. Its purpose is twofold: first, to weigh the effectiveness of litigation in furthering the goals of the gay community; second, to assess the degree to which the courts have engaged in judicial activism by opposing prevailing public opinion or negating the policy decisions of the other branches of the national and subnational governments. In discussing countermajoritarianism, the focus of attention has typically been on the federal courts, but although the appointed-for-life federal judges have long been assailed as judicial activists—most commonly by those who disapprove of their decisions—more recently, state court judges, many of whom are also appointed, have been painted with the same brush, largely for their role in the same-sex marriage debate.[15]

GAY RIGHTS AT ISSUE

In examining gay rights litigation over the last five decades, this book explores the courts' answers to such questions as the extent to which erotic material for a gay audience should be censored, whether the right to privacy should be broad enough to encompass same-sex sexual activity, whether private organizations should be permitted to exclude gays from membership or participation in their activities, whether same-sex marriages should be legally recognized and granted the full panoply of rights adhering to marriage, whether gay men and lesbians should be permitted to serve openly in the military, and whether laws against employment discrimination should apply to gays as they do to other minority groups.

Focusing on the legal issues involved in such questions, the study discusses whether the courts perceive a distinction between homosexual orientation and conduct, whether they view gays as an identifiable minority group and the extent to which they believe discrimination on the basis of sexual orientation is as objectionable as discrimination on the basis of race or sex, and the extent to which they are willing to override decisions made by other branches of government at the state and federal level in adjudicating claims of substantive and procedural constitutional violations.

THE PLAN OF THE BOOK

Chapter 1 sets the stage for these inquiries by placing gay rights activism in a historical context, discussing the gay rights movement from the 1920s through the end of the Reagan and Bush presidencies (the legal and political events during the Clinton and second Bush administrations are covered in depth in subsequent chapters). Chapter 2 reviews United States Supreme Court decision making in equality and privacy cases. Chapter 3 revolves around the controversy over same-sex marriage. Chapter 4 examines the exclusion of gays from military service in the context of presidential and legislative policymaking. And chapter 5 explores discrimination in employment, also addressing the role of the legislative and executive branches.

The cases, comprising the primary material for the analysis, were gathered through searches of computerized legal databases, yielding opinions published in bound reporters as well as those reported only to Westlaw or

LexisNexis. In addition to the judicial rulings, the primary source materials for this study include legal briefs, congressional committee reports, congressional testimony, presidential papers, and government documents such as the Federal Register, the United States Code, and the Code of Federal Regulations, as well as polling data available from Gallup, Harris, and the Pew Research Center, to mention just a few.[16] Scholarly books, legal journals, and myriad newspapers and periodicals make up the secondary source material.

A NOTE ABOUT TERMINOLOGY

The terminology in the discourse of social reform movements is always important, and gay rights policymaking is no exception; additionally, the significance of labels for the actors involved cannot be overestimated. Among other things, the gay rights movement has been characterized as the "queer civil rights movement" (Paris 1998, 43). The term *queer*, as appearing in the title of the book, was initially intended as an insult to members of the gay community; however, "more recently this term has been reclaimed by some lesbians, gay men, bisexual people, and transgender people as an inclusive and positive way to identify all people targeted by heterosexism and homophobia" (Griffin and Harro 1997, 162–3). That the purpose has been achieved is demonstrated by a literature with books variously entitled *Queer Theory*, *Queer Cowboys*, *Queer Astrology*, and *Queer Blues*.

Another term often used to denote the inclusivity of the gay community is *LGBT*. In explaining their use of LGBT—an abbreviation for lesbian, gay, bisexual, and transgender—Smith and Haider-Markel (2002, 3–5) observe that *gay* was originally used to depict male homosexuals and is often perceived as a generic "he" (see also Bruce 1996). However, although they refer to the movement as LGBT to emphasize broader inclusivity, for the most part, Smith and Haider-Markel's analysis addresses the concerns of lesbians and gay men.

Rimmerman (2002, chap. 1) uses the term *lesbian and gay movements* to suggest the diversity of interests in the gay community, noting that women, regardless of their sexual orientation, have interests that diverge from those of men as a group. MacKinnon (2003, chap. 8) agrees, suggesting that although *gay* may appear to be gender neutral, it implicitly refers to men, and *gay and lesbian* is the preferred phrase to denote inclusiveness. Distinguishing between the sexes, she believes, sends the proper signal that sex makes a difference, regardless of sexual orientation.

Initially supporting the aims of the homophile movement, lesbians began to feel their interests were subsumed within the male-dominated hierarchy of gay rights activists (see D'Emilio 1983, chap. 6). Just as women in the antiwar and civil rights movements of the 1960s complained of their male colleagues treating them as subordinates, lesbians began to resent their unequal status in the movement. At the same time, although Gartner (2004, 4) notes that many leaders of the feminist movement strongly supported the cause of lesbian rights, lesbians felt marginalized within the feminist movement as well as within the gay rights movement. They found themselves caught between the male-dominated gay liberation movement and the straight-dominated women's liberation movement, at odds with men in the former and nonlesbian women in the latter (see Hertzog 1996, chap. 2; Schroedel and Fiber 2000). And to complicate matters even further, Smith and Haider-Markel (2002) note that some women even prefer to be called gay rather than lesbian.

Racial and ethnic divisions add another layer of complexity to the terminology of the LGBT movement. Just as the rhetoric of inclusion erroneously assumes an absence of sex differences within the gay community, it also presupposes the irrelevance of racial differences. Boykin (2000), however, argues that African Americans have been marginalized within the gay rights movement, and that "terms such as gay and lesbian are perceived as vestiges of white Eurocentric dominance." In his view, a more acceptable term that has recently begun to replace gay, lesbian, or queer is *same-gender-loving*, a phrase that has come to be identified with members of the non-white community (91–2).

It is not my aim to explore such differences in the goals or status of individuals within the gay community, significant as they may be. Obviously, as with other social movements, its members stress different priorities and urge different strategies. Without intending to minimize distinctions among those who identify themselves as members of the LGBT community or oversimplify a complex set of attitudes and behaviors, I use the term *gays* or *gay community* to denote lesbians and homosexual men— as well as bisexual and transsexual persons when appropriate. For the most part, it appears that no matter how divergent the interests of individuals within the movement may be, outsiders generally perceive the LGBT community as an undifferentiated whole, without recognizing distinctions among them in the policymaking process. Finally, although the term *homosexual* is generally disfavored today because of its clinical connotation and its earlier identification with same-sex sexual orientation as a pathology, it is often necessary to use it for purposes of historical accuracy, especially in discussing judicial opinions and legislation where it is almost always used (see Bruce 1996). I refer to "gay rights advocates" or "gay rights activists" to signify the individuals and groups who favor equality for members of the gay community, broadly defined, and "anti–gay rights advocates" or "anti–gay rights activists" to depict those who oppose some or all of these goals. This shorthand approach does not mean to suggest, however, that the motives and tactics of individuals within these two broad groupings are identical.

NOTES

1. Button, Rienzo, and Wald (1997, chap. 1) discuss the debate over the gay community's attempt to produce social change through the use of law.

2. In discussing the complexity of religious opposition to homosexuality, Green (2000, 122–3) notes that while most religions do not approve of it, there are differences in the degree of their opposition.

3. See Endean (2006, appendix C) for members of the Congressional Black Caucus who have cosponsored and supported gay rights legislation in addition to other African American leaders who have been supportive.

4. Feldblum (2000) discusses the difficulties of gay rights groups in gaining acceptance in the civil rights community.

5. Jacobs (1993, 728) refers to this as "affirmation/scourge opposition in gay rights discourse."

6. The HRC began as the Human Rights Campaign Fund (HRCF); in 1995, the word *Fund* was omitted from the name (www.hrc.org).

7. In 1957, the ACLU released a position paper in which it accepted the constitutionality of sodomy laws as well the legitimacy of denying security clearances to gays (Pacelle 1996, 201).

8. Among judicial scholars, the sides of this debate are typically represented by McCann (1994), arguing for the effectiveness of the courts, and Rosenberg (1991), making the opposite claim.

9. The more common term to describe the countermajoritarian role of the courts, *judicial activism*, has been used as a pejorative term by both liberals and conservatives over time. Until the late 1930s and 1940s, activism was used mostly to advance conservative goals; from the 1950s until 1970, the courts' activism was largely in a liberal direction, and the term is more commonly used by conservatives to denounce decisions that protect the rights of minorities. According to Kmiec (2004, 1442), there were almost four thousand references to the terms *judicial activism* and *judicial activist* in journal and law review articles in the 1990s. Between 2000 and 2004 alone, he adds, these terms have appeared in almost two thousand articles. He notes as well that the terms have become part of the popular culture in discussing the role of the courts, surfacing in the press as well as on the Internet.

10. Stone's analysis in *Carolene Products* has often been credited as a principal factor in the development of the notion of "strict scrutiny" in equal protection cases; see chapter 2.

11. Given the myriad ways in which the executive and legislative branches are unrepresentative of the people, it is not always accurate to characterize their decisions as representing the majority will.

12. Kramer (2004) challenges the wisdom of allowing the Court to define the nation's constitutional values, preferring a system of "popular constitutionalism." Chermerinsky (2004) disagrees, arguing that the Court and its power of judicial review play a crucial role in protecting minority rights; see also Tushnet (1999).

13. See Hutchinson (2005) for a discussion of the Supreme Court and public opinion.

14. The *Bowers* Court, in a 5–4 decision, came within one vote of striking the Georgia sodomy law; see chapter 2.

15. In Hawaii, Alaska, Vermont, Massachusetts, and New Jersey—where same-sex marriage cases were decided largely in the plaintiffs' favor—state court judges are appointed by the governors of the states.

16. Most of these data were obtained from the research organization's website; some of the data were taken from PollingReport.com and cited as such.

CHAPTER 1

Forging Gay Rights Activism

THERE are myriad accounts of the origins of the gay and lesbian rights movement in the United States and abroad (see, for example, D'Emilio 1983; Duberman 1993; Marotta 1981; Adam 1995). Gay rights organizations were initially a European phenomenon dating back to the mid- to late 1800s. The Scientific-Humanitarian Committee, founded in Berlin on May 15, 1897, was the first modern gay rights group and became the model for future organizations.

Across the ocean, gay rights activity evolved more slowly. In the United States, the struggle for gay rights was marked by a transformation from sexuality as a private affair to its current prominent place on the nation's political agenda. D'Emilio (1983, chap. 1) chronicles the emergence of homosexual identity in the United States from the time of the early settlers to the 1980s. For more than a century, although there were reports of same-sex sexual activity, such behavior was well hidden.[1] He dates the rise of distinct homosexual and lesbian identities to the middle of the nineteenth century with the advent of the Industrial Revolution and urbanization. Beginning in the 1870s, it was not uncommon for similarly minded people of all classes to congregate in urban areas and form social groups, all the time attuned to the hostility of the outside world.

During the 1920s, members of the gay community began to develop the determination and confidence to challenge the prevailing homophobia within American culture. The Chicago-based Society for Human Rights, incorporated in 1924, represented the first "known" gay rights organization in the United States. Established by Henry Gerber, it was disbanded shortly after the arrest of several members of the group, following a tip to the Chicago police department. Although they were eventually released without being charged, the organization fell victim to the climate of repression that pervaded the nation following World War I (Cain 1993; Smith and Haider-Markel 2002, chap. 3).

The disruption to the social order caused by World War II had a marked influence on the formation of explicit gay identities as awareness and opportunities to act increased. Many of the ties formed during the war years remained in place after the cessation of hostilities, allowing greater openness of sexual identification, including the publication of literature focusing on homosexuality. The post–World War II era also gave rise to gay bars as retreats for gays and lesbians, allowing them to share experiences and seek out sexual relationships. Their importance cannot be overstated as they "were seedbeds for a collective consciousness that might one day flower politically" (D'Emilio 1983, 33; see Cain 2000, chap. 3).

Society's awareness of homosexuality was spurred by the 1948 publication of Alfred Kinsey's *Sexual Behavior in the Human Male*, followed by the 1953 publication of his *Sexual Behavior in the Human Female*; Kinsey revealed that homosexual sexual activity was more prevalent than most believed.[2] But although more became known about homosexuality in the late 1940s, the heterosexual world still had little understanding of it and even less tolerance for it. The social conservatism of the times merged with the anticommunist Cold War mentality to produce an antigay fervor, leading, among other things, to arrests, denials of security clearances, and disqualification from federal employment (Kameny 2000, 189). During the Truman and Eisenhower administrations, gay men and lesbians, along with suspected communists, were driven out of jobs at every level of government and discharged from the military in ever-increasing numbers (Adam 1995, chap. 4).

With increasing awareness and manifestation of a gay consciousness, there was an accompanying backlash of repression and harassment fueled by the fear of a national security threat in government work and the military. D'Emilio, depicting the hazards of living a gay life during the 1950s, writes that the linkage between homosexuality and communism was brought to light in February 1950 when John Peurifoy, a State Department undersecretary, testified in a Senate Appropriations Committee hearing "that most of the ninety-one [federal] employees dismissed for moral turpitude were homosexuals" (1983, 41).

Republicans, anxious to paint the Truman administration with a broad unpatriotic brush, sought to take advantage of the public's fear of homosexuality and communism to exploit this information. Letters were sent to

Republican party workers, alerting them to the danger, and more important, impressing them with their duty to disseminate the news. The disregard for civil liberties that characterized inquiries into suspected communist activity was evident in the attempt to ferret out gay men and lesbians, including pressure to provide names to the investigators. Intertwined with communism, homosexuality was believed to be "an epidemic infesting the nation, actively spread by communists to sap the strength of the next generation" (D'Emilio 1993, 44).

Exacerbated by the onset of the Korean War, the anticommunist fervor of McCarthyism (after Senator Joseph McCarthy, Republican from Wisconsin), led, in 1947, to President Harry Truman's Executive Order No. 9835, permitting executive branch agencies to refuse employment to individuals believed to be "disloyal." Soon after, in 1949, the Department of Defense declared that "known homosexual individuals were military liabilities and security risks who must be eliminated" (quoted in M. Lewis 1990, 138).

Gay men and lesbians were caught up in the government's efforts to secure loyalty oaths and other methods of achieving conformity, including sexual conformity (D'Emilio 1992, chap. 3; Cain 1993). There were charges that gays abounded in the State Department, with the chair of the Republican National Committee asserting that "perhaps as dangerous as the actual communists are the sexual perverts who have infiltrated our government in recent years" (Walzer 2002, 32).

Senate committees held hearings on gays in the federal civil service, concluding that they were unfit for federal employment. A report issued in 1950 in the 81st Congress entitled *Employment of Homosexuals and Other Sex Perverts in Government*, by the Investigations Subcommittee of the Senate Committee on Expenditures in the Executive Department, warned of character deficiencies, saying "Those who engage in overt acts of perversion lack the emotional stability of normal persons," and because of their propensity to seduce others "to engage in perverted practices . . . one homosexual can pollute a government office." Additionally, it cautioned about gays' susceptibility to blackmail, warning that "gangs of blackmailers" make "a regular practice of preying upon the homosexual" and that foreign agents "can use the same type of pressure to extort confidential information." The report made it clear that faced with the choice of betraying their country or suffering exposure, targeted employees would choose the former (quoted in D'Emilio 1983, 42–3; Cain 1993).

The report claimed that from 1947 until 1950, "there were 4,954 cases involving homosexuality in the federal government, of which 88 percent involved military personnel" (Haggerty 2003, 20). Republicans took special aim at Truman's State Department, accusing it of harboring communists and homosexuals. According to Kameny (2000), these witch hunts against gay federal workers resonated throughout all of society, and employment discrimination in the private sector mirrored that of the federal government, continuing long after it was finally halted in the federal government.

In addition to arousing fears about federal employees generally, "sexual McCarthyism" conjured up frightening scenarios of the consequences of gays receiving security clearances for sensitive work.[3] Witnesses testifying in McCarthy's Senate committee hearings in 1953 asserted that homosexuals were unfit because they were vulnerable to blackmail by communists who would force them to reveal government secrets (Haider-Markel 1999). The concern about gays and national security was reflected in Executive Order No. 10450, issued by President Dwight Eisenhower on April 27, 1953, a version of the Truman administration's loyalty policy. It ordered all government workers to be investigated, citing several grounds for evaluation, including "any criminal, infamous, dishonest, or notoriously disgraceful conduct, habitual use of intoxicants to excess, drug addiction, or sexual perversion" as well as "any facts that furnished reason to believe that the individual might be subjected to coercion, influence, or pressure that might cause him to act contrary to the best interests of the national security."

As Kameny notes, these reasons "were used specifically to target gays . . . [turning the] security clearance program into an open war against gay Americans that went on for some four decades" (Kameny 2000, 197; see Duong 2003/2004). For the first sixteen months, the Eisenhower security program removed at least forty suspected homosexuals from employment a month, not counting those who decided to leave quietly and avoid being discharged (D'Emilio 1983, 44). But evidently despite the intensive efforts to find evidence of disloyalty, there was never any proof that any blackmail actually occurred (D'Emilio 1992, 64).[4] By the end of 1955, although more than 650 gays had been discharged from government jobs, as a government report later indicated, there was no relationship between homosexuality and security violations among government employees (M. Lewis 1990, 139).

THE HOMOPHILE ERA

Attempting to counter the pervasive witch-hunt atmosphere, the Mattachine Society was founded in Los Angeles in 1951, largely at the instigation of Henry Hay, a gay leftist living in California.[5] Trained as an actor, Hay had been unable to secure work and turned to labor agitation, joining the Communist Party. During the 1930s, when homosexuals were persecuted in the Soviet Union, and he was advised to repress his homosexuality, he married. In 1948, he worked for the Henry Wallace campaign, hoping to organize a gay artistic group to support Wallace. Although nothing much came of this plan, it led to his realization that he was no longer willing to turn his back on homosexuality, and he applied his professional organizing skills to building a homosexual rights organization. In November 1950, Hay called a group of five men to a secret meeting at his house to discuss his proposal for achieving "the heroic objective of liberating one of our largest minorities and guaranteeing them self-respecting citizenship" (D'Emilio 1992, 18; D'Emilio 1983, chap. 4).

Following the model of the Communist Party in the 1940s and 1950s, membership in the gay organization was secret, the participants feeling vulnerable to harassment, arrest, and dismissal from their jobs for their radical political views as well as their sexual orientation. Eventually joined by others without the current membership's Communist Party leanings, the group soon dropped its Marxist orientation and aimed at raising group consciousness among the members, emphasizing their identification as an oppressed minority.[6]

A few years after its founding, with a substantial increase in membership, the group began to lose its focus and early radicalism. In 1953, a new leadership assumed power and adopted a strategy of seeking assimilation and societal acceptance; they stressed the similarities between gay and non-gay people and were intent on proving themselves respectable members of society. But in attempting to fit into mainstream society, the group lost its focus and ultimately most of its members (Adam 1995, chap. 4; D'Emilio 1993, chap. 2).

Although the Mattachine Society had some lesbian members, it was predominantly male. In 1955, Del Martin and Phyllis Lyon launched the first lesbian group, the San Francisco–based Daughters of Bilitis (DOB), which split off from the Mattachine Society. The story behind the founding of the DOB was quite different from that of the Mattachine Society, but both groups experienced similar difficulties of organization and direction (see Walzer 2002, chap. 1; D'Emilio 1983, chap. 6).

Martin, who had been married, divorced her husband and moved to Seattle, where she met Lyon. Their relationship gradually became physical and, in 1953, they moved back to San Francisco to make a life there.[7] It was "the desire to socialize with gay women [that] propelled the Daughters of

Bilitis into existence" (D'Emilio 1983, 102). But once established, the membership soon became divided over the direction the organization should take. Martin and Lyon wanted it to assume a broader outlook and attempt to change societal attitudes about lesbianism, looking to the newly formed Mattachine Society as a model. Others disagreed and, wanting it to remain a social club, split off from the group. Those remaining joined with the Mattachine Society to become part of the homophile movement; they established their own newspaper called the *Ladder*. For a period of time, the two organizations gained from their association with each other, sharing a common goal of public education and combating the antipathy and discrimination directed toward them.

LITIGATING AGAINST CENSORSHIP

From the 1950s to the 1970s, the bulk of the litigation activity affecting the gay community revolved around First Amendment challenges to the censorship of reading materials and films through postal regulations and obscenity laws. Regardless of the rulings, however, the opinions in these cases frequently reflected the justices' evident distaste for sexual conduct they considered beyond the pale of decency and normalcy.

The Court became involved in shaping the nation's obscenity laws when it was asked to interpret postal restrictions barring mail delivery of obscene material. Such literature, often intended for a homosexual audience, fell within the boundaries of the obscenity statutes, usually based on a postal employee's judgment that it failed to meet the standards of "normal" sexuality. When ruling on such cases, the justices often appeared conflicted about whether to declare such material beyond the protection of the First Amendment, their aversion to the subject matter battling with their antipathy to the image of themselves as modern-day Anthony Comstocks. Consequently, the rulings were often inconsistent, with the Court at times upholding the First Amendment guarantee and, at other times, refusing to do so, usually without making clear distinctions between what was acceptable and what was unacceptable. The constant in these cases, even from justices who were staunch protectors of First Amendment freedoms, was their discomfort with what they termed "deviant sex."

The high court struggled with the constitutionality of laws restricting obscenity for almost two decades—beginning in the late 1950s.[8] In *Roth v. United States* (1957), its first case applying a federal obscenity standard, the Court affirmed a conviction under federal law punishing the mailing of

material considered "obscene, lewd, lascivious, or filthy" (480 n1). Five justices agreed that obscenity was "utterly without redeeming social importance" and "not within the area of constitutionally protected speech or press"
(484–5). The definition of obscenity was a broad one: "whether to the average person, applying contemporary community standards, the dominant
theme of the material taken as a whole appeals to prurient interest" (489).

Roth led to greater tolerance for gay literature, as evidenced in the
Supreme Court's ruling in *One, Inc. v. Olesen* (1958). The case arose when
the Los Angeles postmaster banned the magazine *One: The Homosexual
Magazine*, a publication initially tied to the Mattachine Society but later
becoming independent.[9] The founders of *One* intended it to provide an
opportunity for members of the gay community to air their ideas to the
public and to each other (D'Emilio 1983; Murdoch and Price 2001). On
October 1, 1954, federal postal authorities seized it, informing the publisher
that the postmaster considered it "obscene, lewd, lascivious and filthy" and
thus "non-mailable" under an almost century-old provision of the United
States Postal Code (*Olesen* 1957, 773).[10] The publisher sued, claiming a violation of the First Amendment and the Fourteenth Amendment's equal protection and due process clauses. Both sides agreed that the decision revolved
around the narrow question of whether the October 1954 issue of the magazine was obscene.[11]

The trial court upheld the postmaster, finding the magazine obscene
because it consisted of stories and poems that were "lustfully stimulating
to the homosexual reader," contained "filthy language," and provided information on how to obtain obscene material (another criterion of "non-
mailability") (774).

On appeal, the Ninth Circuit stressed that its decision must be based on
the impact of the words on the reader, insisting that it was not "its brother's
keeper as to the type of reading to be indulged in" (774). Speaking for the circuit panel, district court judge Ross, sitting by designation, noted that although
the magazine's stated intent was to provide educational and informative material, it "has a primary purpose of exciting lust, lewd and lascivious thoughts
and sensual desires in the minds of the persons reading it. Moreover, such
articles are morally depraving and debasing. The articles mentioned are sufficient to label the magazine as a whole, obscene and filthy" (778).[12]

The appellate court indicated that it believed the only proper discussion of homosexuality was from a "scientific, historical and critical point
of view." It described one of the articles entitled "Sappho Remembered,"
about a twenty-year-old woman's choice of living as a lesbian or having "a

normal married life with her childhood sweetheart" as "nothing more than cheap pornography calculated to promote lesbianism." Finding articles such as this "morally depraving and debasing," the court characterized the magazine as a whole as "obscene and filthy" and affirmed the trial court's finding that the postmaster was justified in determining it "non-mailable" under the statute (777–8).

A week after it voted to grant certiorari, without hearing oral argument, the Court issued a per curiam opinion in *Olesen* (1958), reversing the appellate court's ruling and citing *Roth* (see Murdoch and Price 2001).[13]

A few years after *Roth*, in *Manual Enterprises v. Day* (1962), the Court was again asked to rule on the Post Office Department's determination that three magazines written for, and read almost entirely by, homosexuals were obscene. Four hundred and fifty copies of the magazines had been sent to the Alexandria, Virginia, post office for shipment to Chicago. Based on his belief that they were obscene, the Alexandria postmaster sent sample copies to the general counsel of the Post Office Department. The department's hearing officer found that the magazines, which largely featured nude male models, violated the law because the content was obscene and because they provided information on where to obtain obscene material. The publishers unsuccessfully sought injunctive relief in the trial court, and the appellate court upheld the lower court's dismissal of their complaint.

The Supreme Court reversed the courts below, but, although the ruling was 6–1 (Justices Felix Frankfurter and Byron White did not participate), there was no majority opinion. Justices John Marshall Harlan and Potter Stewart believed that the magazines were not obscene because they were not patently offensive and because the government had failed to show that the publisher was aware that the advertising promoted obscene material. Justice Hugo Black concurred in the result, as did Justices William Brennan, William Douglas, and Chief Justice Earl Warren; the latter three voted to reverse the conviction on procedural grounds because they believed that the statute did not authorize the Post Office Department to determine that the material was nonmailable.

In writing for himself and Stewart, Harlan noted that the magazines were aimed primarily at a homosexual audience. He indicated that there was "substantial evidence" to support the Post Office Department's determination that they "would appeal to the 'prurient interest' of such sexual deviates, but would not have any interest for sexually normal individuals" (481). Although the lower court had been preoccupied with whether the magazines should be judged by their impact on the average person or the average homosexual, Harlan said that their audience was irrelevant to the outcome of the case. The lower courts had read *Roth* incorrectly, he said, and found the magazines obscene because they appealed to the reader's prurient interest. *Roth*, however, required the court to find that material was also patently offensive to reach a finding of obscenity. In his view, these magazines were not obscene because they were not patently offensive.[14] In most cases, he noted, the criteria are joined in that material that appeals to a prurient interest in sex will also be patently offensive; but because this material was aimed at a special audience, the reviewing court must assess the offensiveness factor independently.

Assessing the material as a whole, Harlan stated that although the magazines were "dismally unpleasant, uncouth, and tawdry," they were no "more objectionable than many portrayals of the female nude that society tolerates" and therefore were not obscene under the law (*Manual Enterprises* 1962, 490). He also found there was insufficient evidence that the publishers knew that the advertisers were offering obscene material.

Justice Tom Clark dissented, charging that despite the split in the majority, the "ultimate holding of the Court today . . . requires the United States Post Office to be the world's largest disseminator of smut and Grand Informer of the names and places where obscene material may be obtained" (519). He did not even address the question whether the material in the magazines was obscene. In his view, simply because they provided information about where obscene material may be obtained, the post office was justified in refusing to mail them.

Almost a decade after *Roth*, the Court decided a trio of cases on the same day; in two of them, it addressed the effect of obscenity laws on material directed at a homosexual audience. The proliferation of cases and fractured rulings added to the confusion in the lower courts about the proper test for obscenity for any audience.

In *A Book Named "John Cleland's Memoirs of a Woman of Pleasure" v. Attorney General of Massachusetts* (1966), Brennan, speaking for himself, Warren, and Justice Abe Fortas, reformulated the *Roth* test; proof of obscenity, he said, requires three findings: "It must be established that (a) the dominant theme of the material taken as a whole appeals to a prurient interest in sex; (b) the material is patently offensive because it affronts contemporary community standards relating to the description or representation of sexual matters; and (c) the material is utterly without redeeming social value" (418). The three-justice plurality voted to reverse the conviction because the prosecution had failed to show it met the last prong of the test.

Despite the book's appeal to prurient interests and its seeming offensiveness, in their view, because the lower court had found that the book was not devoid of literary value, it could not be found obscene.[15]

In *Ginzburg v. United States* (1966), a 5–4 Court, with Fortas, Warren, Clark, Brennan, and Justice Byron White in the majority, upheld the federal conviction of Ralph Ginzburg for attempting to send three publications, including *Eros* magazine, through the mail.[16] Speaking for the Court, Brennan characterized the issue as whether the lower court judge had correctly applied the *Roth* standard in determining the material obscene. Ginzburg argued that the prosecutor had improperly presented evidence of how the material was marketed, including the advertising campaign, to secure the conviction. The majority, however, found that a court may "view the publications against a background of commercial exploitation of erotica solely for their prurient appeal" (*Ginzburg* 1966, 466). Given the circumstances, the Court held, the lower court judge had correctly determined the material obscene.

Writing in dissent, Black faulted the majority for establishing "vague and meaningless" standards for determining criminal liability in obscenity cases (478). Douglas's dissent argued against the use of subjective criteria based on "normal" sexuality in deciding whether individual "ideas and tastes" are obscene. However, although he criticized the government for imposing the majority's values on individuals, he also characterized homosexual sex as "deviant" (489). Stewart charged that although the majority "appear[ed] to concede that the materials Ginzburg mailed were themselves protected by the First Amendment," it upheld his five-year sentence because he "was guilty of 'commercial exploitation,' of 'pandering,' and of 'titillation'" (500).

In the third case, *Mishkin v. New York* (1966), the justices again revealed that they shared society's prevailing view of homosexuality as sexual deviance. The defendant was convicted under New York law for publishing and possessing obscene books and sentenced to three years in prison and a $12,000 fine. After explaining that states may establish their own standards for obscenity as long as they are consistent with *Roth*, the Court interpreted the state's definition of obscenity, revisiting one of the issues left open in *Manual Enterprises*.[17]

The Court described the content of the books, which were intended for a homosexual audience, as "portray[ing] sexuality in many guises. Some depict relatively normal heterosexual relations, but more depict such deviations as sado-masochism, fetishism, and homosexuality" (*Mishkin* 1966, 505). It rejected the defendant's claim that the terms *sadistic, masochistic,* and *obscene* were vague and turned to his argument that the materials were not obscene because they did "not appeal to a prurient interest of the 'average person' in sex," that "instead of stimulating the erotic, they disgust and sicken" (508).

The "prurient interest" element, the Court stated, must be judged in terms of the audience at which it was aimed, including a homosexual audience. Citing the 1959 *American Handbook of Psychiatry's* characterization of homosexuals as "deviant sexual groups," the Court ruled that because the books appealed to the prurient interest of a homosexual population, the government satisfied its burden of proving the *Roth* requirement (*Mishkin* 1966, 509 n8).

These cases show that, as Black observed, the justices were conscripted into performing "the irksome and inevitably unpopular and unwholesome task of finally deciding by a case-by-case, sight-by-sight personal judgment of the members of this Court what pornography (whatever that means) is too hard core for people to see or read" (516–7).[18] In reversing obscenity convictions, the justices indicated their discomfort in their role as the nation's censor. Yet, at the same time, most of them reflected the prevailing view of sexuality by regarding homosexuality as deviant, that is, not "normal," behavior. In 1973, the Court finally reached consensus on a test for obscenity upon which a majority agreed. With a new definition of obscenity, proclaimed in *Miller v. California* (1973), it signaled that it was unwilling to continue acting as the ultimate censor of the nation's reading material and visual arts.[19]

THE RISE OF GAY CONSCIOUSNESS

During the 1950s, gays were largely focused internally, devoting themselves to sharing views on collective problems, adopting the consciousness-raising model of the women's liberation movement (Brewer, Kaib, and O'Connor 2000). The next two decades encompassed the rise and decline of the homophile movement, generally considered to have ended in the late 1960s, with the emergence of a new gay consciousness and the creation of the gay liberation movement. During this time as well, a litigation strategy for social reform was being formulated by gay rights activists.

The changes were evident as early as the beginning of the 1960s with the more aggressive leadership in the Mattachine Society. Much of the change was credited to Kameny, founder of the Mattachine Society of Washington, who adopted the civil rights rhetoric of the African American civil rights movement. Kameny organized the Washington organization shortly after he was fired from his government job as an astronomer with the Army Map Service in 1957 (Rimmerman 2002; Cain 2000). Through this organization, he played a leading role in the attempt to use litigation to fight discrimination against gays in federal employment and, in particular, to seek his own reinstatement. However, his own lawsuit was unsuccessful; after losing in the lower courts, the Supreme Court ultimately refused to hear his case (*Kameny v. Brucker* 1961).[20]

The more militant face of the gay rights movement gradually spread to other cities, leading to demonstrations and demands for recognition, and in San Francisco, the formation of the Society for Individual Rights (SIR), which until 1969 was the largest gay rights organization in the nation (Cain 1993, 1563).[21] The movement owed much to the spirit of the 1960s and the radicalism of the "New Left" antiwar and civil rights movements.[22] By the end of the sixties, although the "New Left" began its demise, it had a lasting impact on U.S. politics because it "empowered and mobilized millions of people and gave voice to new categories of the powerless and oppressed. [And] out of the decay of the New Left came the modern feminist and gay liberation movements" (Adam 1995, 78).

The Stonewall Rebellion of June 1969, following the police raid on the Stonewall Inn—a bar on Christopher Street—in Greenwich Village, New York, is commonly viewed as the match that sparked the birth of the gay liberation movement, akin to Rosa Parks's historic refusal to step to the rear of the bus that triggered the Montgomery, Alabama, bus boycott.[23] Before Stonewall, no antidiscrimination legislation existed to protect gays in the private or the public sector (Button, Rienzo, and Wald 2000, 271). Moreover, for the most part, a litigation strategy had not yet evolved to challenge the myriad restrictions on gay and lesbian lives (Pacelle 1996).

Although gay rights (or homophile) organizations had existed before 1969 as local chapters of the Mattachine Society and the Daughters of Bilitis, a new era of gay rights consciousness and radicalism emerged from the events of June 27, 1969 (Rimmerman 2002, chap. 2; Smith and Haider-Markel 2002, chaps. 1, 3; see Carter 2004; Alexander 2002). Jacobs (1993, 726) calls Stonewall the "catalyst" and "milestone" of gay rights activism for two reasons: "First, it was active, collective, public action by gays and for gays. Second, it energized lesbians and gays across the country to spontaneously form political associations and to publicly demonstrate in affirmation of gayness" (see Gartner 2004; Cain 2000).

Police raids on gay bars, with accompanying arrests, were fairly commonplace during the 1960s (see Faderman 1991 on gay bars and the lesbian community). In an atypical "gay bar" case, and, according to Rimmerman

(2002), perhaps the first legal victory for gay rights advocates, the California Supreme Court held in *Stoumen v. Reilly* (1951, 971) that the state could not suspend indefinitely the liquor license of a restaurant merely because it was a "'hangout' for homosexuals." Reversing the lower court ruling, Chief Justice Gibson said there was no evidence that the Black Cat was "used as a disorderly house or place 'to which people resort for purposes which are injurious to the public morals'" as the statute required (971). However, the more common experience during the pre-Stonewall era entailed situations in which patrons of gay bars were harassed by the police and the authorities frequently succeeded in closing the establishments (Cain 2000).

The Stonewall Rebellion is almost universally "marked as the start of the modern-day gay rights movement" (Murdoch and Price 2001, 27). However, although all acknowledge the importance of Stonewall to the gay liberation movement, in writing about the rise of gay consciousness, D'Emilio (1983, 251) emphasizes that "gay and lesbian life didn't start with Stonewall; rather there was a rich history of social experience and political struggle" preceding it. Cain (1993, 1580–1) argues that Stonewall reflected society's increasing tolerance of radicalization evidenced by the civil rights and feminist movements, and its major effect was to allow gay people—especially those who looked and acted differently—to add their claims for civil rights to those in other movements, borrowing legal arguments as well as tactics. Bawer (1994, 24) also concedes the importance of Stonewall yet points to decades of gay political activism preceding it and urges the gay community to get beyond the "Stonewall sensibility" and stop treating the events of June 1969 as "sacred."

The night the Stonewall riot began, the patrons—"homosexuals, drag queens, and transsexuals"—were unwilling to go quietly when the police appeared (*San Francisco Chronicle* June 27, 1994). The apparent catalyst for the protest was a patron who resisted arrest by throwing a bottle at a police officer (*Washington Post* June 27, 1994). As Duberman (1993, 182) explains, Stonewall had been "an oasis" to its gay clientele, a "safe retreat from the harassment of everyday life."[24] Ostensibly provoked by the law enforcement authorities, the customers began throwing coins at the police and soon escalated to rocks, bricks, and beer bottles; the police retaliated, swinging their nightsticks. When they went inside to make arrests, the police became trapped in the building, with demonstrators hurling burning trashcans and other objects; the disturbance was eventually quelled in the middle of the night by the arrival of carloads of riot-control police (Introduction: Stonewall at 25 1994, 277; see Bruce 1996).

One analysis of Stonewall claims that the rioters were not politically motivated and that gay activists took advantage of the events surrounding the Stonewall Rebellion to build momentum for a gay rights movement (Introduction: Stonewall at 25 1994, 278). Twenty-five years later, there was still speculation about the cause of the riot, that is, whether it was planned or spontaneous. Some have argued that it was a reaction to the death of Judy Garland, a gay icon, whose funeral took place that afternoon (*The Independent* [London] June 23, 1994). Another account describes "the Stonewall Army" as a "mix of homeless teen-age prostitutes who sold themselves in a little park across the street, a few middle-class gay men who came to dance, transvestites, poor Hispanic, black, and white gay men, college boys, a few lesbians, and uncounted passers-by who were swallowed up in the frenzy" (*New York Times* June 23, 1994). Whatever the motivation, one of the immediate effects of Stonewall was that New York City police ceased their raids on bars frequented by gays and ended the practice of entrapment as well.[25]

THE GAY LIBERATION MOVEMENT

For many gay people, Stonewall began a decade of freedom, ending "years of repression and paranoia, and [coming] before AIDS" (*New York Times* June 23, 1994). Shortly after the events at Stonewall, the Gay Liberation Front (GLF) was launched in New York City. Although it represented an off-shoot of the essentially moderate Mattachine Society, it presaged a new era of radicalism. During this time as well the designation *homosexual* was replaced with the term *gay*, and gay pride parades became commonplace in municipalities around the nation. Jacobs (1993, 726) believes the name change allowed gays to assume a more public identity, making themselves and their political agenda visible to the rest of the nation.

The success of the gay liberation movement can be measured by the degree to which it was able to portray gays and lesbians as a minority group and the extent to which it established a gay rights rhetoric that corresponded to the rhetoric of comparable civil rights organizations (see Jacobs 1993). To this end, GLF organizations spread throughout the country, "attack[ing] the consumer culture, militarism, racism, sexism, and homophobia" (Rimmerman 2002, 24). GLF chapters were created in urban areas and sought to make common ground with a series of left-progressive groups engaged in Vietnam War protests as well as African American and feminist movement activities (Brewer, Kaib, and O'Connor 2000).

Soon the GLF foundered amid internal disputes about the strategic soundness of its broad-based societal criticisms. Dissension among the members grew, in part because of the identification with the Black Panthers and antiwar radicals, and the GLF morphed into the somewhat more conservative Gay Activists Alliance (GAA). The GAA focused its attention on the issues directly relating to the gay community, committing itself to "militant but nonviolent homosexual civil rights struggle" (Rimmerman 2002, 26). Also unable to hold its membership together, the GAA had a short life span and disbanded in 1972, ultimately replaced by the National Gay Task Force, later renamed the National Gay and Lesbian Task Force (NGLTF). Among other things, the Task Force is credited with helping persuade the American Psychiatric Association (APA) to remove homosexuality as a mental disorder in the *Diagnostic and Statistical Manual of Mental Disorders* (*DSM*), in which it had been listed since the 1950s (Rimmerman 2002, chap. 2).

GAY RIGHTS SUCCESSES

Establishing themselves as a civil rights movement, gay rights activists across the nation created organizations representing a range of political and strategic approaches, such as lobbying, litigation, public education, electoral activity, and grassroots organizing; some of the more well-known are the HRC, Log Cabin Republicans, Lambda, the NGLTF, the National Black Lesbian and Gay Leadership Forum, and the Gay and Lesbian Victory Fund (Rimmerman 2000).

During this time, there was a flurry of grassroots activities in large urban areas and liberal university communities, such as Palo Alto and Berkeley, California; East Lansing and Ann Arbor, Michigan; Austin, Texas; Madison, Wisconsin; and Boulder, Colorado. Because the political and social environment in such communities made them more receptive to gay rights advocacy, the local governments in these municipalities led the way in enacting antidiscrimination measures, especially in housing and employment.

In addition to laws against discrimination in public employment, municipalities began to enact ordinances banning discrimination in private employment (see Marcus 2002, part 5). For the most part, this was accomplished by including sexual orientation as a prohibited category within existing antidiscrimination employment, public accommodations, and housing laws. Not surprisingly, because of their increased tolerance for diversity, many of these efforts were also concentrated in university communities. In March 1972, East Lansing had become the first community to include a ban on discrimination in private employment on the basis of sexual orientation in a civil rights ordinance.

In writing about these grassroots efforts, Button, Rienzo, and Wald note that such victories were made possible by the absence of "organized resistance," aside from some "modest opposition" from the Catholic Church (2000, 272). With the gay community becoming increasingly visible and mobilized, gay rights issues began to occupy a greater role in politics at all levels of government. An important part of the mobilization effort occurred on October 14, 1979, when mounting its "biggest cultural success to date," the gay community celebrated the tenth anniversary of Stonewall with the first national March on Washington for Lesbian and Gay Rights. Although the media put the number of participants at 100,000, gay activists say it was closer to 200,000 (Vaid 1995, 67).[26]

Dozens of city and county antidiscrimination ordinances were soon enacted around the nation. Eventually, during the 1980s, suburban communities began to follow the lead of the nearby urban areas in enacting protective legislation (see Button, Rienzo, and Wald 1997; Eskridge 1999; Keen and Goldberg 2003; Rimmerman 2002). By the early 1990s, because of state and local antidiscrimination acts, a significant proportion of workers (about 23 percent) were employed in jurisdictions with legislation banning discrimination against gays. By the end of the century, a majority of workers was likely covered—either through constitutional protections or antidiscrimination legislation. More recently, a number of municipalities have conditioned the award of city contracts on the contractor's provision of benefits to the same-sex partners of gay employees (Leonard 2004/2005).

State legislatures followed more slowly in enacting laws against discrimination in private employment; those that did generally added sexual orientation as a forbidden category of discrimination in existing laws. On the national level, Congress has had repeated opportunities to ban employment discrimination on the basis of sexual orientation, but although its support for such a measure seemed to be increasing, it has consistently refused to enact an antidiscrimination law. And despite numerous attempts by litigants, most courts have been unwilling to include sexual orientation within the sex discrimination provisions of Title VII of the 1964 Civil Rights Act. Thus, by the end of the twentieth century, although a substantial number of private and public employees are protected by state and local antidiscrimination legislation, and federal workers are covered under President Bill Clinton's 1998 executive order against discrimination, there is no national law prohibiting discrimination against gays in employment, public accommodations, or housing.

BACKLASH

The gay community's success in persuading government officials to enact antidiscrimination laws led to a backlash that often took the form of state and local ballot initiatives and referenda urging voters to nullify the policies. As recently as 2000, Maine voters defeated a ballot measure that would have included a prohibition on discrimination on the basis of sexual orientation in the state's civil rights law. Executive orders banning discrimination in Iowa, Ohio, and Louisiana were nullified in a variety of ways (Wood 2003, 526).

The first major antigay political crusade was organized around efforts to repeal the Dade County antidiscrimination ordinance in 1977; after a brief hiatus, a second wave of backlash arose with the ascendancy of the "New Right" in 1980. Although both were infused with overtones of Christian fundamentalism, the latter represented a concerted effort by national political groups to enter the policy arena to deny equal treatment to gay people (Note 1993). By 1992, a total of thirty-three antigay initiatives and referenda had appeared on the ballot in local elections, almost one a year since 1974 (Keen and Goldberg 2003, 5).

There was a flurry of such initiatives from 1978 to 1988, asking voters to retract antidiscrimination policies passed by city or county governments. For the most part, these were aimed at reversing laws or policies that prohibited discrimination in housing and employment (Donovan, Wenzel, and Bowler 2000, 162–3).[27] Most of the antigay measures succeeded, reflecting the influence of right-wing Christian groups that mobilized to turn back the gay rights protections. Perhaps the best known effort to repeal a gay rights law took place in Dade County, Florida, in 1977, fueled by Anita Bryant's Save Our Children campaign.

On January 28, 1977, in a 5–3 vote, the Dade County Commission amended the county's equal employment and fair housing law to ban discrimination on the basis of "affectional or sexual preference" in housing, public accommodations, and employment. The action was quickly followed by a series of newspaper ads aimed at its repeal. The ads sought to counter the popular belief that "homosexuals are gentle and non-aggressive." "The other side of the homosexual coin," one ad said, "is a hair-raising pattern of recruitment and outright seductions and molestation" (*Washington Post* June 7, 1977). Bryant not only "argued that 'homosexuality is immoral and against God's wishes,' but also charged that the gay rights law would encourage people to cross-dress, molest children, and rape animals" (quoted in Eskridge 1999, 131).[28]

In the end, the Dade County electorate overwhelmingly voted to revoke the ordinance in a 202,319–83,319 vote (Adam 1995, 111).[29] Both sides agreed that the result was attributable largely to Bryant's personal intervention. According to her husband, Bob Green, who called the repeal effort a "defensive measure," Bryant, a former Miss Oklahoma, was "the first person with a name to come out and speak on this issue" (*Washington Post* March 27, 1977).

The Dade County victory by antigay forces created a national momentum that had enormous success in repealing antidiscrimination measures around the nation over the next twenty years (Eskridge 1999, 132). After Dade County, Bryant took her crusade to Wichita, Kansas; Eugene, Oregon; and St. Paul, Minnesota, as well as other cities with antidiscrimination laws on the books (Keen and Goldberg 2003, 5).[30] Her efforts in Dade County and elsewhere were furthered by support from the Christian Right, which, aided by the business community, mobilized itself around opposition to gay rights and helped bring about the repeal of antidiscrimination ordinances around the nation (Rimmerman 2002, chap. 5).

The backlash against gay rights was also manifested in outbreaks of antigay violence across the nation; the murder of San Francisco supervisor Harvey Milk and Mayor George Moscone was in part associated with this violence. Milk was the first openly gay member of the board of supervisors, and indeed, was the first openly gay elected official in the United States. A transplanted New Yorker, Milk was a leader of the gay liberation movement, housed largely in San Francisco's Castro neighborhood, and elected to the board in 1977 (see Shilts 1982). Shortly after his election, he became involved in the battle against—and helped defeat—Proposition 6 (known as the Briggs Initiative after its sponsor, state senator John Briggs), which aimed at removing gay and lesbian schoolteachers from California schools.[31]

Milk was assassinated by former supervisor Dan White on November 27, 1978. Riots broke out in the city when a jury refused to convict White of murder and instead convicted him of the lesser charge of voluntary manslaughter. White, who killed Moscone before killing Milk, was sentenced to seven years and eight months in prison and served only five years (Shilts 1982, 267–72; Shilts 1993, 313; Adam 1995, 114). According to Shilts (1993, 313) White was "the city's most outspokenly antigay politician," and many gays believed that the killing and the verdict "were acts of homophobia, plain and simple."

THE POLITICS OF AIDS

With the election of Ronald Reagan and the new Republican majority in the Senate in 1980, the gains made by the gay community slowed to a virtual halt. At the same time, gay rights activists were forced to turn their attention to the medical condition known as acquired immune deficiency syndrome or AIDS (see Haider-Markel 1999; D'Emilio 2000; Campbell and Davidson 2000). "The appearance of the AIDS epidemic . . . wholly unexpected and unanticipated" was a radical shock to gay politics (Smith and Haider-Markel 2002, 45). The disease that would take thousands of lives, especially in New York and San Francisco, was first identified in 1981 as the "gay cancer," and then named AIDS later that year. By the late 1980s, the number of AIDS-related deaths was higher than the number of soldiers who had been killed in Vietnam, and by the middle of 1991, almost 100,000 had died (Cruikshank 1992, 181).

Awareness of AIDS brought the subject of homosexuality to the forefront of the nation's public policy agenda and changed the politics of gay rights forever. But notwithstanding the ferocity of the disease, the Reagan administration's policy toward AIDS was characterized largely by indifference and an unwillingness to commit resources for research and treatment, hardly surprising given its overall hostility to gay rights (see Turner 2000).

Vaid (1995, chap. 3) writes that the emergence of AIDS created two political dilemmas for the gay community: first, how to get a response from an unconcerned administration; and second, how to mobilize members of the community into action. Before the infectious nature of the disease was fully known, the gay community was split on the best method of coping with it. Some argued for more restrained sexual activity; others viewed exhortations to limit high-risk sexual encounters as discriminatory and antithetical to the maintenance of the gay culture. Often the debate revolved around whether public officials, especially in San Francisco and New York, with their high concentration of gay citizens, should shut down public bathhouses—a favorite gathering place. As the disease continued, most of those stricken with it saw little need to focus on prevention, and this task fell to public health officials. The federal government, dominated by Republicans during the 1980s, seemed to make little effort to halt the spread of the disease beyond promoting sexual abstinence. Thus, with little support for prevention within and outside the gay community, few federal resources were devoted to it (Rom 2000).

The illness and the search for a cure took on political dimensions in a way that no other medical condition has before or after. To build coalitions to fight the disease, the gay community deemphasized rights issues and focused on its universality, stressing that its tentacles reached beyond gays. Originally conceived as caused by homosexuality, AIDS was first known as "gay related immune deficiency." Discussing the relationship between the politicization of the lesbian and gay movement and AIDS, Blasius (1994, 158 n16) notes that one of the first tasks the gay community accomplished was to decouple the disease from homosexuality, demonstrating that it affected the nongay population as well.

Vaid (1995, 74) argues that the gay community made strategic errors by "degaying, desexualizing, decoupling AIDS-specific reform from systemic reform and direct action" in response to the AIDS crisis. The results, she maintains, produced "short-term, quick-fix strategies that yielded dramatic but short-lived gains" that failed to transform society and promote equality. Notwithstanding the long-term implications of these strategic choices, she notes that the onset of the epidemic catapulted the gay community into the national political playing field. Blasius (1994, 157) also observes that the "politicization" of the disease allowed members of the gay community "to empower themselves as individuals, and their organizations as political actors, to shape the future development of the epidemic."

As with other social movements, differences within the gay community had emerged as it matured. At first, the rifts developed between lesbians and gay men, followed by racial divides in the late 1970s. An unanticipated consequence of the AIDS epidemic was the healing of these rifts and the emergence of greater unity among gay rights activists (D'Emilio 2000). In writing about the effects of AIDS, Cruikshank (1992, chap. 7) observes that members of the gay community, devastated by the spread of the disease and drained of resources by caring for its ill and dying members, became more unified in their effort to combat it and force the government to reverse its initial attitude of indifference to it. Additionally, there was support from parents of gay men afflicted with the disease as well as from the medical profession. AIDS also raised awareness among civil rights activists of discrimination on the basis of sexual orientation.

Despite its effect on forging solidarity within the gay community, public awareness of the disease led to increased homophobia and discrimination, including incidents of violence that often went unpunished (see Clendinen and Nagourney 1999, chap. 33). Fueled by its antipathy to the gay lifestyle, the administration was slow to react and loathe to commit resources to fighting the disease. Cruikshank (1992, 181–2) argues that the Reagan administration was indifferent to the deaths of gay men and drug users and did not take action against AIDS until heterosexuals were affected by the disease. Some Reagan administration officials such as Surgeon General C. Everett Koop were sympathetic to the concerns of the gay community, according to Vaid (1995, 99), but most were not. It was said that Reagan himself never spoke the word *AIDS* until 1987.

CONGRESS ACTS

Congress finally began appropriating funds to fight AIDS in 1985. But in October 1987, the Helms amendment (after Senator Jesse Helms, Republican from North Carolina) banned federal funds for AIDS education that "promotes or encourages homosexual behavior" (Vaid 1995, 85; Haider-Markel 1999). Helms had proposed the amendment after erroneously claiming that a comic book promoting safe sex was produced with federal funds. The Senate voted 98–2 to add the Helms amendment to the AIDS appropriation bill currently before it. And although it was attenuated in later versions, a form of the Helms amendment was subsequently added to each appropriation bill, thereby eliminating the use of federal dollars for programs designed to prevent the spread of AIDS (Vaid 1995, 139–40).

Viewing it as a political campaign, AIDS activists empowered themselves by becoming enmeshed with existing gay rights organizations to exert pressure on the federal government to commit resources to fighting the disease. Before this happened, however, the gay community had to overcome its suspicion of the federal government and its reluctance to seek assistance from it (Andriote 2000, 411). At the same time, its members were conflicted because of their concern that attention to the disease would ultimately weaken their community and its institutions.

Members of the gay community were divided among themselves over how much information about the disease should be released to the public, fearing that it would lead to a backlash and diminished support for civil rights (see Clendinen and Nagourney 1999, chap. 33). Vaid (1995, chap. 3) explains this double-edged sword: Fighting AIDS transformed the gay community into a player on the national political scene, with its successful lobbying efforts forcing government officials in Congress and the executive branch to deal with openly gay individuals as a group for the first time. However, because these interactions tended to be more narrowly focused on AIDS, rather than on gay rights, the effect of their activism in achieving broader equality aims was blunted. But at the same time, there is no doubt that fighting AIDS also energized the gay liberation movement and led to increased activism in fighting for antidiscrimination laws at all levels of government: at the state and local level in housing and employment laws and at the federal level in the 1990 Hate Crimes Statistics Act and the 1990 Americans with Disabilities Act (ADA). Moreover, during the 1990s, there was more openness about sexual orientation in the media, in political campaigns, and on the public policy agenda (D'Emilio 2000).

Numerous organizations sprang up to lobby for greater government involvement in fighting the epidemic. The most visible groups, with each emphasizing a different strategy or activity in the fight against AIDS, were the Gay Men's Health Crisis, HRC, and Lambda, the latter specializing in test case litigation against discrimination related to AIDS. A fourth group, the AIDS Coalition to Unleash Power (known as ACT UP), was launched in March 1987 after Larry Kramer had proclaimed to his New York City audience of mostly gay men that as many as two-thirds of them could be dead within five years (Rom 2000; see also Vaid 1995). Noted for its "in-your-face" confrontational style, ACT UP adopted a militancy that made many uncomfortable but achieved results (see Cruikshank 1992; Clendinen and Nagourney 1999; D'Emilio 2000). Lastly, the AIDS Action Council and its offshoot, the National AIDS Network, played crucial roles in obtaining federal support for AIDS-related activities and services (Andriote 2000). Although the debate over whether the government devoted sufficient resources to combating AIDS will undoubtedly continue, these organizations were the heart of the effort to increase funding for AIDS research and education.

The primary vehicle for committing funds to fight AIDS was adding amendments or inserting supplemental funding provisions into pending legislation (Rom 2000). Because of this, government expenditures to fight AIDS increased during the 1980s, but the issue was rarely discussed in Congress. On those occasions when there were attempts to enact explicit AIDS-related legislation, leading opponents of AIDS funding and education programs, such as Helms, threatened to block or encumber them.

It was not until 1990 that the first major piece of federal AIDS legislation was finally enacted with the passage of the 1990 Ryan White Comprehensive AIDS Resources Emergency (CARE) Act as P.L. No. 101-381. The law represented the first instance in which Congress created a federal program to appropriate money for a single disease (Rom 2000, 235).

The act was named after the teenager who died a few months before the bill was passed in August 1990. He first became known to the public when he contracted the disease at thirteen and was barred from his junior high school; he eventually won the right to attend.[32] Naming the bill after young Ryan was intended to assuage conservatives who feared that supporting an AIDS-related bill would label them pro-gay; they wanted the law associated with a boy who died from a tainted blood transfusion. Thus, the first explicit AIDS bill came at the cost of "de-gaying" or "mainstreaming" the disease, offending some members of the gay community who objected to this strategy (Andriote 2000, 413).[33]

The Ryan White Care bill, amending the Public Health Service Act, arose in the Senate Labor and Human Resources Committee. In April 1990, the committee unanimously approved a bill authorizing $300 million for fiscal 1991 and 1992 and "necessary" amounts for fiscal 1993–1995 to assist areas with more than 2,000 cases of AIDS. Among other things, the funds could be used for hospital care and clinics, as well as outpatient services in these hard-hit areas; another $300 million was authorized to provide grants to states to provide care for those with HIV. Thirteen cities would be eligible for emergency grants under this measure. By February 1990, the AIDS epidemic had reached mammoth numbers in these cities: almost 75,000 cases since 1981, representing 61 percent of the total number of cases (*Congressional Quarterly Weekly* April 7, 1990, 1079).

When the bill reached the floor, Helms repeatedly reminded the Senate about the connection between AIDS and homosexuality. He emphasized that young Ryan was an innocent victim of the disease, distinguishable from the other AIDS sufferers, and he accused the "AIDS lobby and its allies in the media and in the political arena" of covering up the fact that "Ryan White would never have contracted AIDS had it not been for the perverted conduct of people who are demanding respectability" (*Congressional Record* 1990, S6127). Helms insisted there were really only two causes of the disease, which he characterized as a "behavioral epidemic"—"homosexuals and IV drug users"—and if they "would stop their abnormal practices," there would be no new AIDS cases (*Congressional Record* 1990, S6128). He repeatedly stressed the need to attribute blame to those who were responsible for transmitting the disease to innocents such as Ryan, urging that "it was about time the Senate addressed the moral issue." He was the only one, he stressed to his colleagues, who wanted to deal with "who caused it [the epidemic] from the very beginning" (*Congressional Record* 1990, S6128).

During House debate, some raised questions about the confidentiality of the results of AIDS and HIV testing. William Dannemeyer, Republican from California, proposed an amendment that would have required the names and addresses of those testing positive for HIV to be reported to state health authorities. One member of the House, Indiana Republican Dan Burton, proposed that all Americans be tested for AIDS—at a cost of $11 billion. More generally, some members of Congress complained that the law would be perceived as providing support for the gay lifestyle.

The final bill was approved in the House on August 3, 1990, and in the Senate a day later.

And despite his objections to the "narrow disease-specific approach" of the law, President George H. W. Bush signed the measure into law on August 18, 1990. With its passage, hundreds of millions of dollars were funneled to provide for a multitude of AIDS-related services, including medical care, food, housing, and prescription drugs.

As approved, the law authorized $875 million in fiscal 1991 (*Congressional Quarterly Weekly* June 16, 1990, 1891–5; August 4, 1990, 2527; August 25, 1990, 2720). Among other things, the law provided grants for emergency relief for metropolitan areas with a high number of AIDS sufferers (Title I); grant funds to states for care of persons with HIV (Title II); funds for early intervention services, including testing, counseling, and referrals (Title III); and funds for research and evaluation programs (Title IV). Five years later, it was reauthorized for another five years—through fiscal 2000.[34] Again, Helms, who had protested that the disease is transmitted by "deliberate, disgusting conduct," was unsuccessful in blocking the measure (*Congressional Quarterly Weekly* July 29, 1995, 2277; May 4, 1996, 1228).

Aside from funding issues, the onset of AIDS raised numerous questions about the confidentiality of treatment, the right to privacy, and the permissible limitations on people affected with the disease in employment and educational settings; another crucial question was the extent to which insurance companies were required to extend coverage to people with AIDS or HIV (see Cruikshank 1992, chap. 7).[35] Despite its success in achieving passage of the Ryan White Act, the gay community was aware that the bill was well received in part because of the natural sympathy for the child and because his illness was caused not by a "gay lifestyle" but by the unfortunate circumstance of a tainted blood supply. The nation's outpouring of grief for the tragedy of Ryan's death was not matched by its attitude toward other AIDS sufferers. According to a media report, about one-third of Americans supported tattooing HIV-positive individuals, and one-fifth expressed no sympathy for people who contracted AIDS through homosexual conduct or use of drugs (*U.S. News and World Report* April 16, 1990, 8).

Another significant event in the battle against AIDS-related discrimination was Congress's refusal to exempt persons with AIDS or HIV from the reach of the ADA. Passage of the ADA illustrates the intersection of medicine and politics involved in the AIDS epidemic.[36] During the debate over the ADA, most of the discussion in the House of Representatives revolved around whether alcoholism, drug addiction, and homosexuality should be classified as disabilities—none were (Mezey 2005; Craig 1999). Dannemeyer proposed several amendments barring coverage of homosexuals regarded as having AIDS or HIV, excluding communicable diseases from the reach of the act and specifying that the law does not create rights based on sexual orientation. He said the latter was intended to avoid having the ADA "turned into a homosexual bill of rights" (*Congressional Quarterly* May 5, 1990, 1335). These amendments were defeated.

One of the most hotly contested issues in the House was an amendment proposed by Representative Jim Chapman, Democrat from Texas, that would have permitted a food service facility "to refuse to assign an employee with an infectious or communicable disease of public health significance to a job involving food handling" (*Congressional Record* 1990, S7437). After much debate, on May 22, 1990, the amendment narrowly passed the House in a vote of 199 to 187 (*New York Times* May 23, 1990).

The House approved the final bill in a 403–20 vote.

On May 24, the House requested a conference, and the Speaker appointed twenty-two conferees to represent the House side. When the Senate met on June 6, Helms sought to have the Senate conferees include the language of the Chapman amendment in the final version of the bill, replacing a Senate version that offered broader protection to food service workers with AIDS or HIV. Admitting there was no evidence that AIDS or HIV was transmittable though food or casual contact, Helms nevertheless termed this a key vote in support of small businesses because of the consequences of the public's perception of the health risk of such workers. "You can call it hysteria all you want to," Helms said, "but you better believe that the vast majority of people who eat in restaurants do not want to have their food prepared or handled by people who have AIDS or who are HIV positive" (*Congressional Record* 1990, S7437).

Arguing against the motion to instruct, Tom Harkin, Democrat from Iowa, pointed out that the Senate-passed measure already removed "an individual with a currently contagious disease" who poses "a direct threat to the health or safety of other individuals" from the protection of the law (*Congressional Record* 1990, S7437). The Chapman amendment proposed to strike "the words 'poses a direct threat to others'" from the act, allowing a worker with a communicable disease that was not transmittable through food or other casual contact, such as AIDS, to be excluded from the ADA's protection. Harkin cited medical evidence indicating "that there is not one case of AIDS or HIV ever coming from food handling or from airborne substances." Accepting this amendment, he warned, would undermine the integrity of the law, allowing employers to act "on ignorance, based upon fear, based upon mythology" (*Congressional Record* 1990, S7438).

In remarks made to the business leadership on March 29, 1990, Bush also spoke out against the amendment (*Congressional Record* 1990, S7442), saying "our goal is to turn irrational fear into rational acts." Amid procedural wrangling, the Senate adopted, in a voice vote, Helms's motion to instruct the conferees.

There were countervailing pressures at work during the Senate-House conference over the bill. Although a majority of both houses favored the Chapman amendment, representatives of the disability community announced that they would withdraw their support for the law if it were included. With pressure from the disability community, the majority of conferees from each house voted against it.

A second trip to conference provided Helms another opportunity to have the conferees accept the Chapman amendment. This attempt failed, and another attempt by Dannemeyer to recommit the bill to conference for a third time to restore the amendment language also failed to secure a majority (*Congressional Quarterly Weekly* July 14, 1990, 2227–8).

The 1980s and 1990s were a time of upheaval for the gay community. Marked by the terrible onslaught of the AIDS epidemic and an accompanying rise of gay-bashing, these years also witnessed greater mobilization of gay rights activists, ironically, in part as a response to AIDS. Despite the setbacks, gay rights advocates succeeded in getting laws enacted in numerous municipalities and suburban areas and, although at a much slower pace, even managed to achieve the passage of about a dozen statewide laws (Button, Rienzo, and Wald 2000).

A NEW ERA FOR GAY RIGHTS

The end of the Reagan-Bush years and Clinton's election in 1992 led to a more supportive atmosphere as gay rights candidates and issues were more openly accepted, and gay political appointees became more commonplace. And even though Clinton disappointed many with his retreat on ending discrimination against gays in the military, the White House proclaimed itself on the side of equality in a number of ways. Additionally, it seemed as if more of the American people were willing to declare their opposition to discrimination. By the end of the decade, according to the results of a Harris Interactive (1998) poll conducted in July 1998, about half of American adults (52 percent) responded that they "favor laws that make it illegal to discriminate against gays and lesbians"; 41 percent of the respondents were opposed.

The election of George W. Bush in 2000 made it clear that the White House was no longer interested in appealing for the support of the gay community. Indeed, the Bush administration paid little attention to gay rights during its first three years in office, in part because the events of September 11, 2001, and the Iraq war riveted the nation's attention. The issue of same-sex marriage, first arising in 1996, resurfaced at the end of Bush's first term in office and continued through the second, in addition to occupying a great deal of attention during the 2004 election; it gave the president an opportunity to mobilize support for his party by engaging in battle with the gay community, providing ammunition for a new antigay backlash.

Notes

1. In many of the American colonies, homosexuality was punishable by death (Fotopoulos 1994, 619).

2. Kinsey reported that "37 percent of white adult males had had at least one homosexual encounter" (Murdoch and Price 2001, 35–6).

3. "Sexual McCarthyism" also affected private-sector employment. Police and postal authorities conducted raids at the homes of known or suspected homosexuals, looking for illegal pornography. In traditional McCarthy style, in at least one notorious case, the subjects of the raids were charged and convinced to produce the names of other homosexuals (*New York Times* February 20, 2006).

4. Marion Lewis (1990, 143) notes that there were fifty "significant" espionage prosecutions since World War II; gays were implicated in only two, neither of which involved blackmail.

5. Hay preferred the term *homophile* to homosexual because of the negative image and "baggage" associated with the latter (Cain 2000, 54).

6. D'Emilio (1992, chap. 2) notes that the Mattachine Society's consciousness-raising efforts were similar to those of the women's liberation movement in the 1960s.

7. In February 2004, the two founders of the Daughters of Bilitis, in their eighties at the time, were one of the first lesbian couples married in San Francisco (Gartner 2004, 1).

8. For over a decade, the Court was unable to agree upon a definition of obscenity, and most rulings were plurality decisions based on ad hoc decision making, with the justices split on the reasoning.

9. According to D'Emilio (1992, 34–35), *One* was intended to be "a real magazine." The name and masthead slogan were drawn from the following quote by Thomas Carlyle: "A mystic bond of brotherhood makes all men one."

10. At issue was 18 U.S.C. §1461, which provides that "every obscene, lewd, lascivious, indecent, filthy or vile article, matter, thing, device or substance . . . is declared to be non-mailable matter and shall not be conveyed in the mails or delivered from any post office or by any letter carrier."

11. The government's efforts to suppress *One* was part of its campaign against homosexuals and communists, often viewed interchangeably as perverts and traitors, during the 1950s (Murdoch and Price 2001, 34–5).

12. The three-judge circuit court panels frequently include a district court judge "sitting by designation."

13. The Court's opinion in *Oleson* (1958) simply stated, "The petition for writ of certiorari is granted and the judgment of the United States Court of Appeals for the Ninth Circuit is reversed. *Roth v. United States* (citation omitted)."

14. The elements of "patent offensiveness" and "appeal to prurient interest" were necessary for a finding of obscenity under 18 U.S.C. §1461.

15. The Court later criticized this formulation in departing from *Roth* by requiring the prosecutor to prove the worthlessness of the material instead of presuming, as the Court had in *Roth*, that obscenity was "utterly without redeeming social importance" (*Miller* 1973, 21–2).

16. In addition to *Eros*, the material included *Liaison*, a biweekly newsletter, and a book entitled *The Housewife's Handbook on Selective Promiscuity* (*Ginzburg* 1966, 466).

17. Section 1141 of the New York State Penal Code made it a misdemeanor to have in one's "possession . . . any obscene, lewd, lascivious, filthy, indecent, sadistic, masochistic or disgusting book."

18. More recently, despite increasing First Amendment protection, the Supreme Court rejected a First Amendment challenge by an adult bookstore that sought to reverse a New York State district attorney's decision to close it for a year when the police found homosexual activity taking place on the premises (*Arcara v. Cloud Books, Inc.* 1986).

19. The *Miller* Court revised the formula for finding material obscene. It announced that "the basic guidelines for the trier of fact must be: (a) whether the 'average person, applying contemporary community standards' would find that the work, taken as a whole, appeals to the prurient interest . . . ; (b) whether the work depicts or describes, in a patently offensive way, sexual conduct specifically defined by the applicable state law; and (c) whether the work, taken as a whole, lacks serious literary, artistic, political, or scientific value" (24).

20. The story of Kameny's arrest and dismissal, as well as his futile efforts to seek reinstatement, is told in Murdoch and Price (2001, chap. 2).

21. The Society for Individual Rights was founded by gay activist Jim Foster, a San Franciscan who was discharged from the military in the 1950s for being gay.

Foster's efforts on behalf of George McGovern, Democratic candidate for president in 1972, were largely responsible for his appointment as one of the two openly gay delegates to the 1972 Democratic Convention (Vaid 1995, 109–10).

22. See Rimmerman (2002, chap. 2) for a discussion of the aims and strategies of the major national gay rights organizations.

23. Some members of the gay community credit the events at Stonewall with the decision to acknowledge their sexual orientation, that is, to "come out" (*San Francisco Chronicle* June 27, 1994).

24. One of the best accounts of the events of June and July 1969 is in Duberman (1993).

25. Because sodomy was illegal, those arrested were typically charged with the intent to commit a crime (*The Independent* [London] June 23, 1994).

26. Subsequent Marches on Washington were held in October 1987 and April 1993.

27. In a number of states, largely in the West, policy issues are placed on the ballot for voters' approval with a requisite number of signatures. Although this form of direct democracy was begun as a reform measure, more recently, it often provides an opportunity for a backlash against minority rights to assert itself (Donovan, Wenzel, and Bowler 2000).

28. According to Culhane and Sobel (2005), Florida's current ban on adoption by same-sex couples stems from the antigay backlash that fueled Bryant's campaign against the Dade County ordinance in 1977.

29. Another antidiscrimination ordinance, enacted in 1998, was subjected to the same campaign as Bryant's. This time the repeal effort lost in a 53–47 percent vote (*Miami Herald* September 12, 2002; September 11, 2002).

30. Partially as a result of the negative publicity she received in her drive to repeal similar ordinances around the nation, Bryant lost her endorsement deals and lucrative contract with the Florida Citrus Commission to advertise Florida orange juice (*Washington Post* May 12, 1996; *New York Times* December 2, 1998).

31. In the tradition of California politics, after his unsuccessful attempt to pass a bill in the state legislature, Briggs sought to achieve his result through the initiative process.

The Briggs Initiative would have allowed the removal of "any employee 'for advocating, soliciting, imposing, encouraging or promoting . . . private or public homosexual activity directed at, or likely to come to the attention of, schoolchildren and/or other employees'" (Vaid 1995, 113). After a vigorous public relations campaign, it was defeated in the November 1978 election in 58–42 percent vote (Adam 1995, 113).

32. See Bodine (1986) for discussion of suits based on the Education of All Handicapped Children Act to fight the exclusion of children with AIDS from schools.

33. The relationship between AIDS and gay male sex is complex (see Vaid 1995, chap. 3).

34. Some criticize the AIDS activists for their failure to seek reform of the health care system more widely; such critics charge that the AIDS activists are most concerned with improving care for middle-class people, maintaining the flow of funding to that group rather than the poor through the Medicaid system (see Andriote 2000).

35. Plaintiffs with AIDS or HIV brought claims against insurance companies under Title III of the ADA, challenging benefit restrictions imposed by the company. Most courts have held, however, that insurers are not forbidden from discriminating in the content of policies, rejecting plaintiffs' arguments that Congress intended to foreclose disability-based distinctions and benefit caps, absent actuarial data to justify them. In the Seventh Circuit decision of *Doe v. Mutual of Omaha* (1999, 558), the court upheld the insurer's right to limit benefits for policyholders with AIDS even though the company was unable to show it was "consistent with sound actuarial principles, actual or reasonably anticipated experience, bona fide risk classification, or state law."

36. *Henrietta D. v. Giuliani* (2000), a class action suit against the City of New York, raised the question of how support for AIDS victims intersected with the ADA. The plaintiffs were indigent city residents with AIDS or HIV who charged that the city—specifically, the Division of AIDS Services and Income Support (DASIS)—had failed to enable them to access public benefits, thereby violating the ADA as well as numerous state and federal laws. Recognizing the myriad physical, mental, and emotional problems confronting people with AIDS and HIV, DASIS had been established to assist such individuals in receiving government benefits, including Medicaid, food stamps, and Social Security, as well as such services as emergency shelters, transportation, and food assistance. In addition to charging the agency with assisting its clientele in negotiating through an often opaque bureaucratic structure, the law under which DASIS was created included intensive case management, expedited review of applications, and lower ratios of case managers to clients.

In September 2000, following a bench trial, district court judge Johnson found the city guilty of violating Title II of the ADA in addition to other statutory and constitutional provisions and ordered injunctive relief. He noted that the assistance provided by DASIS was merely an accommodation to allow people with disabilities meaningful access to existing services and benefits. The judge rejected the city's argument that the plaintiffs were seeking extra benefits and services not required by the ADA. "To the contrary," said the court, they "seek meaningful access [only] to the very same benefits and services . . . and only the modifications—such as intensive case management and low case manager-to-client ratios—required to ensure meaningful access to the same benefits and services" (212). The court added that without these modifications, people with disabilities would be unable to achieve the equality of services that the ADA required the city to provide. After much procedural wrangling over the next several years, the Second Circuit upheld the lower court in *Henrietta D. v. Bloomberg* (2003).

CHAPTER 2

Litigating Equality and Privacy Rights

DURING the 1970s and 1980s, as gay rights advocates began to develop a more sophisticated litigation strategy, the United States Supreme Court was forced to confront many of the issues raised in gay rights claims. But although the plaintiffs in these cases differed from the earlier civil rights litigants, their claims were based on the familiar right to privacy, due process, and equal protection as well as gender discrimination (see Koppelman 2002a).[1] Additionally, gay rights litigants sought constitutional protection under the First Amendment's guarantee of free expression.[2]

CRIMINALIZING SEXUAL CONDUCT

In one of the first cases in which it was forced to confront a gay rights claim, the Court demonstrated its discomfort with homosexuality. The case arose from an Immigration and Naturalization Service (INS) decision to deport Clive Michael Boutilier, a Canadian immigrant, under a provision of the Immigration and Nationality Act of 1952 that labeled homosexuals as "afflicted with a 'psychopathic personality' " who may be excluded or deported from the United States (*Boutilier v. Immigration and Naturalization Service* 1966, 490).[3]

When he applied for U.S. citizenship in 1963, Boutilier submitted affidavits admitting he had homosexual relations prior to his entry into the country and, since 1959, had been living and having sexual relations with a man. Based on this information, a physician for the Public Health Service found that he "was afflicted with a class A condition, namely, psychopathic personality, sexual deviate, at the time of his admission to the United States for permanent residence," and the INS ordered him to be deported (491).

With one judge dissenting, the three-judge panel of the Second Circuit dismissed Boutilier's petition to reverse the deportation order.[4] Judge Kaufman found that the term *psychopathic personality* was not unconstitutionally vague and that Congress had intended to include homosexuality within it. The court held that Boutilier's sworn statement of his homosexual activities in Canada sufficiently demonstrated his existing personality defect when he entered the United States to justify the deportation.

The Supreme Court affirmed the appellate court in a 6–3 ruling, with Clark delivering the opinion for the majority. Reviewing the legislative history of the law, he stressed that Congress did not intend it to have a strictly clinical meaning; the original language of the bill had referred to barring aliens who were "homosexuals and other sex perverts" from the country. The Senate report accompanying the bill had explained that this language was eliminated because the Public Health Service advised that the term *psychopathic personality* included "homosexuals and sex perverts." Quoting from the committee report, Clark emphasized its warning that *"this change of nomenclature is not to be construed in any way as modifying the intent to exclude all aliens who are sexual deviates"* (*Boutilier* 1967, 121, emphasis in the original).

Douglas's dissent argued that the term *psychopathic personality*, like *communist* or *Bolshevik*, refers only to "an unpopular person" and is "much too vague" to serve as a basis for punishment (125). He quoted extensively from psychological experts to show the range of meaning in the term *psychopathic personality*, insisting that it was particularly inappropriate to apply it to sexual conduct. And because of these uncertainties, he argued, it violates due process to apply it to an individual who engages in homosexual conduct. Based on his interpretation of the legislative history, he disputed the majority's view that Congress had intended the statute to be broadly applied. Rather, he said, Congress "meant to refer to lifelong patterns of action that are pathologic and symptomatic of grave underlying neurosis or psychosis" (135).

The modern era of Supreme Court decision making in gay rights cases began with the Court's review of sodomy laws (see Cain 1993). After the high court formalized a right to privacy in *Griswold v. Connecticut* (1965), it was inevitable that it would be asked to rule on the constitutionality of laws criminalizing certain sexual conduct for, as late as 1968, every state but Illinois punished acts of sodomy.[5]

Andersen (1998) notes that such laws, most applying to consenting adults, with many covering heterosexual conduct as well, were rarely prosecuted.[6]

Regardless of the lack of enforcement, however, she argues, such laws critically affected members of the gay community because "they served as the cornerstone for criminalizing homosexuality and legitimating discrimination against lesbian, gay, and bisexual people" (288). Indeed, state sodomy laws were considered by some as a "cause of the second-class citizenship inflicted upon gay and lesbian Americans" (Leslie 2005, 189). Koppelman (1988, 145–6) adds, "Perhaps equally significant is the insult that the statutes imposed." Moreover, because sodomy arrests had a domino effect on litigation in other areas of law such as employment and housing discrimination and family law (especially in child custody and adoption cases), advocates realized that without sodomy laws, it would be easier to win lawsuits brought to vindicate other rights (see Cain 2000).

Not surprisingly, following *Griswold*, the gay rights community focused on challenging sodomy laws as unconstitutional violations of their right to privacy (see Kimball 1996). One of the first federal court cases, *Doe v. Commonwealth's Attorney for Richmond* (1975), arose when two gay men challenged a Virginia law referring to sodomy as a "crime against nature." Although they were not arrested or threatened with prosecution, they sought a declaratory judgment that the law violated their rights under the First, Fifth, Eighth, Ninth, and Fourteenth Amendments by intruding on the "privacy of the incidents of marriage, upon the sanctity of the home, or upon the nurture of family life" (1200).

In a 2–1 vote, a three-judge district court ruled against them, distinguishing *Griswold* because it was based on marital privacy.[7] The opinion by Judge Bryan cited Justice Arthur Goldberg's concurrence in *Griswold* in which he referred to homosexual activity as an example of conduct that may be forbidden by the state. Goldberg had based his opinion on Harlan's dissent in *Poe v. Ullman* (1961, 553), in which Harlan characterized homosexuality as an activity "which the law has always forbidden and which can have no claim to social protection." Harlan had likened it to adultery, fornication, and incest, saying none were protected merely because they took place in private.

Tracing the Virginia law back to 1792 and citing biblical text for support, the district court held that the state may criminalize private as well as public homosexual conduct to preserve "morality and decency." And, it continued, such a law may merely rest upon a belief that the behavior may lead to "moral delinquency" (*Commonwealth's Attorney* 1975, 1202). Without hearing oral argument, the Supreme Court summarily affirmed the lower court ruling (*Commonwealth's Attorney* 1976).[8]

Although summary affirmances are binding on lower courts, their precedential value is not equivalent to opinions on the merits (*American Jurisprudence* 2d 2005, §170). The ambiguity of the Court's summary affirmance in *Commonwealths' Attorney* (1976) left the lower courts divided on the constitutionality of sodomy laws. The New York State Court of Appeals (the state supreme court) held in *New York v. Onofre* (1980) that the state cannot constitutionally punish private sexual conduct between consenting adults.[9] A few years later, in *New York v. Uplinger* (1983a), the same court dismissed a charge against a defendant who was convicted of "loitering 'in a public place for the purpose of engaging, or soliciting another person to engage, in deviate sexual intercourse'" (62). It held that the statute was a "companion" to the sodomy law declared unconstitutional in *Onofre*, and because the underlying conduct was not illegal, the loitering charge must be dismissed.

The United States Supreme Court granted certiorari in *Uplinger* (1983b), but after a full briefing and oral argument, it dismissed the writ as "improvidently granted" (*Uplinger* 1984). The high court explained that because the lower court opinion "is fairly subject to varying interpretations," there was doubt "as to the precise federal constitutional issue the court decided"; therefore, the "case provides an inappropriate vehicle for resolving the important constitutional issues raised by the parties" (*Uplinger* 1984, 248–9). Thus, by declining to rule in *Uplinger*, the high court again passed up the opportunity to address the constitutionality of state sodomy laws and resolve the conflict among the lower courts.

Similarly, in *Pennsylvania v. Bonadio* (1980), without mentioning *Commonwealth's Attorney* (1976), the Pennsylvania Supreme Court held that the "Voluntary Deviate Sexual Intercourse Statute" exceeded the state's police power and violated the defendants' rights to equal protection (48). And in *Baker v. Wade* (1982), Texas district court judge Buchmeyer held that a Texas statute criminalizing "deviate sexual intercourse with another individual of the same sex" violated the plaintiffs' rights to privacy and equal protection under the state and federal constitutions (1124). The Fifth Circuit, sitting en banc, reversed the lower court and upheld the Texas law (*Baker* 1985), reasoning that the United States Supreme Court's summary affirmance in *Commonwealth's Attorney* (1976) controlled its decision, and hence the law was constitutional.[10]

After a decade, the Court finally returned to the issue it had left open in *Commonwealth's Attorney* (1976) by ruling on the constitutionality of a sodomy law in *Bowers v. Hardwick* (1986).

Bowers unceremoniously began on August 3, 1982, when a police officer appeared at Michael Hardwick's home to serve a warrant for failing to appear in court to answer a charge of drinking in public, specifically, for carrying an open bottle of beer.[11] In response to the officer's knock, a guest opened the door. When the officer went to look for Hardwick, he found him in the bedroom engaged in oral sex with another man and arrested him on a felony charge of violating the 1816 Georgia sodomy law, a offense applying to heterosexual conduct as well, that was punishable up to twenty years in prison.[12]

After a municipal court hearing, Hardwick was bound over for trial in superior court and released on bond. However, when the county prosecutor declined to put the case before the grand jury, attorneys of the Georgia affiliate of the ACLU persuaded Hardwick to challenge the law in federal court.[13] His complaint stated that he was a "practicing homosexual" who was in imminent danger of arrest under the statute (Irons 1990, chap. 16; see Bruce 1996). Adding a married couple, the Does, as plaintiffs, they sought a declaratory judgment that the law was unconstitutional.

The lower court dismissed the complaint, ruling that the Does had no standing and, citing the Supreme Court's summary affirmance in *Commonwealth's Attorney* (1976), held that Hardwick had no legal claim.[14]

On appeal, the Eleventh Circuit panel affirmed that the Does lacked standing, but it reversed the lower court's dismissal of Hardwick's complaint (*Hardwick v. Bowers* 1985). Speaking for the court, Judge Johnson devoted most of the decision to discussing how the Supreme Court's affirmance in *Commonwealth's Attorney* (1976) affected the constitutionality of consensual sodomy laws. He explained that although a summary affirmance has precedential value, it does not indicate that the Supreme Court agrees with the reasoning of the lower court. Because the plaintiffs in the Virginia case had not been arrested (or even threatened with arrest), they clearly lacked standing to bring the case, and the high court could have merely affirmed the lower court's ruling on those grounds.

As the Court had explained in *Hicks v. Miranda* (1975), summary affirmances or dismissals are binding on future courts only if the issues in the two cases are sufficiently related and no later cases have undermined the precedential value of the affirmance (Fuller 1985). In addressing the question whether doctrinal developments after *Commonwealth's Attorney* (1976) attenuated the precedential value of the high court's summary affirmance, the Eleventh Circuit pointed to a footnote in *Carey v. Population Services International* (1977), a case involving limitations on the sale of nonprescription contraceptives to adults by other than licensed pharmacists. In that footnote, the *Carey* majority had stressed that it was not answering "the difficult question whether and to what extent the Constitution prohibits state statutes regulating [private consensual sexual] behavior among adults" (*Hardwick v. Bowers* 1985, 1209, quoting *Carey* 1977, 689 n5). The circuit court also noted that the Supreme Court's dismissal of the writ of certiorari in *Uplinger* indicated that it considered the constitutionality of sodomy laws an open question that it would rule on in the appropriate case.

Based on these principles, the Eleventh Circuit concluded that the Georgia law infringed on Hardwick's fundamental right to privacy under the Ninth and Fourteenth Amendments. "The activity he hopes to engage in," the court held, "is quintessentially private and lies at the heart of an intimate association beyond the proper reach of state regulation" (*Hardwick v. Bowers* 1985, 1212). Citing the long line of cases affirming the right to privacy, the court remanded the case, holding that because a fundamental right was implicated, the law must be reviewed under strict scrutiny, and the state must present a compelling reason to justify it.

The state appealed and, with the Does no longer in the case, the only issue before the Supreme Court was the constitutionality of the Georgia law as it applied to acts of "consensual homosexual sodomy" (*Bowers v. Hardwick* 1986, 188).[15]

Speaking for a 5–4 majority including Chief Justice Warren Burger and Justices Lewis Powell, William Rehnquist, and Sandra Day O'Connor, White announced the opinion of the Court. He began by stating that the issue presented was "whether the Federal Constitution confers a fundamental right upon homosexuals to engage in sodomy and hence invalidates the laws of the many States that still make such conduct illegal and have done so for a very long time" (190). Presenting the issue in these terms signaled the outcome of the case, for although the law did not single out homosexual sodomy, the Court focused on its application to same-sex conduct, rather than treating the case as a facial challenge to a gender-neutral law. Had it done so, it would have been forced to evaluate whether the state was justified in invading the privacy rights of all persons, including married couples (see Halley 1993).

The Court did not rule on whether the statute would be constitutional if it were applied to heterosexual sodomy. Moreover, White emphasized that the case was not about the wisdom of the Georgia law in outlawing sodomy, nor, he said, did it address decisions by state courts to strike such laws on state constitutional grounds. The only question here, he stressed, was the extent to which a law such as Georgia's conflicted with the fundamental right to privacy guaranteed in the United States Constitution. After reviewing the long line of privacy cases preceding and following *Griswold*, White declared that the right to privacy had been extended only to certain types of activities, broadly grouping them under the rubric of family relationships, procreation, and marriage.[16] And because these spheres of human interaction are distinguishable from homosexual sodomy, he concluded that these prior cases cannot be interpreted as "confer[ring] a fundamental right upon homosexuals to engage in sodomy" (*Bowers v. Hardwick* 1986, 190).

After rejecting precedent as a source of Hardwick's right of privacy, White assessed the substantive protection offered by the due process clause.[17] Rejecting the lower court's analysis that the due process clause of the Fourteenth Amendment guaranteed a fundamental right to engage in homosexual sodomy, he warned that the Court must be cautious about expanding the substantive reach of the due process clause. Seeking to avoid the accusation that the Court imparts its own values into the Constitution, he said it must be exceedingly cautious in declaring a right fundamental and should do so only if the right is "deeply rooted in this Nation's history and tradition" or "implicit in the concept of ordered liberty" (192).[18]

To demonstrate that homosexual sodomy does not fit within either of these two formulations, White detailed the history of state sodomy laws from 1791 to the present.[19] "Against this background," he asserted, "to claim that a right to engage in such conduct is 'deeply rooted in the Nation's history and tradition' or 'implicit in the concept of ordered liberty' is, at best, facetious" (194).[20]

Hardwick also argued that he was entitled to constitutional protection under the Fourth Amendment, citing *Stanley v. Georgia* (1969), a case allowing the private possession of obscene material in the home. White, however, distinguished *Stanley*, noting that it was decided entirely on the freedom of speech clause of the First Amendment, not on the right to privacy. Illegal behavior, he continued, does not become legal merely because it takes place in the home. If it did, courts would have difficulty in drawing lines between the act of consensual homosexual sodomy and acts of incest and adultery.

Finally, White addressed Hardwick's contention that even if the right to privacy is not implicated, the statute must be struck because it lacks a rational basis, stemming from the "presumed belief of a majority of the electorate in Georgia that homosexual sodomy is immoral and unacceptable" (*Bowers v. Hardwick* 1986, 196). Not at all, White said; states are within their authority to enact laws encapsulating citizens' views of morality.

Burger concurred with the majority, writing to emphasize his opinion of the offensive nature of homosexual sodomy. Citing "Judeao[sic]-Christian moral and ethical standards," and quoting from Blackstone's *Commentaries*, which characterized it an "infamous crime against nature" and "a crime not fit to be named," Burger charged that "to hold that the act of homosexual sodomy is somehow protected as a fundamental right would be to cast aside millennia of moral teaching" (196–7).

Powell's concurring opinion represents the most intriguing aspect of the decision. When the Court had met in conference after hearing oral argument, Powell, a strong supporter of privacy rights, expressed his willingness to vote with Justices Harry Blackmun, John Paul Stevens, Thurgood Marshall, and Brennan to strike the Georgia statute. Powell disliked sodomy laws, saying they were unenforceable and, indeed, were never enforced. But although he seemed reluctant to extend the right to privacy to include homosexual conduct, he was sufficiently concerned about the constitutionality of the law to be willing to join with them to create a majority. Based on the initial vote, Brennan, the senior justice in the majority, assigned the opinion to Blackmun, who seemed prepared to issue a sweeping rejection of sodomy laws, with White writing a dissent (Leonard 2000, 64).

A few days later, however, Powell circulated a memo indicating he would join White and the others to create a 5–4 majority to uphold the law, saying, "I cannot say that conduct condemned for hundreds of years has now become a fundamental right." His concurring opinion suggested that one of the reasons for his shift was that Hardwick had not been prosecuted for the crime, but instead had initiated the action by filing a civil suit against the state (*Washington Post* July 13, 1986). Rejecting Hardwick's fundamental rights claim, he observed that the Georgia law, imposing a possible twenty-year sentence, might well offend the Eighth Amendment's prohibition against cruel and unusual punishment. However, because Hardwick had not been sentenced under the statute and had not raised the Eighth Amendment issue himself, Powell was unwilling to address it.

Powell retired in 1987, and three years later, he reversed himself again. During a question and answer session with students at New York University School of Law on October 18, 1990, he was asked how he reconciled his position in *Bowers* with his support for privacy rights and his vote in *Roe v. Wade* (1973). Referring to *Bowers*, he said, "I think I probably made a mistake in that one." A few days later in an interview, he elaborated, saying, "I do think it was inconsistent in a general way with *Roe* [and] when I had the opportunity to reread the opinions a few months later, I thought the dissent had the better of the arguments" (*National Law Journal* November 5, 1990).[21]

Blackmun's dissent, joined by Brennan, Marshall, and Stevens, sharply criticized the Court for its "almost obsessive focus on homosexual activity" (*Bowers v. Hardwick* 1986, 200). Blackmun argued that Hardwick's sexual orientation was irrelevant because the Georgia law applied to both sexes (although the state showed no inclination to apply it to heterosexuals). Charging that the majority had mischaracterized the case by casting it in terms of "a fundamental right to engage in homosexual sodomy," he insisted that the real issue was whether "individuals [have] the right to decide for themselves whether to engage in particular forms of private, consensual sexual activity" (199).

Blackmun concentrated on the fundamental rights claim, reprising many of the themes from the Court's rulings in the abortion cases.[22] He criticized the Court "for refus[ing] to recognize . . . the fundamental interest all individuals have in controlling the nature of their intimate associations with others" (206). This refusal was even more distressing, he pointed out, because the behavior in question took place in the home, a space accorded special protection under the Fourth Amendment.

Blackmun also charged that the majority accepted the state's justifications for the law too readily: first, by equating incest and adultery with private consensual behavior between adults; and second, by relying on a centuries-old view of morality and religious beliefs, specifically referring to Burger's invocation of Judeo-Christian values. He concluded by expressing the hope that "the Court soon will reconsider its analysis and conclude that depriving individuals of the right to choose for themselves how to conduct their intimate relationships poses a far greater threat to the values most deeply rooted in our Nation's history than tolerance of nonconformity could ever do" (214).

Stevens's dissent, joined by Brennan and Marshall, made two essential points. First, he argued that a state cannot simply rationalize a law by claiming it offends a traditional view of morality.[23] Second, he noted that the statute as written, applying to both heterosexual and homosexual conduct, is unconstitutional because it invades the privacy of married couples. Moreover, he said, the selective application of the statute to homosexuals raises additional questions about an equal protection violation.

Despite the Court's firm rejection of the challenge to the Georgia law in *Bowers*, gay rights litigants fared better in the state courts of Tennessee, Montana, and Kentucky, which struck sodomy laws on state constitutional grounds (Andersen 1998). Ironically, in *Powell v. Georgia* (1998), the

Georgia Supreme Court struck the state sodomy law as it applied to "a non-commercial sexual act that occurs without force in a private home between persons legally capable of consenting to the act" (23–4). The court ruled that the law conflicted with the "right to be let alone," an integral component of the right to privacy in the Georgia constitution (22). In judging whether there was a compelling state interest justifying the infringement on the right to privacy, the court found that "the sodomy statute's raison d'etre can only be to regulate the private sexual conduct of consenting adults, something which Georgians' right of privacy puts beyond the bounds of government regulation" (24–5).

At the time, *Bowers* was rightly perceived as disastrous; it was a devastating blow to the gay community because it reinforced the stigma of arrests for violation of sodomy laws.

Gay rights advocates likened it to the *Dred Scott* (1856) case, the infamous decision denying citizenship to black Americans (Duong 2003/2004, 564). Moreover, despite the Supreme Court's insistence that it was expressing no view on the wisdom of the state's sodomy law, the majority's condemnation of homosexuality in *Bowers* was manifest.

GAY RIGHTS AND EQUAL PROTECTION

Bowers had a far-reaching effect on gay rights litigation for almost two decades. And with the right to privacy essentially declared out of bound for gays, litigants challenged discriminatory laws largely on equal protection grounds.[24] Their initial task in such cases was to convince the courts to treat discrimination on the basis of sexual orientation as they do laws discriminating on the basis of race or sex, that is, to apply a heightened scrutiny, or at least to persuade them that such laws arise from irrational bias and stereotypical views of gays.

Many scholars have addressed the often-mystical role of scrutiny in equal protection cases; the difficulty of understanding it is made more acute because of the Court's long-standing record of applying it inconsistently and often without satisfactory explanation. The level (or rigor) of scrutiny used by the courts when adjudicating the constitutionality of a statute under equal protection analysis depends upon their view of the class of people affected by the law (see table 2.1 in note 25 for levels of scrutiny in equal protection cases).[25]

The Supreme Court initially formulated a two-tier level of scrutiny for determining the constitutionality of laws challenged on equal protection grounds. In cases involving a suspect classification (such as race) or a fundamental right (such as privacy), the Court applies strict scrutiny, with the burden of proof on the state to show a compelling interest in the law and demonstrate that the means are necessarily related to the ends sought to be achieved and are narrowly tailored to those ends. The standards for suspect class status include having a history of discrimination, possessing the immutable (innate) characteristics of a distinct group, and political powerlessness; racial minorities are considered the prototypical suspect class. Alternatively, in due process analysis, the Court applies strict scrutiny to laws infringing on a fundamental right, such as the right of privacy, interstate travel, voting, and equal access to the courts.

Under the Court's two-tiered formulation, it applies minimal scrutiny to laws affecting nonsuspect classes and merely asks whether there is a legitimate reason for the law and whether the classification is rationally related to the goal sought to be achieved. However, even when applying minimal scrutiny, the Court examines the purpose and effect of the law more carefully if it appears to be based on dislike of, or a desire to harm, a particular group. Some call this higher-level minimal scrutiny "rational basis with bite" or "active rational basis review," but the Court has never formally acknowledged this approach and appears to use it on an ad hoc basis, thus depriving lower courts of a rationale for determining when and how to use it (see Callahan and Kaufman 2004).

In 1976, the Court added intermediate (or heightened) scrutiny in equal protection cases for laws involving sex-based classifications and illegitimacy. To survive a constitutional challenge, a law reviewed under intermediate scrutiny must further an important governmental objective and be substantially related to that objective (Mezey 2003; see Tribe 1988).[26]

The concept of strict scrutiny in equal protection analysis stems in part from footnote 4 in *Carolene Products*, in which Stone suggested the courts must look more closely at laws affecting "discrete and insular minorities" who lack adequate representation in the political branches to seek redress of their grievances. The literature is replete with analyses of the Court's use of strict scrutiny; one of the earliest and perhaps the most famous is Gunther's (1972, 8) oft-quoted characterization of the Warren Court's "aggressive 'new' equal protection, as scrutiny that is 'strict' in theory and fatal in fact."

Determining the appropriate level of scrutiny and the characterization of the class alleging discrimination is more than mere legal gymnastics; it is crucial to the outcome of the case. A statute reviewed under minimal scrutiny almost always receives the Court's approval. Conversely, over the years, a mystique has surrounded the use of strict scrutiny, a mystique that springs up not only from the language and mind-set accompanying the Court's strict scrutiny analysis but also, and perhaps even more important, from a strong presumption against the constitutionality of the law under review. The outcome is more uncertain when the Court applies intermediate scrutiny, primarily in laws involving sex-based classifications.[27]

Gerstmann (2003, 9) accuses the Court of using the terms *suspect class* and *suspect classification* inconsistently in a way that disadvantages gays. On the one hand, it refuses to accord gays the status of a suspect class (and apply strict scrutiny to laws affecting them) on the grounds that they are not politically powerless. However, he maintains, when whites complain that they have been subjected to discrimination as a result of an affirmative action program, the Court applies strict scrutiny because race is a suspect classification.

PARADING GAY PRIDE

Almost a decade after *Bowers*, the Supreme Court decided its next gay rights case, *Hurley v. Irish-American Gay, Lesbian and Bisexual Group of Boston* (1995). The issue in *Hurley* was whether the South Boston Allied War Veterans Council, organizer of the annual South Boston St. Patrick's Day–Evacuation Day Parade, had a First Amendment right to exclude the Irish-American Gay, Lesbian and Bisexual Group of Boston (GLIB) from marching in the parade, notwithstanding the state public accommodations law prohibiting discrimination on the basis of sexual orientation.[28]

GLIB, formed in January 1992, sought to march in the traditional St. Patrick's Day Parade, in part to show its members' dual identity as Irish Americans and gay Americans.[29] Its attempt to register for the parade was rebuffed by the Veterans Council, claiming security concerns and insufficient knowledge of the group.[30] At the preliminary injunction hearing, the council maintained that GLIB's participation would block the expression of "traditional family values" in the parade (Van Ness 1996, 643). GLIB obtained a temporary injunction from Massachusetts Superior Court judge Zobel and marched in the 1992 parade (*Irish-American Gay, Lesbian and Bisexual Group of Boston v. City of Boston* 1992). The next year, following another refusal by the council (this time on the grounds that "sexual themes" were excluded), GLIB sought and obtained another injunction that permitted it to participate in the 1993 parade (*Irish-American Gay, Lesbian and Bisexual Group of Boston v. City of Boston* 1993a).[31]

In the third year, GLIB alleged at trial that the council violated the provision of the state public accommodations law that prohibited discrimination on the basis of sexual orientation. On December 15, 1993, Judge Flannery of the Massachusetts Superior Court issued a permanent injunction against the council, finding that the parade was a public event and therefore a public accommodation within the meaning of the law.[32] Based on the testimony of the council's representative, John Hurley, Flannery held that members of GLIB were being discriminated against on the basis of their sexual orientation.

The judge addressed the council's argument that its rejection of GLIB's application was protected by the First Amendment. But because the parade consisted of a multitude of messages and there was little or no selectivity in deciding which groups were permitted to march and little or no attempt to inquire into or censor their messages, the council did not have a First Amendment right to exclude GLIB. Moreover, he held, even if forcing the council to include GLIB in the parade was a minor invasion of its First Amendment right, it was outweighed by the state's interest in eradicating discrimination on the basis of sexual orientation (*Irish-American Gay, Lesbian and Bisexual Group of Boston v. City of Boston* 1993b).

The council sought direct review from the Supreme Judicial Court (the state supreme court), which ruled for GLIB on March 11, 1994. In response, the council canceled the 1994 and 1995 parades (see Greyerbiehl 1996). In its written opinion delivered on July 11, 1994, by Justice Liacos, the state supreme court affirmed the lower court judge in all respects (*Irish-American Gay, Lesbian and Bisexual Group of Boston v. City of Boston* 1994). The council appealed the Massachusetts high court decision to the Unites States Supreme Court, arguing the injunction was inconsistent with its First Amendment right.[33]

Speaking for a unanimous Court in *Hurley v. Irish-American Gay, Lesbian and Bisexual Group of Boston* (1995), the outcome was clear when Justice David Souter began by characterizing the question presented as whether the council can be forced to include an unwanted message in the parade without violating its First Amendment rights.[34] After recounting the century-old history of the St. Patrick's Day Parade, Souter contemplated the nature of a parade, likening it to a group of private citizens engaged in a protest march and characterizing it as "a form of expression" protected by the First Amendment (568).

Souter's approach to the state public accommodations law differed from the state courts' approach. In his view, the gay, lesbian, and bisexual individuals were not barred from the parade as individuals; rather, the council's opposition to members of GLIB was directed solely at their participation as a marching unit under the GLIB banner, not on the basis of their sexual orientation. In framing the issue this way, Souter had simply overlooked the antigay bias motivating the council, as indicated in the testimony of its representative at trial.

Addressing the First Amendment issue, Souter indicated that forcing the council to include GLIB in the parade would have "the effect of declaring the sponsors' speech itself to be the public accommodation" (573). Although GLIB's message consisted only of its marching banner identifying it as the Irish-American Gay, Lesbian and Bisexual Group of Boston, the Court held that this would conflict with the sponsors' First Amendment right to determine the message they wished to convey and to bar a message they did not wish to convey. The Court found that the Council's willingness to allow a wide-ranging assortment of messages (groups) to participate in the parade did not negate its right to exclude GLIB's message if it believed it would signal the council's acceptance of homosexuality. But whatever the reason, Souter maintained, the decision is wholly within its discretion—without interference from the state.[35] The state's aim of preventing discrimination in public accommodations, he concluded, cannot override the organizers' First Amendment right to determine the content of their message.

Unlike the trial court, the Supreme Court did not rest its decision on the council's right of expressive association but instead based its opinion on its right of speech (see Duncan 1996).[36] Nevertheless, Souter briefly distinguished it from the three cases (*United States Jaycees v. Roberts* 1984, *Board of Directors of Rotary International v. Rotary Club of Duarte* 1987, and *New York State Club Association v. City of New York* 1988) that established the limits of an expressive association defense against antidiscrimination laws. In the three cited cases, the Court upheld public accommodations laws in the face of challenges by men's clubs that excluded women. But, Souter emphasized, in those cases, even though the Court held that the state's interest in preventing discrimination outweighed the organization's First Amendment right of expressive association, it did not require them to admit individuals who disagreed with their message. Unlike the women who sought admission to the men-only clubs, he said, GLIB espoused a message that was contrary to the Veterans Council's message (see Zaleskas 1996).

In focusing on the parties' conflicting messages, the Court minimized the significance of the Massachusetts public accommodations law and gave short shrift to the state's interest in preventing discrimination on the basis of sexual orientation (see Van Ness 1996). *Hurley* represents another example of the Court's failure to equate discrimination against gays with discrimination against other minority groups. Yet despite the outcome in *Hurley*, there was a discernible change in the Court's language compared with its earlier rulings in gay rights cases. There were no references to "pathologies," "deviance," "immorality," or "depravity," and the tone of Souter's opinion was respectful of the gay community. *Hurley* thus "gave a hint of changes in the air" (Leonard 2000, 65); perhaps a new era was dawning. The next year, it appeared that the new era may have arrived with the Supreme Court's decision in *Romer v. Evans* (1996).

"SPECIAL RIGHTS" OR "EQUAL RIGHTS"

By 1993, at least 139 jurisdictions had adopted antidiscrimination policies in various sectors, including education, housing, and employment (Note 1993, 905). Following the lead of other localities, several Colorado municipalities enacted ordinances prohibiting discrimination in housing, employment, education, public accommodations, and health and welfare services. The backlash began in Colorado Springs, the center for Christian right-wing organizations committed to antigay activism. As the staff counsel of the HRC charged, "through careful appropriation of the popular fear of AIDS and the anti-affirmative action sentiment of the late 1980s and early 1990s, these conservative organizations successfully established an environment that was distinctly suspicious of the gay movement as militant, radical, contagious, unhealthy, and essentially unfair" (Alexander 2002, 273).

Spurred by the right-wing Colorado for Family Values, antigay activists denounced the "homosexual agenda" and characterized antidiscrimination laws as "special rights" for gays and succeeded in placing an initiative—Amendment 2—as a proposed constitutional amendment on the November 1992 ballot (Kimball 1996; Alexander 2002).[37] Amendment 2 claimed to deprive persons with a "homosexual, lesbian, or bisexual orientation" of a "special status" in the law, preventing them from bringing claims of discrimination on the basis of sexual orientation, and barring communities from enacting laws to ban discrimination on the basis of sexual orientation.[38]

Richard Evans and eight others, as well as several Colorado municipalities and a Boulder school district, filed suit in state district court, seeking a preliminary injunction against Amendment 2 on the grounds that it conflicted with the United States Constitution. They alleged that it would deprive them of equal protection by denying them the right to participate equally in the political process as well as the freedom under the First Amendment to seek relief for discrimination.

At the hearing, the plaintiffs testified that the amendment would foreclose the passage of new antidiscrimination laws as well as the enforcement of laws already on the books in Aspen, Boulder, and Denver; they also argued it would lend state approval to acts of private discrimination and deprive them of the opportunity to seek relief from the government for such discrimination.

Addressing himself only to the equal protection claim, Judge Bayless said strict scrutiny should be applied because the law burdened the "fundamental rights of an independently identifiable group" (*Evans v. Romer* 1993a, at 9). He identified the fundamental right as "the right not to have the State endorse and give effect to private biases" (at 11).[39] To defeat the plaintiffs' claim at a trial on the merits, he said, the state must provide a compelling reason to enact Amendment 2. And with this heavy burden on the state, he felt it would likely be found unconstitutional.

The defendants appealed to the state supreme court, arguing that the lower court had improperly granted the injunction. And although Bayless had not addressed the plaintiffs' contention that Amendment 2 violated their right to equal protection by denying them the fundamental right of equal participation in the political process, this argument became the basis of the state high court's ruling (*Evans v. Romer* 1993b).

Announcing the opinion for the en banc court, Colorado Supreme Court Justice Rovira devoted most of his ruling to discussing the appropriate level of scrutiny. Citing the line of Fourteenth Amendment cases involving voting rights and participation in the policymaking process, Rovira analogized Amendment 2 to the provision declared unconstitutional by the United States Supreme Court in *Hunter v. Erickson* (1969). In *Hunter*, the high court had held that an Akron, Ohio, charter amendment that required electoral approval for passage of fair housing ordinances was unconstitutional because it specially burdened racial minorities.

Rovira rejected the state's argument that the United States Supreme Court reserved strict scrutiny for laws affecting equality in the political process when they burdened racial minorities or, more generally, politically powerless groups. Extrapolating from the principles articulated in those Fourteenth Amendment cases, the court held that those rulings did not rest solely on race but encompassed all groups lacking political power. "The Equal Protection Clause of the United States Constitution," Rovira said, "protects the fundamental right to participate equally in the political process, and . . . any legislation or state constitutional amendment which infringes on this [fundamental] right by 'fencing out' an independently identifiable class of persons must be subject to strict judicial scrutiny" (*Evans v. Romer* 1993b, 1282).[40]

In deciphering the meaning of Amendment 2, the court noted that although the parties disagreed over its breadth, there was a consensus that it invalidated existing state and local antidiscrimination laws and barred the passage of such laws in the future unless the electorate approved a new constitutional amendment. In doing so, it singled out the gay community by erecting a barrier to antidiscrimination legislation and eliminating their opportunity to challenge laws discriminating against them. The justice conceded that Amendment 2 reflected the views of a majority of Colorado's citizens and therefore merited respect, but popular support, he said, was an insufficient reason to justify invading the plaintiffs' constitutional rights.

Rovira concluded that the lower court judge had not erred in granting the preliminary injunction and remanded the case back to him to determine whether the state had a compelling interest in Amendment 2 and whether that interest was sufficiently narrow.[41]

In his initial ruling, Bayless had made it clear that he applied strict scrutiny because the fundamental right of equal access to the political process was involved. At the same time, he denied the plaintiffs' motion to treat homosexuals and bisexuals as a suspect or semisuspect class because, in his view, they were not politically powerless, the indicia of a suspect class.[42] In its briefs and through testimony at trial, the state's position was that Amendment 2 was essential to avoid the effects of a "militant gay aggression" in validating a "homosexual agenda" (*Evans v. Romer* 1993c, at 4). Its justifications for Amendment 2 included "preserving the integrity of the state's political functions," "preventing the government from interfering with personal, familial and religious privacy," and "promoting the physical and psychological well-being of our children" (at 2). With one exception, Bayless was not persuaded that these reasons were compelling. But although he found the state's interest in promoting religious freedom compelling, he believed it could be accomplished simply by adding a religious exemption to the antidiscrimination law as two Colorado communities had done. After duly considering the state's elaborate rationales, many of which appeared to be based on blatant prejudice, the judge found Amendment 2 unconstitutional and issued a permanent injunction against it.

On appeal again, the state supreme court affirmed Bayless's ruling, echoing most of his analysis (*Evans v. Romer* 1994).

When the case reached the United States Supreme Court, the state abandoned much of its earlier strategy and introduced the "special rights" theme into the argument (Alexander 2002). Controversy over whether antidiscrimination laws afforded gays "special rights" or "equal rights" was part of the national debate, reaching all the way to the 1996 presidential campaign.[43] During the televised town meeting in San Diego, California, that served as the site of the second presidential debate, Republican candidate Bob Dole was asked to explain his position on the federal law that would have prohibited discrimination on the basis of sexual orientation in employment. Dole (1996) proclaimed his opposition to discrimination, yet characterized antidiscrimination legislation as special treatment. He said,

> Well, I'm opposed to discrimination in any form but I don't favor creating special rights for any group. That would be my answer to this question. And I'm, you know—there would be special rights for different groups in America. But I'm totally opposed to discrimination. I don't have any policy against hiring anyone; whether it's lifestyle or whatever, we don't have any policy of that kind, never have had in my office or will we have in the future. But as far as special rights, I'm opposed to same-sex marriages, which the President signed well after midnight one morning in the dark of night.

As Dole's response indicates, the language of "special rights" suggests that gays seek privileges others lack (see Schacter 1994). Alternatively, it suggests that antidiscrimination legislation unfairly privileges the group seeking equality over the group seeking to maximize an opposing goal, such as freedom of association.[44]

Speaking for a six-justice majority, Justice Anthony Kennedy announced the opinion of the Court for O'Connor, Souter, and Stevens as well as Justices Stephen Breyer and Ruth Bader Ginsburg. Justice Antonin Scalia dissented, joined by Rehnquist (now Chief Justice) and Clarence Thomas.

The high court did not address the plaintiffs' argument that homosexuals constituted a suspect or semisuspect class, thereby necessitating strict scrutiny; nor did it discuss the state supreme court's fundamental rights rationale (see Wilson 1997). And although the state court had applied strict scrutiny because a fundamental right was involved, the United States Supreme Court applied the lower level of scrutiny more common in equal protection cases.

Kennedy set the stage by quoting from the first Justice John Marshall Harlan's dissent in *Plessy v. Ferguson* (1896) that "the Constitution 'neither knows nor tolerates classes among citizens'" (*Romer v. Evans* 1996, 623, quoting *Plessy* 1896, 559). The outcome of the case became apparent when Kennedy unceremoniously rejected the state's argument that Amendment 2 only denied gays and lesbians special privileges, merely placing them on the same level as all other citizens. He called this interpretation of Amendment 2 "implausible" (*Romer v. Evans* 1996, 626). Instead, he cited the state supreme court's finding that Amendment 2 would repeal all existing antidiscrimination laws and prevent the passage of new legislation. Moreover, as the state court had also recognized, Amendment 2 would legitimize private discrimination by foreclosing sexual orientation as a classification in public accommodations laws. Its effect on equal rights would be sweeping for it would bar laws against discrimination in housing, education, employment, health and welfare, real estate, and insurance, as well as policies against discrimination in the public employment sector and the public education system.

Kennedy noted that Amendment 2 might also have implications for laws of general applicability that prohibit arbitrary treatment or unfair discrimination against all citizens for it would negate such laws if public officials or judges determined that they were being treated "arbitrarily or capriciously" on the basis of their sexual orientation (630). But because the state court did specifically rule on this issue, Kennedy noted that the high court would also not address it.

Sharply denouncing the special rights rhetoric, Kennedy declared, "We cannot accept the view that Amendment 2's prohibition on specific legal protections does no more than deprive homosexuals of special rights. To the contrary," he emphasized, "the amendment imposes a special disability upon those persons alone" (631). Unlike other Coloradans, he noted, the gay community's struggle for equal rights would require them to secure the support of a majority of the state's citizens to approve a constitutional amendment negating Amendment 2. He ended by saying, "We find nothing special in the protections Amendment 2 withholds. They are protections taken for granted by most people either because they already have them or do not need them; these are protections against exclusion from an almost limitless number of transactions and endeavors that constitute ordinary civic life in a free society" (631).

Turning to the Fourteenth Amendment analysis, Kennedy did not address the issue of whether gays constituted a suspect or semisuspect class.[45] He explained, however, that normally, absent a suspect classification or the presence of a fundamental right, the Court upholds a law if it bears a rational relationship to a legitimate state objective. But Amendment 2, he stressed, defied typical equal protection analysis by "confound[ing] this normal process of judicial review. It is at once too narrow and too broad. It identifies persons by a single trait and then denies them protection across the board." He called the policy "unprecedented in our jurisprudence" and outside "our constitutional tradition" (633). The government, he emphasized, cannot create inequalities by singling out a group of citizens and depriving them of the access to the government's protection to which others are accustomed.

Kennedy branded "laws of the kind now before us" as "rais[ing] the inevitable inference that the disadvantage imposed is born of animosity toward the class of persons affected" (634). Giving short shrift to the state's purported justifications for the law—to protect the freedom of others, particularly landlords and employers, who objected to homosexuality—and to conserve resources to fight discrimination against others, he found that "the breadth of the Amendment is so far removed from these particular justifications that we find it impossible to credit them" (635). Because he could find no legitimate state goals or objectives in the law, he declared that "we must conclude that Amendment 2 classifies homosexuals not to further a proper legislative end, but to make them unequal to everyone else" (635).

In a scathing dissent, Scalia rejected the majority's characterization of the law, declaring that "the Court has mistaken a Kulturkampf [culture war] for a fit of spite" (636). In his view, the amendment was simply a reasonable effort by the citizens of Colorado "to preserve traditional sexual mores against the efforts of a politically powerful minority" (636). Cultural battles over the status of homosexuals should be resolved through democratic means, he insisted, including the process of amending the state constitution.

Scalia took exception to Kennedy's assertion that Amendment 2 was motivated by animosity toward homosexuals and for equating opposition to homosexuality to racial and religious bigotry. He also sharply criticized the majority for omitting mention of *Bowers* entirely and disregarding its holding that states are allowed to outlaw homosexual conduct.[46] If they can criminalize such conduct, he argued, surely they can merely register their disapproval of it as Colorado had done.[47] But, in any event, although Colorado residents may legitimately dislike homosexuality, he said, Amendment 2 does not demonstrate any such disapproval; it merely prevents the state from furnishing them with special advantages. He pointed out that in repealing its sodomy law, the citizens of the state had demonstrated that they had no animosity against homosexuals. Amendment 2, he asserted, was simply the result of a democratic process by which the citizens of Colorado sought to constrain the special rights and privileges that members of the gay community had achieved through their high socioeconomic status, their political power, and their success in manipulating the political agenda to their advantage.[48]

A public opinion poll taken a few years after *Romer* was decided suggests that Kennedy's opinion was more consistent with the views of the electorate than Scalia's. A nationwide NBC News/*Wall Street Journal* poll conducted in June 1999 showed that the country as a whole disagreed with the voters of Colorado about the "special rights, equal rights" debate. When asked whether "there are too many unnecessary laws that give special rights to homosexuals [or that] current laws are necessary to prohibit discrimination against homosexuals," 49 percent replied that "current laws are necessary," 42 percent believed there are "too many unnecessary laws," and 9 percent were "unsure" (PollingReport.com 2006b).

Romer was "hailed in some quarters as a virtual 'Magna Carta' for gay rights" (Leonard 2000, 74–5). Yet, despite the exultation that greeted it, it proved to be of limited benefit to gay rights litigants in subsequent cases. It is astounding that Amendment 2 failed to survive the deferential minimal scrutiny standard, but although the *Romer* majority sided with the plaintiffs in striking Amendment 2, by failing to elevate homosexuality to a suspect or semisuspect class, the Court deprived future litigants of their most potent weapon in equal protection cases (Dodson 1999; Kimball 1996).

Some argue that despite the use of minimal scrutiny language in *Romer*, the Court actually applied a more rigorous standard, illustrating a type of review called "heightened rationality" review. Although it has never officially acknowledged it, the Supreme Court has occasionally applied this higher level of review to invalidate certain kinds of laws in equal protection cases, primarily when "the right seems fundamental-like, the classification seems suspect-like, or when the law is motivated by animus" (Nguyen 2001, 483).[49]

Gerstmann (2003, 10) discusses the Court's use of "'second-order' rational basis scrutiny" in *Romer*, a type of minimal scrutiny that was first identified by Marshall in *City of Cleburne v. Cleburne Living Center* (1985). In *City of Cleburne*, the Supreme Court had upheld a challenge to a city zoning ordinance that excluded homes for mentally disabled individuals in certain areas. Denying the class of plaintiffs suspect or semisuspect status, the Court nevertheless held that there was no rational basis to believe the home would pose any special threat and that the ordinance appeared to rest on "irrational prejudice" (450). Echoing Marshall, Gerstmann argues that although this analysis means a law is more likely to be struck—resulting in a victory for the plaintiffs—by using this method of decision making on an ad hoc basis without open acknowledgment, the Court offers no principled guidelines for the lower courts to follow in future equal protection cases.

Notwithstanding Kennedy's strong denunciation of the special rights rhetoric in *Romer*, the Sixth Circuit was not convinced that a "special rights" theory had no place in deciding such cases (see Kimpel 1999). After the Colorado State Supreme Court's ruling in *Romer*, in *Equality Foundation of Greater Cincinnati v. City of Cincinnati* (1993), Ohio federal district court judge Spiegel enjoined Issue 3, a measure similar to Amendment 2 that had been approved by Cincinnati voters.[50] Issue 3 had been inspired by two antidiscrimination ordinances that included sexual orientation as a protected classification: The first prohibited the city from discrimination in hiring; the second barred discrimination in public accommodations.

Spiegel granted the plaintiffs a preliminary injunction, applying heightened scrutiny to the ordinance because it implicated the fundamental right of equal participation in the political process and because he considered gays an identifiable group that had been subject to discrimination on the basis of their status and their conduct. Citing the Colorado Supreme Court's holding in *Evans v. Romer* (1993b), he ruled that "states may not disadvantage any identifiable group, whether a suspect category or not, by making it more difficult to enact legislation on its behalf" (*Equality Foundation* 1993, 1241).

Following a trial on the merits, the judge issued a permanent injunction, again echoing the Colorado court's reasoning in *Romer* (*Equality Foundation* 1994). But after the United States Supreme Court granted certiorari in *Romer*, the Sixth Circuit reversed Spiegel's order and vacated the injunction, ruling there was no fundamental right to participate in the political process and that sexual orientation is not a "suspect or quasi-suspect" classification because gays are not an identifiable group (*Equality Foundation* 1995, 270). The panel's opinion, announced by Judge Krupansky, found the policy constitutional, stating that "in any event, the Amendment passes equal protection review *even if* it is read as affecting a status-defined class, in that it imposes no *punishment* or *disability* upon persons belonging to that group but rather merely removes previously legislated *special protection* against discrimination from that segment of the population" (267 n4, emphasis in the original).

After announcing its decision in *Romer*, the Supreme Court vacated and remanded the case to the Sixth Circuit, ordering it to reconsider in light of *Romer* (*Equality Foundation* 1996). On remand, the same panel distinguished *Romer*, in part because it involved a state statute and the Cincinnati charter was a city ordinance, and it again upheld the Cincinnati charter amendment (*Equality Foundation* 1997). A year later, the Supreme Court denied certiorari in *Equality Foundation* (1998), leaving open the possibility that other circuits would also read *Romer* narrowly, as the Sixth Circuit did, and uphold such policies (see Barnett 1999).[51]

There was also speculation about the relationship between *Bowers* and *Romer*, with most scholars predicting that *Romer* was inconsistent with *Bowers* and signaled its upcoming demise (see Papadopoulos 1997). Before the Court addressed this question, however, it decided a case testing the latitude allowed groups to restrict membership on the basis of sexual orientation.[52]

In *Boy Scouts of America v. Dale* (2000), the Supreme Court ruled on whether the Boy Scouts of America (BSA) had a First Amendment right to exclude a gay Eagle Scout from his position as scout leader, despite a New Jersey law prohibiting discrimination in public accommodations on the basis of sexual orientation.

In 1990, James Dale was expelled from the Boy Scouts and removed from his position as assistant scoutmaster after the leadership discovered that he was gay. Dale had come up through the ranks of the Scouts, beginning when he was eight; at eighteen, he was accepted as an adult member, serving as a volunteer assistant scoutmaster for a local troop.[53] The records indicate that Dale was an exemplary scout, earning more than twenty-five merit badges and a number of honors and awards, including the prestigious Eagle Scout Badge in 1988. After being featured in a local newspaper story about gay college students and identified as copresident of the Rutgers University Lesbian/Gay Alliance, his registration (and position as assistant scoutmaster) was rescinded on the grounds that he had "demonstrated his failure to live by the Scout Oath and Law by publicly avowing that he was a homosexual" (*Dale v. Boy Scouts of America* 1998, 275).

The BSA did not inform Dale of the reason for his dismissal until after he inquired. He was told that there was a policy against homosexual scouts as evidenced by a 1978 policy statement that "an individual who openly declares himself to be a homosexual [may not] be a volunteer scout leader [or] . . . a registered unit member." This 1978 policy statement was never disseminated, however. Similar statements, appearing in 1991 and 1993, were written after litigation had begun in other states (*Dale v. Boy Scouts of America* 1999, 1205).

Dale filed suit, claiming, among other things, that the BSA had violated the New Jersey Law Against Discrimination (LAD).[54] A superior court in Monmouth County granted summary judgment to the BSA on a number of grounds. First, the trial judge found that the BSA was not a place of public accommodation and, even if it were, it fell within the "distinctly private" exemption of the act.[55] Second, the court held that the BSA's First Amendment right of expressive association justified Dale's expulsion, finding that the Scouts "had consistently excluded from youth and adult membership any self-declared homosexual and that the BSA considered homosexual conduct neither 'morally straight' under the Scout Oath nor 'clean' under the Scout law" (*Dale v. Boy Scouts of America* (1998, 277, quoting *Dale v. Boy Scouts of America* 1995).

The appeals court reversed the superior court and remanded the case; Judge Havey of the appellate court ordered the BSA to reinstate Dale's membership and restore him to his leadership position (*Dale v. Boy Scouts of America* 1998).

On appeal, the New Jersey Supreme Court unanimously affirmed the appellate court's ruling in Dale's favor (*Dale v. Boy Scouts of America* 1999). Writing for the supreme court, Chief Justice Poritz dwelled at length on the character of the Scouts as an organization, including a lengthy review of its rules, policies, and procedures, followed by recounting Dale's ten-year record of scouting activities, citing his honors and awards. She found that the BSA fell within the LAD for at least two reasons: First, because remedial statutes such as the LAD must be broadly interpreted, following the example set in cases involving the Little League, the BSA must be considered a place of public accommodations; second, the BSA did not fall within the "distinctly private" exception to the LAD because, except for age and sex, it had an essentially nonselective admissions policy.

Concluding that the BSA had violated the New Jersey law by revoking Dale's membership in the Scouts, Poritz assessed the BSA's defense on the charge of discrimination, basing her analysis on the United States Supreme Court's rulings on single-sex private clubs. First, because the BSA's membership numbered nearly 5 million, the court rejected its argument that the LAD infringed on its freedom of intimate association. In determining whether the BSA's right to expressive association outweighed Dale's rights under the LAD, the justice weighed the effect of Dale's membership on the BSA's principles condemning homosexuality. And because "Boy Scout members do not associate for the purpose of disseminating the belief that homosexuality is immoral," she concluded it would not "significantly" affect them (*Dale v. Boy Scouts of America* 1999, 1223).

The BSA pointed to its 1978 position paper as well as other policy statements to demonstrate that the words *morally straight* and *clean* contained in the Scout Oath and Law constituted evidence of the members' shared view that homosexuality is immoral. In a footnote, the court dismissed the significance of these documents because the 1978 opinion had never been distributed and the other policy statements were promulgated after Dale's removal. Nor did it accept the BSA's argument that Dale's expulsion was justified because his moral views differed from theirs. Rather, based on all the evidence, the court found that he was dismissed because of prejudice against him as a gay man, a fact documented by the BSA's letter to him. In sum, the court concluded that Dale's participation in the Scouts did not infringe on the BSA's right of expressive association, but even if it did, any slight infringement was outweighed by the state's compelling interest in eliminating discrimination on the basis of sexual orientation.

The state court also considered the BSA's "compelled speech" claim based on *Hurley*, namely that Dale's presence in the Scouts would be construed as sanctioning homosexuality. *Hurley* was distinguishable, however, said Poritz, because unlike GLIB, Dale did not carry a banner airing his views on homosexuality, nor did he intend to use his position in the Scouts to advance homosexuality. Indeed, scout leaders are instructed not to teach about sex at all; if they are asked about it, they must refer the boys to their families or religious leaders for guidance. Therefore, Dale's membership in the Scouts would not be interpreted as an endorsement of homosexuality.

The BSA appealed. The United States Supreme Court opinion, announced by Rehnquist for O'Connor, Scalia, Kennedy, and Thomas, focused almost entirely on the Scouts' claim that the LAD conflicted with its First Amendment right of expressive association (*Boy Scouts of America v. Dale* 2000). Speaking for the majority, Rehnquist reviewed the private men's club cases, explaining that a private organization's right to exclude members who advocate conflicting views must be balanced against the state's interest in advancing equality. The first step in this inquiry requires a determination that the BSA engages in expressive association protected by the First Amendment. After considering its mission statement, as well as the Scout Oath and Law, Rehnquist concluded that in instilling values and beliefs, including patriotism, reverence, and morality, the BSA engages in expressive activity and is entitled to First Amendment protection.

The Scouts had argued that Dale's membership infringed on its right of expressive association by adversely affecting its ability to disseminate its views disapproving of homosexuality, specifically, its injunction to be "morally straight" and "clean." Although the state supreme court held that excluding Dale was incompatible with the Scouts' stated commitment to diversity and representativeness, Rehnquist chided it, saying courts should not evaluate the coherence of a group's views. Rather, they must accept the group's declaration of its beliefs, in this case, the BSA's claim that it viewed homosexuality as incompatible with being "morally straight" and "clean." And although the group was not required to furnish proof of its beliefs to the court, he noted that the BSA's position on homosexuality was confirmed by a number of internal documents, including the 1978 policy position. Additionally, he continued, courts must defer to the organization's judgment of what type of speech "would impair its expression" (653). In this instance, because he was open about his sexual orientation, "Dale's presence in the Boy Scouts would, at the very least, force the organization to send a message, both to the youth members and to the world, that the Boy Scouts accepts homosexual conduct as a legitimate form of behavior" (653).

Despite the fact that *Hurley* had been decided on the basis of the "compelled speech" doctrine, not on the council's right of expressive association, Rehnquist cited it for support, analogizing Dale's membership in the Scouts to GLIB's participation in the parade. In both cases, he said, the Court believed their presence espoused a particular point of view that was antithetical to the group's.[56] Finally, as was not the case with *Roberts* and *Rotary Club*, Rehnquist noted that the state did not have a compelling interest in ending discrimination against homosexuals that justified the heavy burden on the BSA's right of expressive association.

Concluding, the high court held that Dale's membership burdened the BSA's First Amendment right of expressive association, and the state's interest in the LAD was insufficient to override it.

Writing in dissent for Souter, Ginsburg, and Breyer, Stevens began by extolling New Jersey's history of fighting discrimination. Rather than deferring to the BSA's assertion of its values, Stevens focused his attention on inconsistencies in the Scout's claim that homosexuality conflicted with its beliefs. Parsing the phrases "morally straight" and "clean," he noted that neither term has ever been remotely related to, or expressed an opinion on, homosexuality. Second, he disputed the weight given to the BSA policy statements by the Court; the 1978 statement, for example, was more ambiguous than the BSA asserted. The other statements, written from 1991 to 1993, after Dale's expulsion, had no relevance to the BSA's beliefs in 1990 and had not been the reason for his expulsion. But even these were ambiguous and contradictory, he insisted. At most, they may suggest a policy against homosexual conduct, but Dale was expelled because of his status as a homosexual.

Stevens stressed that the BSA had ample opportunity to proclaim its position on homosexuality. It was aware that since 1984 state public accommodations laws were being used to challenge exclusionary policies because it had participated as amici in two of these cases; moreover, it was being sued in other states for discrimination on the basis of gender and sexual orientation. He criticized the Court for its departure from precedent by merely accepting the organization's claim of expressive association to excuse an exclusionary membership policy.

The Court's private club cases make it clear, he said, that simply engaging in some expressive activity and loosely connecting its exclusionary policy to that activity does not insulate a group from the reach of a public accommodations law. Quoting from earlier cases, Stevens reiterated that "the relevant question is whether the mere inclusion of the person at issue would 'impose any serious burden,' 'affect in any significant way,' or be 'a substantial restraint upon' the organization's 'shared goals,' 'basic goals,' or 'collective effort to foster beliefs'" (*Boy Scouts of America v. Dale* 2000, 683). Stevens charged that the BSA attempted to justify its decision to exclude homosexuals with a latter-day rationalization of its principles, and he was astonished that, contrary to longstanding beliefs and principles, the majority had simply accepted the claims made in the BSA's court documents and briefs, in other words, "its litigating posture" during the lawsuit (686).

Unlike the majority, Stevens discussed the BSA's "compelled speech" claim that Dale's homosexuality would compromise its message against homosexuality. He found this unpersuasive, however, because there was no evidence that Dale intended to advocate homosexuality to the scouts. Echoing the state court, Stevens noted that, unlike GLIB in *Hurley*, Dale had neither a banner nor a message to deliver.

Despite Rehnquist's disclaimer that a claim of "expressive association can[not] erect a shield against antidiscrimination laws simply by asserting that mere acceptance of a member from a particular group would impair its message," (*Boy Scouts of America v. Dale* 2000, 653), *Dale* suggests that a group may successfully defend itself against a charge of violating a public accommodations law simply by proclaiming that individuals in an identified class will negate its message of disapproval of the class.

Not surprisingly, *Dale* was sharply criticized, one scholar deriding the "sheer lunacy of what the Court said" (Koppelman 2002b, 1819). The Court was faulted for merely accepting the BSA's assertion of its views against homosexuality, without independent inquiry into the truth of the matter, as well as its willingness to believe the BSA's claim that Dale would vitiate its ability to deliver its message (see Chermerinsky and Fisk 2001). Speculation has arisen over future cases involving a conflict between free speech and equality about whether the lower courts would follow the *Hurley-Dale* approach, thus diminishing the potency of antidiscrimination laws, or adhere to the principles of the private club cases, thereby promoting equality over the right to exclude (see Troum 2002). Based on *Hurley* and *Dale*, the high court has signaled that it does not consider the state's interest in preventing discrimination on the basis of sexual orientation a compelling justification to prevent the exclusion of gays from public events.

Kelly (2002, 245) calls *Dale* "disappointing," observing that the "Court was willing to accept without criticism the Boy Scouts' unsupported negative generalizations and stereotypes about homosexuality . . . [and] gave little weight to any compelling interest in eradicating discrimination against homosexuals." Thus, despite the Court's apparent turnabout in *Romer*, *Dale* suggests a continuing insensitivity to policies relegating gays to second-class citizenship.

In *Lawrence v. Texas* (2003), the Court responded to a challenge to a sodomy law in a Texas case that, like *Bowers*, began with a routine arrest. After entering their Houston home to investigate a weapons complaint, police arrested John Geddes Lawrence and Tyron Garner for violating the Texas sodomy law.[57] They were convicted in a Justice of the Peace Court and appealed to the Harris County Criminal Court for a trial de novo to challenge the constitutionality of the statute on state and federal constitutional grounds. Their motions to quash the charges were rejected by Judge Ross, who found them guilty and fined them each $200.[58] On appeal to the Court of Appeals for the Fourteenth District of Texas, they claimed the law violated their right to equality and privacy under the federal and state constitutions. In 2000, a panel of the Texas Court of Appeals ruled in their favor (*Lawrence* 2000). The court granted the state's motion for reconsideration, and the court, sitting en banc, reversed the panel's ruling the next year (*Lawrence* 2001).

In deciding whether the statute was a classification on the basis of sexual orientation, the court of appeals found that it applied only to conduct, noting the distinction between homosexual conduct and a homosexual orientation. In a divided opinion for the en banc court, Judge Hudson conceded that the law likely had a disparate impact on those with a homosexual orientation but maintained that it was not limited only to such individuals for "persons having a predominantly heterosexual inclination may sometimes engage in homosexual conduct" (*Lawrence* 2001, 353).

Lawrence argued that the state's repeal of its sodomy law in 1973, replacing it with a same-sex sodomy law, was evidence of intentional discrimination against same-sex couples. However, because sexual orientation was not a suspect classification, the appeals court merely applied minimal scrutiny and accepted the state's contention that the law was rationally related to the legitimate purpose of "preserving public morals" (354). Pleading judicial restraint, the court declined to critique the legislature's judgment about the immorality of same-sex sodomy, concluding that the legislature could have found that same-sex sodomy is more unsavory than other types of sexual conduct.[59]

The state also contended the statute did not discriminate on the basis of sex because both men and women were punished equally, an argument that had been rejected by the United States Supreme Court in a 1965 case involving a Virginia law banning interracial marriage. The appeals court agreed with the state, distinguishing between the two laws by noting that the Virginia law had racist motives while the Texas statute had no comparable sexist overtones. The court held that, on its face, the law was gender neutral, with no evidence of a disproportionate impact on either sex.

Last, the Texas appeals court rejected the claim that the law conflicted with the privacy guarantees of the state and federal constitutions. It echoed much of the United States Supreme Court's analysis in *Bowers*, supplementing it with a discussion of how the world's religions, as well as the entire Western civilization, disapproved of homosexuality, and renewed its commitment to judicial restraint. "Certainly," it said, "the modern national trend has been to decriminalize many forms of consensual sexual conduct even when such behavior is widely perceived to be destructive and immoral, e.g., seduction, fornication, adultery, bestiality, etc." (*Lawrence* 2001, 362). Whatever the wisdom of such policy may be, it continued, the decision is within the legislature's purview, not the court's.

Concluding that the statute did not violate the equal protection or due process clause of the Fourteenth Amendment, the appellate court affirmed the conviction, and the United States Supreme Court granted certiorari (*Lawrence* 2002). Kennedy delivered the majority opinion in which Stevens, Souter, Breyer, and Ginsburg joined. O'Connor concurred in the judgment; Scalia, Thomas, and Rehnquist dissented.

The Court accepted the case to consider whether the arrest and conviction for engaging in private consensual sexual behavior violated the equal protection and due process clauses of the Fourteenth Amendment. But it chose to base its opinion on the due process clause, rather than relying on *Romer* and perhaps striking the law on equal protection grounds. Kennedy expressed concern that striking the law on equal protection grounds would allow other sodomy laws to be upheld if they covered both same-sex and opposite-sex partners. He explained that "equality of treatment and the due process right to demand respect for conduct protected by the substantive guarantee of liberty are linked in important respects, and a decision on the latter point advances both interests" (*Lawrence* 2003, 575).

Because it was clear the lower court correctly followed *Bowers* in denying the due process claim, the Court was forced to revisit it. The outcome was clear when Kennedy explained that "the central holding of *Bowers* has been brought in question by this case, and it should be addressed. Its continuance as precedent demeans the lives of homosexual persons" (575).

Rather than following a traditional fundamental rights approach, he broadly characterized the issue in the case as implicating a liberty with both "spatial" and "transcendent" qualities. The former "protects the person from unwarranted government intrusions into a dwelling or other private places"; the latter "presumes an autonomy of self that includes freedom of thought, belief, expression, and certain intimate conduct" (*Lawrence* 2003, 562).

Kennedy traced the Court's long line of privacy decisions through *Bowers*, variously characterizing each as vindicating privacy and liberty interests guaranteed by the due process clause.[60] He charged that the *Bowers* Court had "failed to appreciate the extent of the liberty at stake" (*Lawrence* 2003, 567). The laws in Georgia and Texas did not merely restrain sexual conduct, he said; they implicated a basic and deeply rooted right to engage in private human relationships in the home without interference from the state. Without precisely defining the contours of the right involved, beyond noting that it was not limited to procreation, marriage, and the family, he asserted that the Constitution equally extends the right to enter into private relationships to homosexual as well as to heterosexual persons.

There were several reasons, he continued, why *Bowers* should be overruled: Its historical analysis was based on faulty premises; it failed to recognize the growing importance of privacy in sexual matters; subsequent cases and scholarly opinion undermined it; it was rejected by courts in other nations; and there was little reliance on it by individuals and society as a whole.

Reflecting the arguments raised by the Stevens and Blackmun dissents in *Bowers*, Kennedy faulted the *Bowers* majority for narrowly framing the issue in the case as whether there is a fundamental right to engage in homosexual sodomy; he questioned as well the majority's interpretation of society's views on homosexuality. The *Bowers* Court, he said, had based its refusal to strike the Georgia law in large part on society's historical antipathy to homosexual conduct. Citing scholarly criticism of this view, he said that a more accurate reading of history showed that "early American sodomy laws were not directed against homosexuals as such but instead sought to prohibit nonprocreative sexual activity more generally" (*Lawrence* 2003, 568). Moreover, he added, throughout history, because there was little enforcement of sodomy laws in private consensual conduct, few prosecutions and convictions resulted from violating these laws. The prohibitions against same-sex conduct did not appear until late in the twentieth century, and many seemed to be aimed at public, as opposed to private, behavior. Criminal prosecutions for same-sex sodomy, he stressed, did not begin until the 1970s and then only in nine states, with some of these states soon repealing their laws.

Turning to the issue of society's more general condemnation of homosexuality, he acknowledged deeply held beliefs about its effect on morality, religion, and the family. Not minimizing the sincerity of these beliefs, however, he questioned whether the state may legitimately enforce them through its criminal laws. He also challenged Burger's sweeping claim in his concurring opinion in *Bowers* that society's censure against homosexuality can be traced back throughout the history of Western civilization. In more recent times, Kennedy stressed, society has displayed greater tolerance of diversity in private sexual behavior and, again criticizing the *Bowers* Court, he said there was evidence of this when *Bowers* was decided as most states had repealed or were simply failing to enforce their sodomy laws. To support his belief that tolerance transcended the borders of the United States, Kennedy cited a 1981 ruling by the European Court of Human Rights holding an Irish law prohibiting consensual homosexual conduct as invalid under the European Convention of Human Rights.[61]

Reiterating that *Bowers* had been undermined, Kennedy cited *Planned Parenthood v. Casey* (1992), an abortion rights case that reaffirmed the principle of liberty and individual autonomy protected by the due process clause, principles that apply to homosexual as well as heterosexual individuals. And although *Romer* was decided on equal protection grounds, he said, it too indicated that the doctrine established in *Bowers* had been eroded.[62] Based on these principles, as well as the fact that reliance on *Bowers* had been minimal so that overruling it would not be detrimental, he found there was insufficient reason to retain *Bowers*. Stare decisis (adhering to precedent) is important, but not absolute, he declared and forcefully proclaimed that "*Bowers* was not correct when it was decided, and it is not correct today. It ought not to remain binding precedent. *Bowers v. Hardwick* should be and now is overruled"(*Lawrence* 2003, 578).

As in *Romer*, the Court applied minimal scrutiny in assessing the constitutionality of the Texas law. Kennedy addressed the state's argument that the law served legitimate interests in furthering its citizens' moral beliefs. He cited Stevens's dissent in *Bowers* approvingly, stressing that this analysis "should have been controlling," and noted that mere disapproval by a majority of people is not a legitimate reason to legislate against a particular form of conduct. Underscoring this principle, he declared that the state had offered *no* legitimate grounds to "justify its intrusion into the personal and private life of the individual" (*Lawrence* 2003, 578). However, Kennedy took pains to point out that *Lawrence* was not about "minors," coercion, or "public conduct or prostitution" and should not be interpreted to signal the Court's rulings on laws involving other same-sex relationships, including, he broadly hinted, marriage laws (578).

O'Connor joined the majority in declaring the statute unconstitutional but refrained from voting to overrule *Bowers*. Instead she argued that the law should be struck on equal protection grounds (see Knauer 2004). She acknowledged that most laws are entitled to a presumption of constitutionality; however, she said, when it appears a statute intends to harm an unpopular group or involves private relations, the Court has "applied a more searching form of rational basis review" to strike laws under the equal protection clause (*Lawrence* 2003, 580). O'Connor seemed most disturbed by the fact that the Texas law punished only homosexual sodomy, which, in her view, emanated from the state's "moral disapproval" of gays (582). She stressed that the law criminalized behavior that is more likely to be performed by those with the same-sex sexual orientation and, although only a misdemeanor, it would result in a criminal conviction that would be far reaching. Emphasizing that moral disapproval was an unacceptable reason to single out a group for punishment, O'Connor said she felt it unnecessary to decide whether a sex-neutral sodomy law would satisfy substantive due process analysis.

Distinguishing *Bowers*, O'Connor pointed out that the Court had not held there that the state's interest in preserving morality justified a statute punishing only homosexual conduct. In her view, such a state interest is not legitimate, and the Court has never held otherwise. She ended by attempting to reassure the state that she did not intend to imply that all laws differentiating between homosexuals and heterosexuals would violate equal protection. A law can survive, she said, if the state can offer a legitimate reason for it, such as "national security or preserving the traditional institution of marriage [for] unlike the moral disapproval of same-sex relations . . .

other reasons exist to promote the institution of marriage beyond mere moral disapproval of an excluded group" (*Lawrence* 2003, 585).

Writing for the three dissenting justices, Scalia condemned the majority for overruling *Bowers* and ignoring the dictates of stare decisis, an important factor in *Casey*'s reaffirmation of *Roe*. He criticized the Court's reasons for overruling *Bowers*, essentially arguing the reverse of his dissent in *Casey*, in which he faulted the Court for *not* overruling *Roe*. Scalia charged the majority with inconsistency in the use of stare decisis, using his dissent to attack the Court for reaffirming *Roe* in *Casey*, while overruling *Bowers* in *Lawrence*.

Scalia particularly objected to the Court's assertion that there was little lost by overturning *Bowers*. In his view, "'societal reliance' on the principles confirmed in *Bowers* and discarded today has been overwhelming," easily justifying the state's ability to regulate in the interests of preserving public morality (*Lawrence* 2003, 589). Moreover, he stressed that although the Court overruled *Bowers*, it did not undermine its central holding that there is no fundamental right to engage in homosexual sodomy. Had it recognized homosexual sodomy as a fundamental right, it would have required the state to present a compelling justification for the law. Instead, he said, the majority regarded homosexual activity as only a liberty interest yet applied a more heightened scrutiny in striking the Texas law. Scalia challenged the premise that the due process clause requires laws infringing on liberty interests to be subjected to heightened scrutiny. Not so, he insisted. Only "fundamental liberty interests" require heightened scrutiny; laws implicating "all other liberty interests" receive minimal scrutiny, requiring the state to show only that they are reasonably related to valid state interests (*Lawrence* 2003, 593).

Continuing to insist that *Bowers* was correctly decided, Scalia attacked the majority for its interpretation that homosexual sodomy was not singled out for criminalization. The *Bowers* Court, he said, had properly relied on evidence that sodomy—whether same sex or not—was widely banned, indicating that it was not "deeply rooted in this Nation's history and tradition," an essential component of a fundamental right.[63] Finally, he challenged the majority's premise that the law has no legitimate basis. Denying a state the right to uphold public morality, he warned, "effectively decrees the end of all morals legislation," including laws regulating "fornication, bigamy, adultery, adult incest, bestiality, and obscenity" (*Lawrence* 2003, 599). He ended, as he had in *Romer*, by accusing the Court of manifesting its elitism by "largely sign[ing] on to the so-called homosexual agenda, . . . promoted by some homosexual activists directed at eliminating the moral opprobrium that has traditionally attached to homosexual conduct" and "tak[ing] sides in the culture war" (*Lawrence* 2003, 602). Scalia briefly dismissed O'Connor's reliance on equal protection to find the law unconstitutional, particularly objecting to what he considered her questionable justification for applying heightened scrutiny. He also raised concerns that *Lawrence* undermined laws against same-sex marriage.

Refusing to distinguish between conduct and sexual orientation, Scalia insisted that many Americans do not wish to be closely associated with those engaging in homosexual conduct in their homes, businesses, schools, and Boy Scout troops (an obvious reference to *Dale*). Although the Court, influenced by the "law profession's anti-anti-homosexual culture," perceives such judgments as discriminatory, he believed that members of society perceive them as simply guarding against contact with a "lifestyle that they believe to be immoral and destructive" (*Lawrence* 2003, 602). He ended with a disclaimer that he harbors no ill will toward homosexuals, but that in a democratic society, the Court must refrain from imposing its views on the majority will of the citizens of Texas. He warned that by refusing to accept moral disapproval as a legitimate state interest, the majority opinion would lead to the ultimate step of striking legislative bans on same-sex marriage.

Thomas joined Scalia's dissent, but wrote separately to underscore his belief in judicial restraint. Although he claimed he would have opposed the Texas law had he been a member of the state legislature, as a justice of the Supreme Court, he said he felt bound to uphold the Constitution, which, in his view, does not guarantee an individual right to privacy.

Bowers to *Lawrence* transcends almost two decades of societal change on gay rights issues. One observer, commenting on the "offensive" manner in which *Bowers* was written, described *Lawrence* as the "Court's apology for that decision" (Schwartz 2004, 233, statement by Kaufman). However, despite the respectful language and the clear vindication of the gay rights claim in *Lawrence*, the ruling left many questions unanswered (see Schwartz 2004; Culhane and Sobel 2005). Hutchinson (2005, 35) argues that much of the elaborate praise and condemnation of the ruling is unjustified. In his view, "rather than undoing societal disapprobation of homosexuality, *Lawrence* moderately advances social justice for gay, lesbian, bisexual, and transgendered individuals, and may ultimately harm political efforts to eradicate heterosexism. *Lawrence*," he continues, "has a restricted reach because it reflects the views of a dominant heteronormative culture concerning sexuality and because the immediate practical implications of the decriminalization of sodomy are themselves limited."

From the perspective of constitutional analysis, the merger of due process and equal protection principles in *Lawrence* added to the doctrinal confusion over gays rights issues (see Note 2005). Additionally, there is a debate over whether *Lawrence* and *Romer* indicate that the Court has de facto applied a higher level of scrutiny to laws involving gay rights, that is, has elevated gays and lesbians to a suspect or semisuspect status. However, even if it has done so, by not straightforwardly announcing this doctrinal shift, it leaves the lower courts without sufficient direction to do the same (Smith 2005). Moreover, by characterizing "autonomy of . . . certain intimate conduct" as a lesser liberty interest, rather than as a fundamental right, the Court may still have left the gay community vulnerable to attack from morals legislation in the future.

Despite Kennedy's and O'Connor's assurances that *Lawrence* was not intended as a precursor of the Court's willingness to strike same-sex marriage laws, the dissent warned that the majority had paved the way for such fundamental alterations in American life. Although Scalia's fear that *Lawrence* signaled the end of morality-based laws against "fornication, bigamy, adultery, adult incest, bestiality, and obscenity" appears overly dramatic, *Lawrence* has spurred challenges to laws implicating adoption, incest, statutory rape, and polygamy as well as same-sex marriage (Bernstein 2004; see Cawley 2004).[64] Such challenges will test the limits of the judiciary's willingness to allow the state to legislate in the interests of preserving public morality.

THE PUBLIC'S VIEW

Surveys show that the Supreme Court's ruling in *Lawrence* coincided with the view of most Americans about the legality of adult homosexual relations. Gallup (2005c) first asked respondents whether they thought "homosexual relations between consenting adults should or should not be legal" in a June 1977 survey; at that time public opinion was evenly split with 43 percent of the respondents saying they should be and 43 percent saying they should not be. When a survey was conducted in early May 2003 (Gallup 2003a), before *Lawrence* was decided, a clear majority of 60 percent of the respondents said homosexual relations should be legal, and only 35 percent believed they should not be. In the same survey, when the question specifically referred to the facts in *Lawrence*, asking "do you think it should be legal or should not be legal for two men who are consenting adults to have sex with each other in their own home," 62 percent said it should be legal, and only 31 percent said it should not be; when the question referred to two women, the comparable responses were 63 percent saying that it should be legal and 30 percent saying that it should not be. As Hutchinson (2005, 43) notes, it is not surprising that the public should take this view, given the absence of sodomy laws in most states at that time.

After *Lawrence* was decided in June 2003, an antigay backlash developed (see Culhane and Sobel 2005; Egan, Persily, and Wallsten 2006). The Gallup data show that when the question was asked in a poll conducted between July 25 and July 27, 2003, the percentage agreeing that homosexual relations should be legal dropped more than 10 percentage points; in the 2003 poll, 48 percent agreed they should be legal, and 46 percent said they should not be (Gallup 2005c). Similarly, there was a decline in support for the statement that "homosexuality should be considered an acceptable alternative lifestyle," which had risen fairly steadily from 34 percent in June 1982 to 54 percent in May 2003, but dropped to 51 percent in May 2005 (Gallup 2005c).

Although *Lawrence* reflected the public's opinion at the time, the Court's action appeared to draw unwelcome attention to the issue of gay rights. The combination of the furor caused by the same-sex marriage debate that surfaced after *Lawrence* and continued into 2004, the media's focus on the issue, and the president's support for an amendment banning same-sex marriage contributed to the public's unease about homosexuality (see Egan, Persily, and Wallsten 2006). Whatever the cause of the decline in support of gay rights, though, the backlash seems to have run its course.[65] The percentage of respondents who agreed with the legality of homosexual relations began to rise again after 2003, and, although the progression has not been steady, by August 2005, 49 percent were agreeing that "homosexual relations between consenting adults should be legal," with 44 percent saying they should not be (Gallup 2006a). Similarly, in a poll conducted in early May 2004, Gallup (2006b) found that respondents saying they considered homosexuality an "acceptable alternative lifestyle" had risen to 54 percent, and when the question was asked in a slightly different way in a May 2005 poll, 60 percent agreed that "gay or lesbian relations should be considered acceptable."

Although there is no direct evidence of the effect of *Lawrence* on the public's views of homosexuality, it was an important event in the struggle for gay rights and, at a minimum, focused the nation's attention on the issue (see Egan, Persily, and Wallsten 2006). Perhaps, as Coles (2005, 56) suggests, before *Lawrence* "questions that had been abstract until then—questions about the proper place of gay people in American society—were suddenly real." It is too soon to know how *Lawrence* will affect the battle for gay rights.

It is clear, however, that the Supreme Court changed the legal and political status of members of the gay community by declaring that gays can no longer be branded as criminals merely to satisfy indeterminate standards of moral disapproval.

NOTES

1. Koppelman (2002a) argues that the sex discrimination analysis, commonly thought of as the weakest of the three, offers the best chance of success in gay rights cases.

2. Ironically, the defendants in such cases also cited the First Amendment to defeat the gay rights claims against them.

3. Section 212(a)(4) of the Immigration and Nationality Act of 1952 prevents "aliens afflicted with psychopathic personality, epilepsy, or a mental defect" from obtaining visas and entering the United States.

4. Most circuit court decisions are made by randomly selected three-judge panels and are considered the law of the circuit. Litigants may seek reconsideration of such rulings from the panel and also review by the entire circuit. If the latter is granted by majority vote of the circuit judges, the circuit court, sitting en banc, will decide the case.

5. In his article discussing the boundaries of status and conduct, Valdes (1994, 389) explains that the term "sodomy has no fixed or universal meaning. It is simply a term of art defined by statute [and] because statutory definitions vary from state to state, the meaning of the word sodomy depends on the specific statutory setting."

6. As of 1993, there were twenty-three laws criminalizing sodomy (including those in the Military Code of Justice); only five were aimed exclusively at same-sex conduct (Halley 1993, 1732).

7. Until 1976 when the law was changed by Congress, three-judge district courts decided cases challenging the constitutionality of state and federal statutes; since then, such courts have been infrequently used.

8. At the time *Commonwealth's Attorney* (1975) was decided, the high court was obligated to review cases arising from three-judge district courts on appeal (as opposed to a petition for a writ of certiorari, which is discretionary). It was common for the Court to dispose of such cases by issuing orders summarily affirming them or dismissing them "for want of a substantial federal question." Congress limited mandatory appeals in 1988.

9. The United States Supreme Court denied certiorari in *New York v. Onofre* (1981).

10. A week after the Supreme Court announced its ruling in *Bowers*, it denied certiorari in *Wade* (1986).

11. Because Hardwick had already paid the fine for the infraction, the warrant was invalid when it was served.

12. Section 16-6-2 of the Georgia Code defined sodomy as "any sexual act involving the sex organs of one person and the mouth or anus of another."

13. According to Cain (1993), prior to *Griswold*, the ACLU did not oppose state regulation of homosexual sodomy.

14. The standing doctrine is based on the "case or controversy" requirement in Article III of the United States Constitution. At a minimum, to have standing, plaintiffs must show that they have suffered an actual injury at the hands of the defendant.

15. Halley (1993) discusses the divergent litigation strategy followed by the two teams of lawyers representing Hardwick, based on a distinction between status and conduct, that is, his identity as a gay man and the act of sodomy.

16. Among the numerous cases White cited were early rulings establishing the right to privacy: *Meyer v. Nebraska* (1923), *Pierce v. Society of Sisters* (1925), and *Prince v. Massachusetts* (1944), as well as the more recent decisions of *Griswold* and *Eisenstadt v. Baird* (1972). The latter struck a Massachusetts law barring the distribution of contraceptives to single people. Although decided on the basis of the Fourteenth Amendment's equal protection clause, *Eisenstadt* is generally considered to have extended the right to privacy to single persons, as opposed to limiting it to the marital bedroom as *Griswold* appeared to do.

17. "Substantive due process" has roots in the early 1900s. Although often derided by the courts and others as judicial activism, it plays an important role in protecting individual rights of autonomy and privacy (see Meyer 2004; Niemczyk 2005).

18. These are two tests commonly used for determining fundamental rights.

19. Although all states had criminal sodomy statutes at one time, by 1986, it was still outlawed in only twenty-four states and the District of Columbia (Irons 1990, chap. 16; see Halley 1993, app. C for discussion of judicial and legislative repeals of state sodomy laws since the 1970s). Andersen (1998, 283) provides an update, reporting that in 1968 every state except Illinois (which repealed its law in 1961) outlawed sodomy, and by 1998, thirty states had joined Illinois, with the status of three other states (Massachusetts, Michigan, and Texas) uncertain.

20. Goldstein (1988) challenges the historical accuracy of the majority's justifications for upholding sodomy laws, asserting that the justices relied on their own values and conceptions of homosexuality.

21. Powell appeared conflicted about the issue of sexual orientation. Well into his seventies, he announced that he had never known a gay person. This was indeed an odd statement to make since, according to Murdoch and Price (2001, 23), he might well hold the record for hiring the largest number of gay men and lesbians as law clerks. They report that during six terms in the 1980s at least one of his four clerks was gay.

22. Blackmun also believed the majority erred by ignoring the conflict between the state law and the Eighth, Ninth, and Fourteenth Amendments. Thornton (1987) discusses cases involving challenges to sodomy laws based on the Ninth Amendment, the establishment and freedom of association clauses of the First Amendment, the cruel and unusual punishment clause of the Eighth Amendment, and the equal protection clause of the Fourteenth Amendment.

23. Koppelman (1988) notes that both Stevens and Blackmun compared the law against sodomy to the Virginia law banning interracial marriage, suggesting parallels between the states' misguided efforts to justify such laws on principles of morality and tradition.

24. In part because of the Court's rejection of privacy rights in *Bowers*, litigants were forced to lessen their reliance on the privacy doctrine and instead employ argu-

ments based on liberty interests (Gartner 2004). The Court typically applies a lower level of scrutiny when liberty interests are involved than when privacy rights are implicated.

25.

TABLE 2.1. Levels of Scrutiny in Equal Protection Cases

Classification	Scrutiny	Ends	Means
Suspect (e.g., race)	Strict	Compelling	Necessarily related
Semisuspect (e.g., sex)	Heightened*	Important	Substantially related
Nonsuspect (e.g., age)	Minimal	Legitimate	Rationally related

*Also known as intermediate scrutiny.

Source: Mezey (2003).

26. The courts are often imprecise in their language and refer to both strict and intermediate scrutiny as heightened scrutiny, meaning scrutiny that is more rigorous than minimal.

27. A study of state supreme court decisions in 416 sex discrimination cases confirms that plaintiffs have a 73 percent likelihood of prevailing in cases in which courts use strict scrutiny, a 20 percent probability in cases in which the courts use minimal scrutiny, and 47 percent probability in cases in which the courts use intermediate scrutiny (Epstein, Martin, Baldez, and Nihiser 2004, 49).

28. Section 272:98 of the Massachusetts General Laws prohibits "any distinction, discrimination or restriction on account of . . . sexual orientation . . . relative to the admission of any person to, or treatment in any place of public accommodation, resort or amusement."

29. GLIB also wanted to demonstrate solidarity with its counterpart in New York, which had been seeking to gain entry to that parade since 1990 under the banner of the Irish Lesbian and Gay Organization (see Yackle 1993).

30. Dwight Duncan (1996, 667) defends the council's reasons for denying GLIB permission to march in the parade; in his view, "GLIB's action in seeking to march can only be called provocative. It was confrontational, in-your-face politics."

31. When the 1993 parade was postponed because of inclement weather, the council returned to court to appeal the injunction to the state appellate and supreme courts; both denied the appeals. The council also sought relief in federal court, but the judge declined to get involved in the state court proceedings (Van Ness 1996, 644–5).

32. Van Ness (1996) discusses the interpretation of the Massachusetts public accommodations law.

33. The council also filed suit in federal court, claiming the state court's order to include GLIB violated its First Amendment right of speech and association (Zaleskas 1996).

34. A number of groups submitted amici curiae briefs urging the Supreme Court to reverse the state court ruling; one of those groups was the Boy Scouts of America.

35. Greyerbiehl (1996) suggests that the Court's reasoning is a victory for the gay rights movement because it extends First Amendment protection to gay pride parades.

36. As the Court explained in *United States Jaycees v. Roberts* (1984, 617–8), it has recognized two types of freedom of association: intimate association and expressive

association. The first, "a fundamental element of personal liberty" involves the free-dom to "enter into and maintain certain intimate human relationships" without "undue intrusion by the State." The latter, arising from the First Amendment, involves "a right to associate for the purpose of engaging in those activities protected by the First Amendment—speech, assembly, petition for the redress of grievances, and the exercise of religion. The Constitution guarantees freedom of association of this kind as an indispensable means of preserving other individual liberties." But, it also indicated, "the right to associate for expressive purposes is not, however, absolute. Infringements on that right may be justified by regulations adopted to serve compelling state interests, unrelated to the suppression of ideas, that cannot be achieved through means significantly less restrictive of associational freedoms" (623). The first case to articulate a constitutional right of expressive association was *NAACP v. Alabama* (1958).

37. Article II is the Bill of Rights provision of the Colorado Constitution. As spec-ified in §2 of Article II, the people have "the sole and exclusive right of governing themselves" and may amend the constitution as long as the change "is not repug-nant" to the United States Constitution. In 1992, there were twenty-nine sections of Article II, many duplicating the Bill of Rights provisions of the federal charter. Amendment 2 became §30 of Article II (*Evans v. Romer* 1993a); it was approved by the electorate in a 53.4 to 46.6 percent vote (*Evans v. Romer* 1993b).

38. Amendment 2 stated,

> No Protected Status Based on Homosexual, Lesbian, or Bisexual Orientation. Neither the State of Colorado, through any of its branches or departments, nor any of its agencies, political subdivisions, municipalities or school districts, shall enact, adopt or enforce any statute, regulation, ordinance or policy whereby homosexual, lesbian or bisexual orientation, conduct, practices or relationships shall constitute or otherwise be the basis of or entitle any person or class of persons to have or claim any minority status, quota preferences, pro-tected status or claim of discrimination.

39. The plaintiffs did not present this theory, thus prevailing in an argument they did not raise (Alexander 2002, 289).

40. The Colorado court identified four types of cases to support its view that a fundamental right, "the right to participate equally in the political process," was at stake: "right to vote cases," "reapportionment cases," "access to the ballot cases," and cases involving "ballot initiatives disadvantaging a particular group." Each would trigger strict scrutiny. The facts in *Erickson*, the last category of cases, most closely resemble those in *Romer* (Collis 1997, 1001–4).

41. Declining to intervene, the Supreme Court denied certiorari in *Romer v. Evans* (1993).

42. At trial, both sides provided expert witnesses, philosophers, and antiquity schol-ars to testify about the morality (or immorality) of homosexual activity, based largely on how it was perceived in ancient Greece (see Keen and Goldberg 2003, chap. 7).

43. Rubin (1998) notes that the charge of special rights is not confined to laws based on sexual orientation; it is frequently used to gain rhetorical advantage against

antidiscrimination laws involving other impermissible classifications. In part, he believes, the rhetoric resonates with the general public because it coincides with its discomfort about affirmative action. Resentment against so-called special treatment may also arise when a majority perceives that members of the group in question are lacking in qualifications or, even worse, are morally deficient—in other words, when it believes the discrimination is warranted. In such circumstances, people "will perceive antidiscrimination law to provide members of the protected group with unjustified deserts, i.e., special treatment" (578). This perception of justifiable discrimination is heightened when the members of the group are thought to have brought it upon themselves by voluntarily choosing to engage in antisocial or "deviant" behavior.

44. It is unclear why protection against discrimination on the basis of sexual orientation constitutes advantage (see Collis 1997; Dubnoff 1997).

45. The trial court had rejected the plaintiffs' scrutiny argument, and it was not raised on appeal (Smith 2005, 2780).

46. Sunstein (1988) argues that *Bowers* did not control in the case of an equal protection challenge to Amendment 2.

47. Scalia was wrong about Amendment 2; by its passage, the citizens of Colorado were expressing their disapproval of homosexual orientation as well as homosexual conduct.

48. Proponents of Amendment 2 argued that because homosexuals had a high socioeconomic status, they did not require protection from antidiscrimination laws (Dubnoff 1997, 283).

49. *Romer* would appear to fit into all three of these categories.

50. Issue 3 states,

> The City of Cincinnati and its various Boards and Commissions may not enact, adopt, enforce, or administer any ordinance . . . which provides that homosexual, lesbian, or bisexual orientation status, conduct, or relationship constitutes, entitles, or otherwise provides a person with the basis to have any claim of minority or protected status quota preference or other preferential treatment.
>
> . . . Any ordinance, regulation, rule or policy enacted before this amendment is adopted that violates the foregoing prohibition shall be null and void and of no force or effect.

51. *Romer* had no effect on *San Francisco Arts & Athletics, Inc. v. United States Olympic Committee* (1987), decided the next year, in which the Court ruled in favor of the United States Olympic Committee's effort to prevent the San Francisco group from organizing "Gay Olympic Games." The gay rights claim appeared only tangential to the ruling, as the Court decided it as a trademark case without citing *Romer*.

52. The Court decided two cases in 1998 that touched on gay rights. In *Oncale v. Sundowner Offshore Services Inc.* (1988), a unanimous Court broadly construed Title VII of the Civil Rights Act of 1964 to encompass same-sex sexual harassment. More indirectly, the Court held in *Bragdon v. Abbott* (1998) that asymptomatic HIV falls within the sphere of protection of the 1990 Americans with Disabilities Act.

53. Adult scouts can become assistant scoutmasters at eighteen and scoutmasters at twenty-one.

54. Section 10:5-4 of the New Jersey Statutes states, "All persons shall have the opportunity to obtain . . . all the accommodations, advantages, facilities, and privileges of any place of public accommodation . . . without discrimination because of . . . affectional or sexual orientation."

55. Section 10:5-5 of the New Jersey Statutes states, "Nothing herein contained shall be construed to include or to apply to any institution, bona fide club, or place of accommodation, which is in its nature distinctly private."

56. Kelly (2002, 273) argues that the Court's reference to *Hurley* in *Dale* provided "gay rights opponents with additional precedent to support discrimination against homosexuals."

57. Section 21.06 of the Texas Penal Code prohibits a person from engaging in "deviate sexual intercourse with another individual of the same sex."

58. Because of Lawrence's and Garner's plea, there was no record of the circumstances leading to the arrest and consequently no grounds for appeal on this issue.

59. The Texas appeals court interpreted *Romer* narrowly, limiting it to protecting the equal right to petition the government and finding it inapplicable to laws prohibiting homosexual conduct.

60. In discussing how *Lawrence* fits into the Court's substantive due process decision making, Coles (2005, 30–1) argues that the "protected liberty" language indicates that the majority used neither strict nor minimal scrutiny, but that "*Lawrence* does not fit neatly into the 'protected liberty' line of cases either." He attributes the "protected liberty" balancing approach used in *Lawrence* in part to the Court's desire to create a more sophisticated type of substantive due process analysis.

61. Two weeks before *Lawrence* was decided, the Ontario Court of Appeals ruled in favor of same-sex marriage (Coles 2005, 49).

62. Although the Court acknowledged that the plaintiffs had raised an equal protection argument, the majority opinion did not address this claim.

63. Scalia cited *Washington v. Glucksberg* (1997), an assisted-suicide case, in which the Court presented a stringent test for substantive due process analysis to determine whether an asserted interest is fundamental, stressing that such a test is necessary to prevent the justices from imposing their own policy preferences. Quoting prior cases, *Glucksberg* announced a two-step analysis in determining if a right is fundamental: It must be "'deeply rooted in this Nation's history and tradition,' ('so rooted in the traditions and conscience of our people as to be ranked as fundamental'), and 'implicit in the concept of ordered liberty,' such that 'neither liberty nor justice would exist if they were sacrificed.' Second, we have required in substantive-due-process cases a 'careful description' of the asserted fundamental liberty interest" (721, citations omitted).

64. In *Utah v. Holm* (2006), the Utah Supreme Court upheld the conviction of a polygamist under the state's bigamy law, rejecting the defendant's argument that the law was unconstitutional under *Lawrence*.

65. These poll results add fodder to the long-standing debate about whether a backlash against a judicial ruling indicates that the Court is ineffective at bringing about social policy reform (see Schultz 1998).

CHAPTER 3

Struggling over Same-Sex Marriage

THE primary locus of same-sex marriage policymaking is at the state level, with gay rights litigants asking the state courts to interpret state and federal constitutional guarantees to allow same-sex marriages, and anti-gay activists attempting to ban same-sex marriages through statutes and constitutional amendments.[1] More recently, local public officials have begun to play a role in the controversy by performing legally questionable same-sex marriages; in doing so, according to the courts, they exceeded their constitutional functions.

For the most part, the state courts rejected the gay community's claims, primarily because they were loathe to interfere with the legislative prerogative to determine marriage policies, and "until the mid-1990s, same sex marriage litigation was always something of a long shot" (D. Duncan 2004, 624; see Rimmerman 2002). When courts in Hawaii, Alaska, Vermont, and Massachusetts began to uphold challenges to same-sex marriage restrictions, state and federal lawmakers feared a trend and sought to offset it through statutes and constitutional amendments, with the approval of the majority of voters.[2]

THE RIGHT TO MARRY

The high court has not yet ruled on the constitutionality of same-sex marriage policy, yet its rulings on the right to marry have provided gay rights litigants with a roadmap to argue for an expansion of the definition of marriage. There has, of course, been widespread speculation that *Lawrence* would open the floodgates to litigation to extend marriage rights to same-sex couples. Although Kennedy stressed that *Lawrence* did "not involve whether the government must give formal recognition to any relationship that homosexual persons seek to enter" (578), the effect of *Lawrence* on same-sex marriage restrictions are still unclear (see Parshall 2005).

Discussions of the judiciary's role in marriage policy traditionally begin with *Loving v. Virginia* (1967), in which the Supreme Court considered the constitutionality of Virginia laws banning interracial marriage. Although the issue was new to the high court, *Loving* was preceded by almost twenty years by *Perez v. Sharp* (1948), a California Supreme Court decision striking a state law prohibiting marriages between whites and nonwhites. The state supreme court ruled that the law violated the equal protection clause of the United States Constitution, also declaring that the right to marry was fundamental.

Plaintiffs Mildred Jeter, an African American woman, and Richard Loving, a white man, were Virginia residents who were married in the District of Columbia in June 1958 and returned to Virginia, thereby violating at least two state antimiscegenation laws.[3] Pleading guilty to the charges, their sentence was suspended for twenty-five years provided they left the state and did not return for twenty-five years. They filed suit several years later, asking a Virginia court to vacate the judgment, arguing that the laws violated the due process and equal protection clauses of the Fourteenth Amendment. The trial court denied their motion, and the appellate court affirmed.

The Lovings also filed suit in federal court, seeking a declaratory judgment against the antimiscegenation laws. When the case reached the Supreme Court, Warren delivered the opinion for a unanimous Court; Stewart concurred, stating that, in his view, a law that subjects a person to criminal penalties on the basis of race is unconstitutional.

The state argued that there was no equal protection violation because the statutes did not single out a race for disfavor, but applied equally to both. It also contended that the Court should apply minimal scrutiny and defer to its judgment to treat interracial marriages differently from other marriages. Warren rejected the state's theory that the laws did not constitute racial classifications because they punished members of both races. Instead, ruling that they involved a racial classification, the Court subjected them to strict scrutiny. Citing *McLaughlin v. Florida* (1964), in which the state also unsuccessfully argued that equal application of a law punishing persons of different races for cohabiting was not racially based, the Court found that the Virginia laws had no purpose beyond "invidious racial discrimination" (*Loving* 1967, 11).

In addition to the equal protection violation, the Court also held that the Lovings were deprived of their due process rights because "the freedom to marry has long been recognized as one of the vital personal rights essential to the orderly pursuit of happiness by free men. Marriage is one of the 'basic civil rights of man,'" the Court continued, "fundamental to our very existence and survival" (*Loving* 1967, 12, quoting *Skinner v. Oklahoma*, 1942, 541). Infringing on this fundamental right for racially discriminatory reasons cannot be justified.

The significance of *Loving* cannot be overstated for, despite the passage of time, it "remains the most important, most coherent, clearest, most frequently cited case explaining the constitutional right to marry" (Wardle 1998, 347). Over a decade later, the Supreme Court again assessed the constitutionality of a state marriage regulation in *Zablocki v. Redhail* (1978). Under Wisconsin law at the time, residents who were legally obligated to support their noncustodial children must obtain a court order permitting them to marry. Because he had not received the court's approval, Roger Redhail's application for a marriage license was rejected. It was agreed that he would have been unable to obtain the court order because he had not fulfilled his support obligations to his daughter, who was receiving AFDC benefits, two conditions the law aimed at preventing.

Redhail filed a class action suit in federal district court, arguing that the Wisconsin statute unconstitutionally infringed on his equal protection and due process rights under the First, Fifth, Ninth, and Fourteenth Amendments. Using strict scrutiny because the law affected the fundamental right to marry, the three-judge district court held that the statute violated the equal protection clause.

With only Rehnquist dissenting, Marshall announced the opinion for the Court. Burger joined Brennan, Blackmun, White, and Marshall in comprising a majority, but he also wrote a concurring opinion, as did Powell, Stevens, and Stewart.

Marshall began by citing *Loving* as "the leading decision of this Court on the right to marry" (*Zablocki* 1978, 383). Although *Loving* involved a racial classification decided on equal protection grounds, Marshall noted that cases following it and *Griswold* "have routinely categorized the right to marry as among the personal decisions protected by the right of privacy" (*Zablocki* 1978, 384) and that laws affecting it required a heightened scrutiny. He reassured states that the Court would not subject all marriage regulations to a higher level of scrutiny, only those that "significantly interefere[d] with decisions to enter into the marital relationship" (386).

Subjecting the Wisconsin statute to the more rigorous analysis, the Court assumed without deciding that the goals of the statute—counseling applicants on meeting their support obligations and protecting the welfare of the child—were legitimate, but that the law did not serve these ends. By unduly impinging on the individual's right to marry, it violated the equal protection clause.

Stewart's concurring opinion argued that the law did not create a classification of persons under traditional equal protection theory. In his view, the statute was unconstitutional because it infringed on the liberty guaranteed by the due process clause. Although the state may constitutionally regulate, or even forbid, marriages, its power is not unlimited. Here, the state's interests were legitimate, but they did not "justify the absolute deprivation of the benefits of a legal marriage" (394). He believed the majority based its ruling on the equal protection clause to avoid the charge of engaging in "substantive due process," but, in his view, it was preferable to candidly admit it rather than attempt to conceal it.

Powell also wrote separately to reaffirm the state's authority over marriage. He agreed that the Wisconsin law violated both the equal protection and due process clauses. His disagreement was over the degree of deference ordinarily owed state marriage regulations, for he was not persuaded that they always implicated a fundamental right and merited rigorous judicial scrutiny.[4] He also criticized the majority for not providing guidance on which type of regulations would "significantly interfere" with the right to marry and trigger the higher form of scrutiny.[5]

Despite the sweeping rhetoric in *Loving* and *Zablocki*, the cases provided little support to litigants in same-sex marriage cases because of the judiciary's unwillingness to supercede legislative judgments and interfere with state marriage policies (Nolan 1998).

EARLY SAME-SEX MARRIAGE CASES

Loving was premised on the discriminatory treatment of interracial couples, yet its strong language affirming the principle of freedom of choice in marriage as a fundamental right became a rallying cry for same-sex couples. It set off a round of challenges to state laws restricting same-sex marriage, in part because it was the first ruling to invalidate a marriage law, forsaking "the long-established emphasis on the ultimate responsibility of the states to regulate marriage in our federal system" (Wardle 1998, 306).

For the most part, however, despite *Loving,* the early challenges to same-sex marriage restrictions were unsuccessful, with most courts interpreting the right to marry narrowly and declining to analogize same-sex marriage laws to miscegenation laws. The major difficulty for same-sex marriage litigants was that the courts typically stopped short of the constitutional analysis, ruling against the plaintiffs on the grounds that they did not satisfy the definition of a marriage. Judges insisted on preserving the prevailing view of marriage as a legal relationship between a man and a woman, often citing dictionaries for support (see Trosino 1993).

In *Anonymous v. Anonymous* (1971), one of the first cases to consider a same-sex marriage issue, a New York trial court ruling illustrated the judiciary's adherence to a traditional definition of marriage when considering whether persons of the same sex could enter into a valid marriage contract. The plaintiff believed he married the defendant in a civil ceremony in Texas. As the court described it, their relationship was murky and infused with alcohol; at the time of the wedding, the plaintiff was unaware that the defendant was a male and that he intended to, and soon would, undergo an operation to become a female.

The plaintiff filed suit, asking the court to rule on his marital status because, among other things, he was being forced to pay the defendant's medical bills and other expenses. In determining whether the parties were legally married, Judge Buschmann cited various dictionary definitions of marriage, all of which specified that a marriage contract required a man and a woman. Based on this, he held that the plaintiff and defendant had not been married within the meaning of the law.

Baker v. Nelson (1971) was one of the first direct legal challenges to a state's ban on same-sex marriage. Richard John Baker and James Michael McConnell applied for a marriage license in Hennepin County, Minnesota. When it was denied, they sought a court order, which was also refused, and they appealed to the state supreme court.

Speaking for the en banc Minnesota Supreme Court, Justice Peterson questioned whether state law permitted same-sex marriage and, if not, whether it was unconstitutional to deny same-sex couples the right to marry. The plaintiffs argued that because the statute lacked a specific prohibition against same-sex marriage, the legislature intended to allow it. Citing dictionary references for support, Peterson found that the legislature intended the "common usage [of marriage], meaning the state of union between persons of the opposite sex" (185–6). He concluded that the legislature had not intended to authorize same-sex marriage.

Rejecting the plaintiffs' argument that they had a fundamental right to marry, the court cited the book of Genesis, as well as case law linking marriage to procreation, and held that opposite-sex marriage was more firmly established than the contemporary social norms the plaintiffs sought to instill. Adverting to the importance of legislative deference, Peterson said he refused to use the due process clause as "a charter for restructuring [marriage] by judicial legislation" (186). He also dismissed their equal protection challenge, saying *Loving* did not apply because the Court's ruling there was premised on the racial discrimination in the Virginia law. By refusing to extend *Loving* to a broader class of litigants, the Minnesota high court signaled that it was unwilling to expand the right to marry beyond the parameters imposed by the legislature.[6]

Shortly after *Nelson* was decided, a Kentucky court of appeals upheld a lower court ruling that Marjorie Jones and her partner were not entitled to a marriage license (*Jones v. Hallahan* 1973). Because state law did not define a marriage, Judge Vance consulted several dictionaries, finding that each referred to a union between a man and a woman. Citing the *Nelson* court's analysis of the right to marry, he dismissed the plaintiff's constitutional arguments out of hand, concluding that the relationship the plaintiffs sought was outside the bounds of marriage.

A year later, a Washington State court of appeals reviewed a marriage policy in *Singer v. Hara* (1974). John Singer and Paul Barwick sought a court order after their application for a marriage license was denied, but the state superior court judge upheld the denial, ruling that they had not shown that Washington law permits same-sex marriage or that withholding a license infringes on their constitutional rights.

On appeal, they claimed that the law discriminated against them on the basis of sex, violating the state ERA as well as the Eighth, Ninth, and Fourteenth Amendments of the United States Constitution. Court of appeals judge Swanson pointed out that the words on the affidavits required to obtain a license were "male" and "female," indicating that the legislature had not intended to authorize same-sex marriage. Unlike *Loving*, in which the United States Supreme Court rejected Virginia's assertion that its antimiscegenation law had no racial implications, the Washington court found that its marriage law was not based on sex because all same-sex couples were denied marriage licenses, regardless of their sex. Echoing the rulings in the Kentucky, New York, and Minnesota courts, Swanson concluded that the link between marriage and reproduction justified the state's position on same-sex marriage.

Swanson also addressed the plaintiffs' argument that the law merited strict scrutiny because it was a sex-based classification and implicated the fundamental right to marry as well. Acknowledging the California Supreme Court's decision in *Sail'er Inn v. Kirby* (1971) and the United States Supreme Court's plurality opinion in *Frontiero v. Richardson* (1973), he conceded that strict scrutiny was warranted if the law were based on sex.[7] However, because the policy was based on marriage rather than sex, it was inappropriate to use strict scrutiny. He also rejected their contention that he should apply heightened scrutiny because the classification was based on homosexuality.

Because the plaintiffs lacked the traditional indicia of a suspect class, the court applied traditional minimal scrutiny analysis and upheld the law as a reasonable legislative classification. The judge acknowledged in a footnote that societal attitudes toward homosexuality were changing, yet he thought it improper to intervene because this was "a question for the people to answer through the legislative process" (*Singer* 1974, 1196n12).

Several years later, the Ninth Circuit also addressed the legality of same-sex marriage in *Adams v. Howerton* (1982a). United States citizen Richard Adams and Australian citizen Anthony Sullivan were married in a religious ceremony in Boulder, Colorado, after Sullivan's visa had expired. The INS rejected their petition to change his immigration status, a decision affirmed by the Board of Immigration Appeals. When they challenged the board's decision, the lower federal court upheld the board, and they sought review in the Ninth Circuit Court of Appeals.

Speaking for the three-judge panel, Judge Wallace first sought to determine whether the Immigration and Nationality Act of 1952 allowed same-sex marriages by consulting Colorado law, which was silent on the matter. He held that such marriages were not permissible under federal law because according to "its ordinary, contemporary, common meaning," several dictionaries defined marriage as "a relationship between a man and a woman" (1040). In deference to Congress's virtual plenary power to regulate citizenship, the court applied the minimal scrutiny typically reserved for immigration matters and found Congress's refusal to recognize same-sex marriage reasonable.[8]

Just two years later, a Pennsylvania superior court ruled on whether same-sex partners could enter into a common law marriage. The case arose when John De Santo sought a "divorce" from William Barnsley, a man he claimed was his common law husband of ten years. Judge DeFuria of the Pennsylvania Court of Common Pleas held that persons of the same sex cannot enter into a common law marriage (*De Santo v. Barnsley* 1982).

On appeal, superior court judge Spaeth focused on the same question
and, citing *Howerton*, *Singer*, and *Jones*, noted the consensus among states
that same-sex partners cannot enter into valid marriage contracts (*De Santo
v. Barnsley* 1984). Although he recognized that the court was not being asked
to adjudicate the constitutionality of a contractual same-sex marriage, the
judge believed that the same principles applied to common law same-sex
marriages.

Like most states at the time, Pennsylvania law did not specify that marriage was restricted to persons of the opposite sex. But citing standard dictionary definitions of marriage, the court ruled that "the inference that
marriage is so limited is strong" in both common law and statutory marriages (954). The court declined to extend common law marriage to include
same-sex partners, reasoning that history, social policy, and considerations of
judicial restraint all militated against it. If courts refashioned state marriage
laws, the judge said, "we should abuse our judicial power: our decision would
have no support in precedent, and its practical effect would be to amend the
Marriage Law—something only the Legislature can do" (956).

SAME-SEX MARRIAGE IN HAWAII

Almost a decade later, the Supreme Court of Hawaii made history in same-
sex marriage policymaking. The case began when three same-sex couples
sued the state after being denied marriage licenses. Arguing that the denial
was based on sex, they sought an injunction against enforcement of the
Hawaii marriage law, claiming it violated their right to privacy and equal
protection under the state constitution.[9] The circuit court ruled in favor of
the state, and the plaintiffs appealed.

With Justice Levinson announcing the opinion for a divided court, the
state supreme court held that their complaint was wrongly dismissed (*Baehr
v. Lewin* 1993).[10] Citing the right to privacy articulated in *Roe*, Levinson
declared that the state constitution explicitly requires the state to demonstrate a compelling interest in a law that infringes on the right to privacy,
that is, the court must use strict scrutiny when the right to privacy is implicated. Reasoning from *Zablocki* that the right to marry is a fundamental
right, the court questioned whether this right also extends to same-sex couples. After reviewing United States Supreme Court rulings on the right to
marry, it determined that "the federal construct of the fundamental right to
marry . . . presently contemplates unions between men and women" (*Baehr
v. Lewin* 1993, 56). And because same-sex marriage was not an essential part

of the nation's traditions and values, the court was unwilling to declare it a fundamental right.

Instead of basing its ruling on the state constitution, the Hawaii court grounded its opinion on the right to privacy within the United States Constitution, adopting the reasoning of the United States Supreme Court in *Bowers* (see Feather 1997). However, in contrast to the prevailing view of most state courts, Levinson recognized that the state's authority to regulate marriages, while extensive, is not plenary. He offered hope to the plaintiffs, explaining that because they had also alleged they were discriminated against on the basis of sex, they were entitled to an evidentiary hearing in which the state would have to show that the law furthered a compelling interest and was narrowly tailored to further that interest, in other words, survive strict scrutiny. He added that the circuit court judge should not have used minimal scrutiny in deciding the case.

The court stressed that, unlike the federal Constitution, the state constitution contains an equal rights amendment that explicitly prohibits sex discrimination.[11] Grounding its decision in *Loving*, it distinguished the cases cited in the state's brief, in part because they had not raised the same constitutional questions.[12] Moreover, Levinson emphasized, the Kentucky court had decided *Jones* on equal protection grounds without even considering how *Loving* affected same-sex marriage. He equated *Jones* and *Singer* to the Virginia court's ruling in *Loving*, saying that all had characterized the sought-after marriages as against God's will. The court concluded that strict scrutiny was the proper standard to judge the constitutionality of sex-based classifications under the Hawaii Constitution and held that the marriage code would be presumed unconstitutional absent proof of a compelling state interest; it vacated the lower court ruling and remanded the case to allow the circuit court to adjudicate the plaintiffs' claim under strict scrutiny.

Judge Heen dissented, voting to affirm the circuit court decision. He distinguished *Loving* and *Zablocki* because neither involved a right to marry a partner of the same sex. Echoing the "equal application" theory propounded by Virginia in *Loving*, Heen rejected the majority's position that the statute might infringe on equal protection. In his view, because the law applied equally to both sexes, it was not a sex-based classification; if anything, it involved only "unmarried persons," a classification that clearly did not merit strict scrutiny. In applying minimal scrutiny, the justice found nothing wrong in the legislative purpose of "fostering and protecting the propagation of the human race through heterosexual marriages." If the plaintiffs believed they were being deprived of the benefits of marriage, their only recourse was to seek relief from the legislature, whose task it is "to express the will of the populace" (*Baehr v. Lewin* 1993, 74).

Before the Hawaii case was heard on remand, gay rights advocates suffered a defeat in a District of Columbia case in which the plaintiffs, Craig Dean and Patrick Gill, challenged the District's refusal to give them a marriage license. They filed suit in the District of Columbia Superior Court, claiming their rights under the District's Human Rights Act were violated; the judge granted summary judgment to the government (*Dean v. District of Columbia* 1992). In a per curiam opinion, with multiple concurring and dissenting opinions, the District of Columbia Court of Appeals affirmed (*Dean* 1995). Although all agreed on the outcome, each judge had a different rationale. Judge Terry's opinion focused on the proper institution to define marriage, stating that the plaintiffs must seek their remedy in the legislature because courts were not permitted to "alter or expand the definition of marriage, as that term has been understood and accepted for hundreds of years" (362).

Meanwhile, the governor of Hawaii, Democrat John Waihee, promised to contest the state supreme court's ruling. "Historically and culturally," he said, "marriage has universally been between a man and a woman" (*ABA Journal* July 1993). The legislature also reacted negatively to the ruling, proposing legislation to reaffirm that marriage was limited to opposite-sex couples. The next year, it created the Commission on Sexual Orientation and the Law to examine issues related to same-sex marriage. There was much controversy surrounding the commission and much dissension within it. Eventually, in a 5–2 vote, it recommended to the legislature that the state allow same-sex couples to marry or, if not, to create domestic partnerships granting them many of the rights and responsibilities of marriage (*New York Times* December 11, 1995; Guillerman 1997).

Further complicating the legal and political landscape, after the supreme court ruled in *Baehr*, clergy members of the Church of Jesus Christ of the Latter-Day Saints (LDS) and the Church sought to intervene in the subsequent court action, arguing that they believed the attorney general would not vigorously counter the plaintiffs' case on remand. When the lower court denied their motion, they appealed to the Hawaii Supreme Court, claiming that they were vulnerable because if they refused to officiate at same-sex weddings, the state could revoke their power to perform marriages; moreover, they argued such action might leave them open to a suit for gender discrimination.

The state high court unanimously held that the circuit court had not abused its discretion by denying their motion to intervene because they had failed to show a sufficient interest in the matter (*Baehr v. Miike* 1996a). The

Hawaii marriage code merely authorizes religious officers to perform marriages; refusing to perform a marriage would not jeopardize their licenses, the court said. Additionally, it reasoned that, as clergy, they could assert a free exercise defense in a gender discrimination suit.

Following a trial, in a decision announced on December 3, 1996, circuit court judge Chang made extensive findings of fact and held there was no compelling reason to justify the discriminatory treatment of same-sex couples. He ruled that the Hawaii marriage law violated the equal protection clause of the state constitution and barred the state from denying marriage licenses solely because the applicants were of the same sex (*Baehr v. Miike* 1996b). Exemplifying the harsh rhetoric often accompanying unpopular judicial rulings, gay rights opponents attacked the decision as "a case of judicial tyranny by another activist judge . . . [and] nothing short of lawlessness" (*ABA Journal* February 1997).

A day after he issued the opinion, Chang stayed his order pending the state's appeal. However, in April 1997, before gay rights advocates were able to celebrate their victory, the state legislature approved a proposal to amend the state constitution that would appear on the November 1998 ballot. The amendment was intended to reinforce the legislature's authority to enact a law restricting marriage to a man and a woman only.[13] Reflecting the compromise between proponents and opponents of same-sex marriage, the legislature also committed to enacting a domestic partnership law, with provisions for hospital visitation, access to workers' compensation and insurance benefits, property ownership, and family leave. Although more extensive than any other domestic partnership law in the nation, members of the gay community found the proposal unsatisfactory and decided to continue to pursue the litigation (Eskridge 2002, chap. 1).

In an unpublished opinion, the Hawaii Supreme Court affirmed Chang's ruling (*Baehr v. Miike* 1997), but the decision would have no effect for the fate of same-sex marriage in Hawaii was sealed in November 1998, when the public overwhelmingly voted to ratify the constitutional amendment. On December 9, 1999, the Hawaii Supreme Court reversed Chang's judgment, ruling that the marriage amendment obviated the equal protection challenge and mooted the case (*Baehr v. Miike* 1999).

Simply dismissing the case did not satisfy Justice Ramil. In his view, the court should have acknowledged that its 1993 opinion was wrongly decided and overruled it. He admonished the court for its involvement in the debate over same-sex marriage, an issue that "involves a question of pure public policy that should have been left to the people of this state or their elected representatives." The plurality opinion, he continued, "amounted to a public policy judgment ordinarily consigned to the people through their elected representatives" (at 10).

The same month that Hawaii voters ratified the constitutional amendment, Alaska voters went to the polls to approve a constitutional amendment restricting marriage to opposite-sex couples.[14] The events leading to this vote were similar to those in Hawaii. In *Brause v. Bureau of Vital Statistics* (1998), Alaska superior court judge Michalski upheld the plaintiffs' challenge to the Alaska law refusing to recognize a same-sex marriage performed in another jurisdiction and denying same-sex partners the benefits of marriage. Refusing to defer to common practice, Michalski noted, "it is the duty of the court to do more than merely assume that marriage is only, and must only be, what most are familiar with. In some parts of our nation mere acceptance of the familiar would have left segregation in place"; he added that "in light of . . . [the plaintiffs'] challenge to the constitutionality of the relevant statutes, this court cannot defer to the legislature or familiar notions when addressing this issue" (at 2).[15]

Michalski disagreed with the Hawaii Supreme Court's refusal to characterize same-sex marriage as a fundamental right. "The relevant question," he said, "is not whether same-sex marriage is so rooted in our traditions that it is a fundamental right, but whether the freedom to choose one's own life partner is so rooted in our traditions" (at 4). Finding that it was, he ruled that under the state constitution's right to privacy, the right to marry was fundamental, and the state was required to show a compelling reason to infringe on it.[16] Michalski stayed his ruling, however, to allow the state to appeal. While on appeal, the legislature proposed, and the voters ratified, a constitutional amendment, effective January 3, 1999, that limited marriage to a man and a woman. As in Hawaii, when the amendment was adopted, the appeal before the supreme court was moot (*Brause v. Department of Health & Social Services* 2001).[17]

DEFENSE OF MARRIAGE ACTS

Although gay rights advocates had scored an important victory in the Hawaii courts in the early stages of the litigation, *Baehr* "provoked the biggest anti-gay backlash since the McCarthy era" (Eskridge 2002, 26). Fearing a domino effect as a consequence of the Hawaii litigation, Congress enacted the Defense of Marriage Act (DOMA) in 1996.[18] The concern was that couples would legally wed in Hawaii and sue to have their marriage recognized in their home state under the Full Faith and Credit (FF&C) clause of Article IV of the United States Constitution (see Koppelman 1996).[19] Senate Majority Leader Trent Lott, Mississippi Republican, claimed DOMA was necessary as "a preemptive measure to make sure that a handful of judges, in a single state, cannot impose a radical social agenda upon the entire nation" (*New York Times* September 11, 1996).

Companion bills with broad support were introduced in the Senate and House in May 1996: H.R. 3396 was introduced in the House by thrice-married Republican Bob Barr of Georgia with 117 cosponsors; S. 1740 was introduced in the Senate by Don Nickles, Republican from Oklahoma, with 24 cosponsors, including Republican presidential nominee Dole. DOMA consists of two main sections: §2 permits states to refuse to recognize same-sex marriages performed in other states;[20] §3 specifies that only opposite-sex marriages are valid under federal law.[21] As explained by the committee report accompanying the bill, "H.R. 3396, the Defense of Marriage Act, has two primary purposes. The first is to defend the institution of traditional heterosexual marriage. The second is to protect the right of the States to formulate their own public policy regarding the legal recognition of same-sex unions, free from any federal constitutional implications that might attend the recognition by one State of the right for homosexual couples to acquire marriage licenses" (United States House Judiciary Committee 1996, 2). Congress also wanted to prevent same-sex couples from claiming entitlement to federal benefits (10–11).[22]

Following traditional rules of comity, most states recognize marriages validly performed in their sister states. However, although its interpretation is subject to some dispute, states would likely cite the judicially derived "public policy exception" to the FF&C clause and refuse to accept same-sex marriages performed elsewhere on the grounds that they conflict with their own public policy (see Holland 1998). The committee report acknowledged that Congress was aware of the role that the "public policy exception" could play in limiting the effect of same-sex weddings performed in Hawaii but was unwilling to leave it to chance (Bossin 2005, 387). Because some believed that *Romer* created the potential for a successful constitutional challenge to DOMA on equal protection grounds, the report also took pains to explain that DOMA was justified by the government's legitimate interest in "defending . . . heterosexual marriage" (United States House Judiciary Committee 1996, 33).

Supporters painted a dire picture of the future without DOMA. During floor debate, Barr warned,

The very foundations of our society are in danger of being burned. The flames of hedonism, the flames of narcissism, the flames of self-centered morality are licking at the very foundations of our society: the family unit. The courts in Hawaii have rendered a decision loud and clear. They have told the lower court: You shall recognize same-sex marriages. What more does it take, America? What more does it take, my colleagues, to wake up and see that this is an issue being shouted at us by extremists intent, bent on forcing a tortured view of morality on the rest of the country? (*Congressional Record* 1996, H7482)

Ironically, DOMA proponents claimed that Congress's authority to enact the law stemmed from the provision in the FF&C clause that "the Congress may by general Laws prescribe the Manner in which such Acts, Records, and Proceedings shall be proved and the Effect thereof." During debate over the bill, Senator Edward Kennedy, Democrat from Massachusetts, inserted a letter into the *Congressional Record* from Harvard law professor Laurence Tribe, who disagreed with this interpretation and warned that DOMA was unconstitutional. Tribe argued that Congress lacked the authority to legislate a specific exemption from the reach of the FF&C clause. Although, he said, there might be debate over the precise meaning of congressional authority, "it is as plain as words can make it" that it does not grant Congress the right to decide exactly which "acts, records, and proceedings" are entitled to full faith and credit and which are not (*Congressional Record* 1996, S5931).

Its supporters claimed that DOMA protected states' rights, yet Tribe contended that it would allow Congress to nullify state policy decisions if they merely "offend a congressional majority." Moreover, he asserted, it was unnecessary because under current judicial interpretations of the FF&C clause, the "public policy exception" permits states to deny full faith and credit to offending acts of their sister states (*Congressional Record* 1996, S5931).[23] However, members of Congress were anxious to take a stand against same-sex marriage (especially in an election year); the bill was overwhelmingly approved in the House in a 342–67 vote on July 12, 1996, and an 85–14 vote in the Senate on September 10, 1996 (*Congressional Record* 1996, H7506; S10129).

After returning from a four-day campaign trip, President Clinton signed DOMA (Public Law 104-199) into law without ceremony on September 21, 1996. His press secretary, Michael McCurry, "acknowledged that Mr. Clinton had signed the bill because 'the President believes the motives behind this bill are dubious and the President believes that the sooner he gets this over with the better'" (*New York Times* September 22, 1996).

Thus far, DOMA has received comparatively little attention from the courts. In *Wilson v. Ake* (2005), Judge Moody, a Florida federal court judge, dismissed a complaint from a lesbian couple who had been legally married in Massachusetts and sought to have their marriage recognized in Florida. The clerk of the court denied their request, and they sued, claiming both state and federal DOMAs violated the FF&C clause, the due process, equal protection, and privileges and immunities clauses of the Fourteenth Amendment, and the commerce clause of the federal Constitution. Moody held that Congress was acting within its authority to enact DOMA under the FF&C clause. Indeed, he believed DOMA was "exactly what the Framers envisioned when they created the Full Faith and Credit Clause" (1303).[24]

In *Smelt v. County of Orange* (2005), a federal court judge in Orange County, California, abstained from deciding the plaintiffs' state constitutional challenge to the California law against same-sex marriage until the state court completed its review, held that they lacked standing to challenge §2 of DOMA allowing states to refuse to accept same-sex marriages performed in other states because they were not married in any state, and ruled that §3 did not violate the due process or equal protection guarantees of the federal constitution. The Ninth Circuit agreed with the lower court that abstention was proper but held that the plaintiffs lacked standing to challenge either §2 or §3 and remanded the case with an order to the lower court to dismiss their claim under §3 (Smelt 2006).

At the state level, legislatures responded to the Hawaii decision by enacting modified versions of DOMA, known as mini-DOMAs, to avert the possibility that their courts would refrain from applying the public policy exception in the case of a marriage performed outside the state or declare the public policy exception unconstitutional. By November 2005, forty states had mini-DOMAs, defining marriage between a man and a woman and precluding recognition of marriages performed elsewhere; three more had laws restricting marriage to a husband and wife (Human Rights Campaign 2005d; Peterson 2005a; American Bar Association Section Family Law Working Group on Same Sex Marriages and Non-Marital Unions 2004, 30).

Both national and state DOMAs have been the subject of endless debate about their constitutionality and their effect on federalist principles. While supporters believed them necessary to avoid the impact of events in Hawaii, critics claimed that both the federal and state DOMAs were politically motivated and largely superfluous. Holland (1998, 395) believes that §2 "must be characterized as nothing more than gratuitous gay-bashing." Whatever the motivation, most legal scholars agree that before DOMA was enacted, states had sufficient authority under the FF&C clause to allow them to refuse to recognize same-sex marriages performed outside their borders if they chose (see Koppelman 1996; Borchers 2005). Once the danger had passed and same-sex marriages were no longer possible to obtain in Hawaii, DOMA essentially lay dormant until seven years later when, in 2003, events in Massachusetts renewed the nation's fears of the legalization of same-sex marriage.

CIVIL UNIONS

Just before the turn of the century, before the furor over Massachusetts arose, the Vermont courts added a new dimension to the same-sex marriage debate. In July 1997, three same-sex couples sued the state of Vermont after they were denied marriage licenses by the clerks in their respective towns. The couples claimed that the state marriage law did not exclude same-sex marriages, and forbidding same-sex marriages violated the state constitution. The superior court judge dismissed their complaint, finding that same-sex couples did not have a fundamental right to marry. Applying minimal scrutiny, she held that the law furthered the state's interest in promoting the link between marriage and children.

On appeal, shortly after the Hawaii court acknowledged that its decision was usurped by the state constitutional amendment, the Vermont Supreme Court handed down its ruling in *Baker v. Vermont* (1999).[25] Speaking for the court, Chief Justice Amestoy rejected the plaintiffs' contention that the Vermont marriage law does not bar same-sex marriage; there was ample evidence, he said, that the legislature intended to limit marriage to a man and a woman. Following the law of most other states, the Vermont high court held that because it treats the sexes the same, the marriage law does not discriminate on the basis of sex.

Focusing the analysis on the common benefits clause of the Vermont Constitution, Amestoy took pains to distinguish it from the equal protection clause of the federal Constitution, in no small measure to justify a more rigorous review of the statute than the minimal scrutiny customarily used by the United States Supreme Court in nonsuspect equal protection cases.[26] Additionally, by grounding its decision in the Vermont Constitution rather than in the equal protection principles of the United States Constitution, the state high court precluded review by the United States Supreme Court.[27]

To survive under the common benefits clause, the state must show the law "is reasonably necessary" to achieve its stated goals (878).[28] In determining whether the Vermont marriage law was reasonably related to the government's aim of strengthening the ties between marriage and children, the court found that same-sex couples were already engaged in child rearing, aided by artificial reproductive technology and legalized adoption. Indeed, it noted, by removing the legal barriers, the state had encouraged same-sex couples to adopt.[29] The court concluded that if the purpose of the marriage law was to protect the interests of children, same-sex couples had the same concerns and needs as opposite-sex couples.

In assessing the marriage-procreation–child rearing link, Amestoy noted that the law extended the benefits and protections of marriage to many persons with no logical connection to children. Opposite-sex couples marry for reasons unrelated to procreation; some never intend to have children, and others are incapable of doing so. "If anything," he said, "the exclusion of same-sex couples from the legal protections incident to marriage exposes their children to the precise risks that the State argues the marriage laws are designed to secure against. In short, the marital exclusion treats persons who are similarly situated for purposes of the law, differently" (882). The court was also not persuaded that the state's traditional opposition to same-sex marriage justified the ban, largely because it believed it was motivated by animosity toward a particular class of individuals.

Accordingly, the supreme court reversed the trial court, holding that the state had not met its burden of offering "a reasonable and just basis" to preclude same-sex couples from enjoying the benefits of a Vermont civil marriage (886). However, rather than fashioning a remedy, the court identified a range of constitutionally permissible options over the objections of Justice Johnson, who charged the court with abdicating its responsibility by not simply directing the state to issue marriage licenses to the plaintiffs.

Amestoy ended by eloquently proclaiming that "the extension of the Common Benefits Clause to acknowledge plaintiffs as Vermonters who seek nothing more, nor less, than legal protection and security for their avowed commitment to an intimate and lasting human relationship is simply, when all is said and done, a recognition of our common humanity" (889).

Despite this broad statement of principle, the relief provided was limited. The court ordered the state to extend the benefits and protections of marriage under Vermont law to same-sex couples, leaving it to the legislature to craft the appropriate means of addressing the constitutional mandate.

Thus, the legislature could choose to allow same-sex couples to marry but was not required to do so.

The public was divided over the ruling, with surveys showing most were opposed. A statewide poll conducted about a month after the decision was announced found that 52 percent of those questioned disagreed with it, 38 percent agreed, and 10 percent were unsure. People were even more divided over what should be done about it; 49 percent favored overturning it by amending the constitution, 44 percent opposed such action (*New York Times* February 3, 2000). However, perhaps in part because of the limited nature of the ruling, the attempt to reverse it by amending the state constitution ultimately failed in the legislature despite extensive debate over it.

In early February 2000, the legislature decided against easing the restrictions on same-sex marriage and began crafting a comprehensive domestic partnership law. The final bill retained the institution of marriage for opposite-sex couples but created a new status for same-sex partners known as civil unions. Couples entering into civil unions were granted many of the benefits and rights of marriage under state law, including judicial termination for dissolution of the union; they remained ineligible for federal benefits and entitlements. After both houses of the legislature approved the Civil Unions bill, Governor Howard Dean signed it into law on April 26, 2000 (*Burlington Free Press* May 1, 2000).

SAME-SEX MARRIAGE APPROVED

Two years after civil unions became a reality in Vermont, seven couples who were denied marriage licenses sued the state of Massachusetts, asking the court to declare that forbidding same-sex marriage violated the state constitution.[30] As in Vermont, the lower court dismissed the complaint and ruled in favor of the state, linking its regulation of marriage to its interest in procreation and child rearing (*Goodridge v. Department of Public Health* 2002).

On appeal, in a 4–3 vote, the state supreme court compared the state constitution with the federal document, noting that the state charter demands a higher standard of liberty and equality than the federal constitution.[31] Speaking for the court, Chief Justice Marshall framed the question as whether an individual who is "barred access to the protections, benefits, and obligations of civil marriage . . . is arbitrarily deprived of membership in one of our community's most rewarding and cherished institutions" (*Goodridge* 2003, 949).

She began by confirming that the legislature had intended to restrict marriages to opposite-sex couples. Citing *Lawrence* four times, Marshall stressed the importance of civil marriage, declaring that "the decision whether and whom to marry is among life's momentous acts of self-definition" (955). She also highlighted the financial and emotional benefits derived from marriage.

The plaintiffs had alleged several constitutional violations, revolving around equal protection and due process.[32] Marshall noted that in such matters as family and marriage, these two principles often converged, and the court would jointly consider the effect of the law on state constitutional guarantees of liberty and equality.

Not surprisingly, the parties differed on the proper level of scrutiny to apply. The court avoided this issue by subjecting the law to its version of rationality review, less than strict, but more rigorous than the minimal scrutiny used by the United States Supreme Court. The state argued that the law furthered its interest in procreation and child rearing, as well as conserving financial resources. The court rejected the first two arguments because the law did not refer to fertility as a condition of marriage, nor did the policy of restricting marriage to opposite-sex couples promote the state's interest in the welfare of children. Indeed, according to the twenty-year-old opinion of *Doe v. Doe* (1983), the parents' sexual orientation or marital status bears no relationship to the best interests of the child. By refusing to allow their parents to marry, the court believed the state was harming children living with same-sex couples.

Marshall also rejected the state's argument that allowing plaintiffs to wed would "undermine the institution of civil marriage," saying that this was far from what the plaintiffs intended (*Goodridge* 2003, 965). Emphasizing its reliance on *Loving*, the court concluded that "recognizing the right of an individual to marry a person of the same sex will not diminish the validity or dignity of opposite-sex marriage, any more than recognizing the right of an individual to marry a person of a different race devalues the marriage of a person who marries someone of her own race" (*Goodridge* 2003, 965). The court ultimately did not resolve the debate over scrutiny, but because the law failed to satisfy the minimal scrutiny test, there was no reason to subject it to a higher level of scrutiny.

Addressing the dissent's claim that its ruling usurped the legislature's authority over marriage policy, Marshall said, on the contrary, the court was duty bound to adjudicate constitutional challenges, especially to laws involving marriage, reproduction, and child rearing. "We owe great deference to the Legislature to decide social and policy issues," she said, "but it is the traditional and settled role of courts to decide constitutional issues" (966). The court was also unpersuaded by the arguments of several amici that it should modify its opinion for the sake of comity among the states.

In the end, the court preserved the marriage license statute but redefined marriage as "the voluntary union of two persons as spouses, to the exclusion of all others" (969). It stayed its judgment until May 2004, giving the legislature six months to respond to the decision. Unclear whether it would be constitutionally acceptable to adopt the Vermont model of civil union, within a month of the decision, the Massachusetts Senate proposed a bill barring same-sex couples from obtaining marriage licenses but allowing them to enter into civil unions. As permissible under Massachusetts law, the Senate brought the matter to the supreme court, asking whether the proposed law "which prohibits same-sex couples from entering into marriage but allows them to form civil unions with all 'benefits, protections, rights and responsibilities' of marriage, comply with the equal protection and due process requirements of the Constitution of the Commonwealth and . . . the Declaration of Rights" (*In re Opinions of the Justices* 2004, 566).

On February 3, 2004, the same four justices who were in the *Goodridge* majority held that the legislature's attempt to suggest equivalency in the terms "civil union" and "civil marriage," while reserving the latter for opposite-sex couples only, failed to satisfy the dictates of *Goodridge*. The court found that creating a separate different legal status for same-sex couples was not rationally related to the state's legitimate goals of procreation and protecting the welfare of children, thereby violating the equal protection and due process clauses of the state constitution. It concluded by saying that "the bill maintains an unconstitutional, inferior, and discriminatory status for same-sex couples, and . . . the answer to the question is 'No'" (*Opinions of the Justices* 2004, 572).

As a result of this decision, on May 17, 2004 (fifty years after *Brown v. Board of Education* [1954]), same-sex couples became eligible for marriage licenses in Massachusetts, the first state in the nation to recognize same-sex marriage.[33]

In an effort to forestall the advent of same-sex marriage, shortly after the court issued its advisory opinion, Massachusetts lawmakers debated a series of constitutional amendments to bar same-sex marriage and allow civil unions instead. The first would have restricted marriage to "the union of one man and one woman" but would have allowed the state to establish civil unions; a second would also have banned same-sex marriage but would have established civil unions in the constitution. Both amendments were narrowly defeated in votes of 100–98 and 104–94. A third proposal, neither requiring nor prohibiting civil unions, also failed in a close 103–94 vote. Finally, on March 29, the legislature approved a compromise amendment to "ban gay marriage and create same-sex civil unions instead," which passed in a 105–92 vote (Crane 2003/2004, 471–3; *Boston Globe* February 13, 2004).

Under Massachusetts law, a constitutional amendment must be ratified by both houses in two successive legislative sessions, followed by approval by the electorate a year later. Thus, the state legislature was required to pass the amendment of March 29 again in the 2005 session, and if it succeeded, the amendment must win approval from a majority of voters in a referendum in November 2006 (*New York Times* March 30, 2004; see K. Miller 2005).

During the legislative debate over the amendment to prohibit same-sex marriage, Governor Mitt Romney had asked state lawmakers to pass emergency legislation allowing him to petition the state high court directly to stay its ruling until the voters had an opportunity to consider the constitutional amendment in November 2006 (the earliest time such a vote was possible). Romney acted, he said, because the state attorney general, Thomas Reilly, had refused to represent him or appoint another lawyer to do so, saying there was insufficient legal justification to ask the court to revisit a question it had already ruled on twice in the last six months.

Another attempt to derail *Goodridge* emerged from a lawsuit filed by a private citizen and eleven state representatives who sued in federal district court to enjoin the enforcement of the state court's decision (*Largess v. Supreme Judicial Court for Massachusetts* 2004a). The plaintiffs argued that because the power to define marriage resided in the legislature, by redefining marriage, the Massachusetts high court had violated the separation of powers principle in the state constitution. They also alleged that in violating the state constitution, the court had simultaneously infringed on their guarantee to a republican form of government, the guarantee clause of the United States Constitution.

District court judge Tauro dismissed their complaint, holding that because the legislature had granted jurisdiction to the supreme court to determine the validity of marriages, the court had not transgressed its jurisdictional boundaries by redefining marriage. "Rather," he said, "it was a legitimate exercise of that court's authority and responsibility to decide with finality all issues arising under the Massachusetts Constitution" (84). In a per curiam opinion, the First Circuit Court affirmed (*Largess* 2004b).[34]

In one more effort to blunt the effect of *Goodridge*, on April 24, 2005, Romney announced that only Massachusetts residents would be permitted to marry in Massachusetts when the six-month stay expired. He cited a forty-eight-word law, enacted in 1913, that prohibited nonresidents from marrying in Massachusetts if the marriage would be "void" in their home state unless they intend to live in Massachusetts. In an interview, the governor said he was interpreting the law as broadly as possible, extending it to states that did not explicitly ban same-sex marriage. Gay rights advocates said that the 1913 law, which was intended to prohibit interracial marriage, was archaic and discriminatory (*New York Times* April 25, 2004).

On May 18, a day after same-sex marriage became legal in Massachusetts, Romney demanded copies of license applications from four cities and towns that he said were defying his order not to marry out-of-state couples. His legal counsel called officials in Somerville, Worcester, Springfield, and Provincetown, ordering them to send the applications to the state capitol (*New York Times* May 19, 2004). As a result, eight couples from Connecticut, Rhode Island, New Hampshire, Vermont, Maine, and New York filed suit, seeking a preliminary injunction to block enforcement of the 1913 statute, claiming it was discriminatory. Judge Ball of the superior court denied the injunction, noting that although she was disturbed that the state began to enforce this law only after *Goodridge*, because it was being applied evenhandedly to both same-sex and opposite-sex couples, she believed it satisfied constitutional standards (*Cote-Whitacre v. Department of Public Health* 2004).

The state supreme court accepted the case for direct appellate review, and on March 30, 2006, the court upheld the lower court's decision to deny the plaintiffs the injunctive relief they sought (*Cote-Whitacre* 2006a). Although there was no majority opinion, there was sufficient agreement among the justices that the 1913 law applied to prohibit the couples from Connecticut, Maine, New Hampshire, and Vermont from marrying in Massachusetts because those states explicitly outlawed same-sex marriage. But because same-sex marriages were not explicitly banned in Rhode Island and New York, those cases were remanded to the lower court to determine the legality of same-sex marriage in those states.[35]

The only dissenter, Justice Ireland objected to the decision, charging that "the Commonwealth's resurrection and selective enforcement of a moribund statute, dormant for almost one hundred years, not only violates the 'spirit' of *Goodridge*, . . . but also offends notions of equal protection. It is, at its core, fundamentally unfair" (660–1).

On September 14, 2005, in a major upset for opponents of same-sex marriage, the Massachusetts legislature voted 157–39 to reject the proposed constitutional amendment to ban same-sex marriage and allow civil unions, the same amendment it had approved in March 2004. The amendment's overwhelming defeat came about in part because fifty-five legislators who had supported it the year before voted "no" this time, and seventeen of the eighteen newly elected members of the legislature voted with the majority. One of the first-year members who voted "no" explained his vote this way: "It is evident that the sky has not fallen [since May 17, 2004]" (*Boston Globe* September 15, 2005). Another said, "Gay marriage has begun and life has not changed for the citizens of the commonwealth, with the exception of those who can now marry who could not before" (*New York Times* September 15, 2005; *Boston Globe* September 15, 2005).[36]

Some opponents of same-sex marriage also voted against the amendment, seeking to replace it with one banning same-sex marriage—without creating an alternative for civil unions. Although supporters of the amendment believe they have enough votes to gain approval in the legislature, they must overcome a number of hurdles before being able to bring it to the voters in 2008 (*Boston Globe* September 15, 2005).

THE NATION REACTS TO GOODRIDGE

After the Massachusetts decision, many same-sex couples succeeded in obtaining marriage licenses, chiefly because local government officials in California, New Mexico, New York, and Oregon acted on their own to issue them despite the questionable legality of their actions.

Perhaps the most interesting and complex events took place in California. Section 300 of the California Family Code, originally adopted in 1977, defines marriage as "a personal relation arising out of a civil contract between a man and a woman." In 1999, the state legislature approved the Domestic Partnership Act, §297 of the California Family Code, granting limited protections to same-sex couples; the benefits were expanded over the years. Then in 2000, California voters approved Proposition 22, which stated that "only marriage between a man and a woman is valid or recognized in California" (Gavin 2004). Also known as the California Defense of Marriage Act, or the Knight Initiative after its principal sponsor, Proposition 22 was approved by voters with a 61–39 percent margin (*Sacramento Bee* September 9, 2005).

Notwithstanding these restrictions, on February 12, 2004, at the direction of newly elected San Francisco mayor Gavin Newsom, San Francisco

County began to issue marriage licenses to same-sex couples. A week later, more than 2,600 marriage licenses were issued in the city (*New York Times* February 18, 2004). In response to questions about his motives, Newsom, who had been considered the conservative candidate in the mayoral election, said, "I did it because I thought it was right" (*New York Times* February 19, 2004). With the courts initially refusing to halt the licenses, despite attempts by opponents to enjoin them, the weddings continued. Rather than waiting for the inevitable lawsuit, San Francisco took the initiative and sued the state in superior court, claiming the California Family Code violated the state constitution. On March 11, 2004, after more than four thousand licenses had been issued, the California Supreme Court ruled on an appeal in a case brought by same-sex marriage opponents and ordered the city to stop issuing marriage licenses to gay couples; the court did not rule on the legality of the marriages that had already taken place (*New York Times* March 12, 2004).

On August 12, 2004, in a 5–2 vote, the California Supreme Court ruled that Newsom had exceeded his authority in determining that the law was unconstitutional and did not have to be obeyed. The marriages performed during February and March were declared "void and of no legal effect" (*Lockyer v. City & County of San Francisco* 2004, 464). But the court ruled only on whether Newsom had the authority to issue the licenses, not on the constitutionality of §300 (*New York Times* August 13, 2004).

Months later, on March 14, 2005, Judge Kramer of the San Francisco County Superior Court ruled in the city's suit against the state and made a "tentative decision" that the opposite-sex requirement in the California Family Code was unconstitutional. Citing *Perez*, the 1948 California Supreme Court decision on interracial marriage, Kramer held that the law was a sex-based classification, mandating strict scrutiny under the California state constitution. The prohibition against same-sex marriage, he said, infringed on the principle that marriage was a profound human choice and found "no rational purpose . . . for limiting marriage in this State to opposite-sex partners" (*Marriage Cases* 2005, at 6). The judge stayed the ruling pending a decision by the state appellate court (see *San Francisco Chronicle* March 15, 2005).[37]

Although the San Francisco marriages captured most of the nation's attention, weddings were taking place in other parts of the country as well. On February 20, 2004, New Mexico's Sandoval County had begun granting marriage licenses to dozens of same-sex couples. The state attorney general, Patricia Madrid, called the issuance of the licenses illegal because, according to her, New Mexico law limited marriage to a man and woman (*New York*

Times February 21, 2004; *Albuquerque Journal* February 28, 2004). Responding to the attorney general's petition, a state district court judge issued a restraining order on March 23, 2004, ordering the town clerk to stop issuing licenses. Shortly thereafter, Madrid filed for a writ with the state supreme court because the district court judge had recused himself from the case, which would make him unavailable to rule on the permanent injunction and therefore allow the restraining order to expire.

In a unanimous opinion, the state supreme court denied the request for a writ but continued the restraining order against the issuance of licenses, putting the matter back in the lower court. Just before the court's decision, the clerk had begun to revise the marriage license application forms, changing them from reading "Male Applicant" and "Female Applicant" to "Applicant 1" and "Applicant 2" (*Albuquerque Journal* February 28, 2004; April 1, 2004). The case was eventually dismissed once the clerk left office, and the attorney general reached an accord with the new clerk. The courts never ruled on the legality of the licenses, and almost a year later, the New Mexico Senate approved a bill limiting marriage to opposite-sex couples (*Albuquerque Journal* March 10, 2005).

About a week after the events in New Mexico began to make the news, the nation's attention was again drawn to the East Coast when, on February 27, 2004, the twenty-six-year-old Green Party mayor of New Paltz, New York, married twenty-five same-sex couples after the town clerk refused to issue them licenses. Mayor Jason West's actions started a series of legal maneuvers, involving several courts, the governor, the state attorney general, and a number of local government officials. Shortly thereafter, in a twenty-eight-page legal opinion, the state attorney general, Eliot Spitzer (elected governor in 2006), advised that although the law does not specifically forbid same-sex marriage, the legislature had not intended to allow them. But, he added, in his view, New York must recognize marriages or civil unions performed outside the state. Spitzer said that his opinion was not binding on West (or on the other mayors closely watching the events who had announced their intention to perform same-sex marriages also) and that the issue should be resolved by the courts.

On March 5, 2004, after a civil suit was filed against him, a state court judge ordered West to stop performing the weddings (*Poughkeepsie Journal* February 28, 2004; March 6, 2004; *Buffalo News* March 4, 2004; March 6, 2004). Meanwhile the Ulster County district attorney charged West in criminal court with nineteen counts of violating the state's domestic relations law by "solemnizing a marriage without a license." After the court had issued the injunction against West, two Unitarian ministers took over the job of marrying unlicensed same-sex couples. The ministers were criminally charged as well, but the charges were subsequently dismissed (*Poughkeepsie Journal* March 7, 2004; July 10, 2005).

When asked whether he was surprised by the criminal charges—for which he could have been fined and sentenced up to a year in jail—West said, "No matter what happens, it would have been worth it. I don't have any regrets at all. Just seeing the looks on these couple's faces was worth any punishment any district attorney and judges could give me" (*Post-Standard* [Syracuse] July 10, 2005). On July 12, 2005, the prosecutor announced he was dropping the criminal charges against West, saying a "trial would be unnecessary and divisive" (*Times Union* [Albany] July 13, 2005).

In the meantime, while attention was focused on New Paltz, more same-sex weddings were taking place on the West Coast. On March 3, 2004, officials in Multnomah County, Oregon, began to issue marriage licenses to same-sex couples after the county attorney, responding to a question from the county board, had stated that he believed that refusing to grant the marriage licenses would likely violate the state constitution. However, when asked by Governor Ted Kulongoski to analyze the applicable Oregon law, Attorney General Hardy Myers took a contrary view. He believed that Oregon law prohibited county clerks from issuing marriage licenses to same-sex couples. Although, he added, the courts would likely find the law unconstitutional under the privileges and immunities clause of the state constitution, the current law must be enforced (*The Oregonian* March 3, 2004; March 13, 2004; March 14, 2004).

Despite the governor's request to stop issuing licenses, officials in Multnomah County continued to do so, and more than 1,500 were issued (*The Oregonian* March 15, 2004). Eventually, all sides to the dispute agreed to have the matter settled in court (*The Oregonian* March 16, 2004; March 20, 2004). The ACLU, several same-sex couples, including four who were married in Multnomah County, and numerous intervenors filed suit in the state circuit court, charging that the state's refusal to accept their marriages violated the privileges and immunities clause of the state constitution.[38] The judge agreed and ordered the state to register the marriages already performed, but he barred the county from issuing future licenses (*Li v. Oregon* 2004). On appeal, the state supreme court reversed, holding that Oregon law limited marriage to opposite-sex couples and that because the county lacked the authority to issue the marriage licenses, they were "void at the time they were issued," thereby nullifying the Multnomah County weddings (*Li* 2005, 102).

Penello (2006, 19) notes that with weddings taking place around the nation, by April 2004, more than 7,000 same-sex couples had married.

THE FEDERAL MARRIAGE AMENDMENT

What appeared to be a rising tide of same-sex marriages around the nation spurred public officials at the state and federal level to enact legislation or propose constitutional amendments to avert similar actions within their borders. Once *Goodridge* was announced, they feared that same-sex couples legally wed in Massachusetts would return to their home states and demand recognition of their marriages. In many states, the amendments merely duplicated existing state DOMAs (Evans 2004, 14). At the federal level, on May 21, 2003, several months before *Goodridge* was decided, Representative Marilyn Musgrave, Republican of Colorado, introduced a resolution that became known as the Federal Marriage Amendment (FMA).[39] Musgrave argued that the amendment was essential because "the trajectory of the courts' decisions is unmistakable" (*Congressional Quarterly Weekly* October 1, 2004).

The original version of the FMA would have restricted marriage to a man and a woman and prevented courts from recognizing other same-sex relationships as marriages. Subsequently, Republican Wayne Allard, also of Colorado, introduced a bill with similar language in the Senate, although his bill purportedly would have permitted state legislatures, but not courts, to recognize civil unions or domestic partnerships (*Congressional Quarterly Weekly* February 28, 2004; July 17, 2004; see Glidden 2004).[40]

The resolutions lay dormant in Congress, but in the wake of *Lawrence* and *Goodridge*, amid a growing public concern over the prospect of same-sex marriage and the fear that DOMA was insufficient to contain the fallout, there was a new groundswell of support for the FMA.[41]

President George W. Bush entered the debate by referring to the FMA during his State of the Union address in January 2004, when he urged the nation to "take a principled stand for one of the most fundamental, enduring institutions of our civilization." After a critique of "activist judges [who] insist on forcing their arbitrary will upon the people, the only alternative left to the people would be the constitutional process. Our Nation must defend the sanctity of marriage," he stated (Bush 2004a).

Shortly thereafter, Bush reacted to *Goodridge*, saying, "Today's ruling of the Massachusetts Supreme Judicial Court is deeply troubling. Marriage is a sacred institution between a man and a woman. If activist judges insist on redefining marriage by court order, the only alternative will be the constitutional process. We must do what is legally necessary to defend the sanctity of marriage" (Bush 2004b). Then on February 24, 2004, citing the developments in Massachusetts, New Mexico, and San Francisco, Bush attacked "activist judges and local officials [who] have made an aggressive attempt to redefine marriage." He urged that "on a matter of such importance, the voice of the people must be heard" and called upon Congress to pass the amendment "defining and protecting marriage as a union between a man and a woman as husband and wife." Alluding to civil unions or domestic partner-ships, he added that states should be permitted to establish legal arrange-ments other than marriage if they chose (Bush 2004c). As the year progressed, and the 2004 election grew nearer, the president discussed the issue almost every month, renewing his support for the constitutional amendment, including a statement on May 17, 2004, the day the Massachusetts same-sex weddings became legal. After reiterating his criticism of "activist judges," he stressed his continued support for the FMA, saying, "The need for that amendment is still urgent, and I repeat that call today" (Bush 2004d).

Amid Republican charges that the courts were destroying the fabric of society and Democratic countercharges that Republicans were capitalizing on a wedge issue in the upcoming presidential election, there was frenetic activity in Congress in the summer and autumn of 2004. On July 14, pro-ponents of the FMA lost a Senate vote of 48–50 to invoke cloture and end the debate on the latest version of the resolution. And on September 30, House leaders bypassed the Judiciary Committee to bring their version of the FMA to a vote; it lost 227–186, almost 50 votes short of the required two-thirds vote needed to approve a constitutional amendment (*Congressional Quarterly Weekly* October 1, 2004; January 17, 2005).

A year later, in February 2006, Senate Majority Leader William Frist, Republican from Tennessee, announced that he would bring a vote on the constitutional amendment, renamed the Marriage Protection Amendment (MPA) in 2005, to ban same-sex marriage to the Senate floor in early June.[42] Frist said the MPA was necessary "to protect the majority of Americans, whom [sic] he said oppose same-sex marriage, from the 'whims of a few activist judges' who seek 'to override the commonsense of the American peo-ple.'" He continued, "'When America's values are under attack, we need to act'" (*Washington Post* February 11, 2006).

When the MPA was brought to the Senate Judiciary Committee in May, it led to a "shouting match" between committee chair Arlen Specter, Republican of Pennsylvania, and Russell Feingold, Democrat from Wisconsin. Feingold stormed out of the committee hearing room after declaring his opposition to the amendment. The committee voted 10–8 along party lines to send it to the Senate floor. Specter, who said he was opposed to the amendment also, nevertheless voted for it. Frist scheduled a vote in the Senate during the week of June 5 (*Washington Post* May 19, 2006; CNN May 19, 2006). Most agree that it was unlikely to receive the sixty votes necessary to invoke cloture (end the debate), and certainly not the requisite two-thirds vote needed for a constitutional amendment.

By the time of the Senate vote, forty-five states had restrictions on same-sex marriage—nineteen through constitutional amendments and twenty-six by statute (*New York Times* June 7, 2006). No state had legalized same-sex marriage since Massachusetts in 2003, and no court of last resort had upheld plaintiffs' challenges to the state or federal bans on it; yet supporters of the amendment sought to alarm the public with the fear that such action was imminent.

On the weekend before the vote would be taken, Bush devoted his Saturday radio address to urging support for the MPA. Speaking on the subject for the first time since his reelection, he again criticized "activist judges and some local officials [who] have made an aggressive attempt to redefine marriage in recent years." He warned that if DOMA "is overturned by activist courts, then marriages recognized in one city or state might have to be recognized as marriages everywhere else. That would mean that every state would have to recognize marriages redefined by judges in Massachusetts or local officials in San Francisco, no matter what their own laws or state constitutions say. This national question," he added, "requires a national solution, and on an issue of such profound importance, that solution should come from the people, not the courts" (Bush 2006a).

Although the White House denied accusations that his actions were intended to shore up his steadily falling poll numbers, many were skeptical, pointing to his need to satisfy his right-wing supporters, who appeared to be losing faith in him (*New York Times* June 4, 2006; CNN June 4, 2006). In his address at the Eisenhower Executive Office Building on June 5, 2006, amid frequent applause, Bush called on Congress to pass the amendment and reiterated the need to "take this issue out of the hands of over-reaching judges and put it back where it belongs—in the hands of the American people (Bush 2006b).[43] At a press conference before the debate, Allard claimed the amendment was needed because "marriage is under attack," warning that "the Constitution will be amended whether we pass this amendment or not. The only question is whether it will be amended through the amendment process or by unelected activist judges" (*Washington Post* June 6, 2006).

Introducing the amendment on the Senate floor, Frist explained that "because same sex marriage advocates cannot win at the ballot box, activists are continuing their campaign to convince State and Federal courts to rewrite traditional marriage laws" (*Congressional Record* 2006, S5393).

When the debate began in the Senate, Minority Leader Harry Reid, Democrat of Nevada, accused the president of attempting "to divide our society, to pit one against another," adding, "This is another one of the president's efforts to frighten, to distort, to distract and to confuse America" (*Washington Post* June 6, 2006).

As predicted, on the day of the vote, amendment supporters were eleven votes short, with only forty-nine of the sixty votes needed for cloture. Senator Sam Brownback, Republican from Kansas, promised supporters, "We're not going to stop until marriage between a man and a woman is protected" (*New York Times* June 7, 2006). Indeed, Allard said, if he were in charge, "we'll have a vote on this issue every year. I think it's important to the American people" (*New York Times* June 8, 2006). House action on the amendment, largely symbolic and obviously futile, was promised for July. On July 18, 2006, despite White House urging, the House voted 237–187 (one member voted present), against it—far short of the two-thirds majority needed for a constitutional amendment. Responding to Democratic criticism that Republicans were ignoring more important issues facing the nation, Representative Phil Gingrey, Republican from Georgia, proclaimed that affirming opposite-sex marriage "is perhaps the best message we can give to the Middle East and all the trouble they're having over there right now" (*New York Times* July 19, 2006).

SAME-SEX MARRIAGE AND THE 2004 ELECTION

Given the prominence of same-sex marriage on the nation's public policy agenda, it was not surprising that the issue would appear on a number of ballots around the nation in the 2004 election. Before 2004, three states— Alaska in 1998, Nebraska in 2000, and Nevada in 2002—had amended their state constitutions to block same-sex marriage. In Nebraska, opponents of same-sex marriage proposed the amendment to ensure that persons who entered into marriages or civil unions in other states would be unable to claim marital status in Nebraska; it was adopted by a substantial majority in the November 2000 election. In a victory for same-sex couples, in *Citizens for Equal Protection, Inc. v. Bruning* (2005), Nebraska district court judge Bataillon declared the amendment unconstitutional.[44] Citing *Romer*, he held that the amendment violated the First Amendment and the equal protection clause of the Fourteenth Amendment.

In August 2004, Missouri voters approved a constitutional amendment banning same-sex marriage. Shortly thereafter, in September, Louisiana voters approved an amendment restricting marriage to a man and a woman and precluding recognition of domestic partnerships and civil unions as well (Peterson 2004). The Louisiana Supreme Court rejected a challenge to the amendment on the grounds that it violated the "single object requirement," in which a proposed constitutional amendment must "be confined to one object" (*Forum for Equality PAC v. McKeithen* 2005, 729).[45] However, in May 2006, Judge Russell of the Georgia Superior Court struck the same-sex marriage amendment approved in November 2004 on the grounds that it violated Georgia's "single subject rule" (*O'Kelley v. Perdue* 2006, at 3).[46] The amendment defined marriage as the union of a man and a woman, banned civil unions, and precluded recognition of marriages performed in other states. The state immediately announced it would appeal her ruling (*Washington Post* May 19, 2006).[47]

During the 2004 election, the electorate in eleven states—Arkansas, Georgia, Kentucky, Michigan, Mississippi, Montana, North Dakota, Ohio, Oklahoma, Oregon, and Utah—went to the polls to cast their votes on the legality of same-sex marriages, and in most cases, civil unions and domestic partnerships as well. In all eleven, the restrictive amendments were approved by substantial majorities: from 86 percent in Mississippi (a 6–1 margin) to 57 percent in Oregon, the state considered least likely to support such an amendment. In all but two states—Oregon and Michigan—the approval ratings were over 60 percent.

The amendments were largely superfluous as most of the eleven states already had state DOMAs on the books. Spurred by *Goodridge*, fearing the courts would declare the existing state DOMAs, and perhaps the federal DOMA as well, unconstitutional, opponents of same-sex marriage sought insurance by inserting prohibitions against same-sex marriage in their constitutions (Bossin 2005, 414). Thus, by the end of 2004, with the voters' enthusiastic approval, thirteen states had amended their constitutions to ban same-sex marriage.[48]

Same-sex marriage loomed large in the 2004 election, but there is disagreement over the extent to which it influenced the outcome of the presidential race. Throughout the year, the media referred to the "values war," a not-too-subtle way of describing the debate over same-sex marriage (see, for example, *New York Times* April 17, 2004). In the months leading up to the election, Republican strategists worked hard to publicize the issue, predicting it would increase turnout and help ensure the president's reelection. Democrats fought back by reminding voters of more important issues in the campaign, such as the war in Iraq and the economy (*New York Times* August 14, 2004; October 30, 2004).

After the election, the media reported that the amendments increased turnout among those "social conservatives" who opposed same-sex marriage and voted for the president (see, for example, *San Francisco Chronicle* November 4, 2004; *New York Times* November 4, 2004; *Washington Post* November 4, 2004; *Chicago Tribune* November 4, 2004; see also Barth and Parry 2005).

Voter exit polls conducted by the National Election Pool, a consortium of news organizations, showed that in responding to a question in which they were given six issues and asked to select the most important, 22 percent of the voters chose "moral values," followed by the economy at 20 percent, terrorism at 19 percent, Iraq at 15 percent, with education, taxes, and health care each in single digits (CNN 2004b). These results led to speculation that the same-sex marriage issue had been responsible for Bush winning the election, especially in Ohio, a closely contested state. This seemed confirmed when it was reported that of the people who chose "moral values" as their most important issue, 80 percent voted for Bush (*New York Times* November 4, 2004).

Many have disputed the significance of these poll results, specifically the influence of the same-sex marriage amendments on the voters' selection of a president (see, for example, Egan, Persily, and Wallsten 2006, 2 n2). Menand (2004), reporting on events at a postelection conference of experts at Stanford University, indicated that it is difficult to obtain accurate information when asking people why they chose their candidate because they often do not really know why. According to Menand, even Jan Van Lohuizen, president of Voter Consumer Research, and one of Bush's chief pollsters, dismissed the importance of these poll results. Kerry voters, Van Lohuizen said, would feel more strongly about more of the choices than Bush voters would and have a more difficult time naming their top choice. Moreover, he said, in the end, only 22 percent, less than a quarter of the respondents, selected "moral values," showing voters were truly divided on the issues.

Some analysts have suggested that the phrase "moral values" has a broad general meaning that encapsulates a multitude of issues. The director of ABC News was quoted as saying that "it could include topics as varied as gay marriage and vulgarity on television." Republican leaders rejected this explanation; they said the voters who selected this choice were aware of its meaning, construing it as being opposed to "gay marriage and abortion." Other independent pollsters pointed out the discrepancy between these results and those in preelection polls. Before the election, when voters were asked to name issues important to them rather than choosing from among a prescribed list, only 1 percent spontaneously identified "moral values" (*New York Times* November 6, 2004).

Analyzing public opinion poll data following the election, Gregory Lewis (2005, 197–8) writes that it was clearly not the most important issue for the voters, being less significant than "the war in Iraq, the economy, and terrorism, all [of which] had larger impacts." He concluded overall that the issue "mattered in the 2004 election, less than some issues, more than most." When analyzing the data at the state level, he found that "popular disapproval of homosexuality" may have played a role in some states, citing New Mexico, New Hampshire, and perhaps Ohio.

Similarly, Hillygus and Shields (2005) criticize the media reports that exaggerate the importance of voters' concerns about morality on the president's reelection. Their study of voter survey data found that other issues, notably the war in Iraq, the economy, and terrorism, were more important in explaining peoples' votes than the values issue. They concluded that "opinions about gay marriage and abortion were far from the most important predictors of vote choice, and had no effect on voter decision making among Independents, respondents in battleground states, or even among respondents in states with an anti-gay marriage initiative on the ballot." Only in the South, they found, did these issues play a role and their effect here was "minimal" (201).

THE BATTLE OVER CONSTITUTIONAL AMENDMENTS AND DOMAS

Whatever the effect of same-sex marriage on the presidential election, voters continued to go to the polls and vote for constitutional prohibitions against same-sex unions after the election. In April 2005, in a 71–29 percent vote, Kansas voters overwhelmingly approved a constitutional amendment to ban same-sex marriage, domestic partnerships, and civil unions (*Topeka Capital-Journal* April 6, 2005). Later in the year, in November 2005, Texas voters went to the polls and approved Proposition 2 with an even larger majority of 76 to 24 percent (*Houston Chronicle* November 15, 2005). The amendment to the Texas Constitution's Bill of Rights extended beyond a ban on same-sex marriage to include "any legal status identical or similar to marriage." Its supporters claimed it was essential to write the prohibition into the constitution to preempt any judicial attempts to nullify the state law against same-sex marriage. The state Republic Party chairwoman broadly proclaimed, "Let there be no doubt that Texans, not liberal activist judges, will decide how best to keep our families and state strong," adding that "campaigns of confusion, lies and deception will go down in blistering defeat" (*Austin American Statesman* November 6, 2005; *Dallas Morning News* November 9, 2005).

Thus, by the end of 2005, eighteen states had constitutional amendments barring same-sex marriage, many with vague and undefined language that went beyond the definition of marriage to include domestic partner benefits as well as civil unions. Additionally, state legislatures in seven states (Idaho, South Carolina, South Dakota, Tennessee, Virginia, Wisconsin, and Alabama) have approved constitutional amendments requiring voter action in the 2006 election.[49] A number of other states have amendments at various stages of progress (Human Rights Campaign 2005d; 2005a; 2005c; Peterson 2005a; 2005b).

Same-sex couples have filed suit in a number of states, asking the courts to enjoin their state's marriage policy; most have been unsuccessful thus far although there continue to be appeals of these cases. Shortly before *Goodridge* was decided, in *Standhardt v. Superior Court* (2003), an Arizona appellate court upheld Arizona laws prohibiting same-sex marriage against a challenge on state and federal constitutional grounds. Similarly, in *Lewis v. Harris* (2005) and *Hernandez v. Robles* (2005), state courts denied plaintiffs' claims against restrictions on same-sex marriage in New Jersey and New York.[50] In *Morrison v. Sadler* (2005), an Indiana appellate court ruled against a couple with a Vermont civil union who argued that the Indiana DOMA violated the state constitution. And later in the year, in *Martinez v. Kulongoski* (2005), a Marion County, Oregon, judge ruled that Measure 36, a 2004 ballot initiative banning same-sex marriage, among other things, did not violate "the separate-vote requirement" for amending the state constitution as the plaintiffs charged (at 3).[51]

Thus far, plaintiffs have successfully mounted challenges to laws restricting same-sex marriage in three states: Washington (*Castle v. Washington* [2004] and *Andersen v. King County* [2004]),[52] California (*Marriage Cases* [2005]), and Maryland (*Deane v. Conway* [2006]); all were decided at the lower state court level, and at least two (*Andersen* and *Marriage Cases*) have been reversed.

At the federal level, in *In re Kandu*, federal bankruptcy judge Snyder upheld DOMA against a challenge on federal constitutional grounds.[53]

Moreover, the plaintiffs' victory in *Bruning* was short-lived when the Eighth Circuit reversed the Nebraska district court in *Citizens for Equal Protection v. Bruning* (2006). Speaking for the unanimous circuit panel, Judge Loken rejected the argument that the Nebraska constitutional amendment deprives gay and lesbian couples of equal protection by precluding public officials from addressing a political issue of great significance to the group. Following the example set by the Colorado Supreme Court in *Romer*, the district court judge had applied heightened scrutiny on the grounds that the amendment deprived Nebraska gays of the fundamental right of equal political access. However, the circuit panel applied rational basis review instead and accepted the state's justification that the amendment rationally linked marriage to procreation.

The opponents of same-sex marriage have also turned to the courts. In Ohio, for example, a Republican member of the Ohio state legislature from Cincinnati sued to block Miami University of Ohio from offering benefits to same-sex domestic partners. The suit alleged that the university policy was inconsistent with the newly adopted provision of the Ohio Constitution that defines marriage only as a "union between one man and one woman" and bars state agencies from acknowledging "a legal status for relationships of unmarried individuals that intends to approximate the design, qualities, significance, or effect of marriage" (*Chronicle of Higher Education* November 28, 2005). Unlike most of the same-sex marriage litigation, the Ohio suit represents an attempt by opponents of same-sex marriage to use the courts to counter liberal policymaking.

By 2005, only Massachusetts, Connecticut, New Jersey, New Mexico, New York, Rhode Island, and the District of Columbia had no laws explicitly prohibiting same-sex marriage (Peterson 2005a; Evans 2004). A number of states, including Alaska, Arizona, California, Connecticut, Delaware, Hawaii, Maine, Minnesota, Nevada, New Jersey, New York, Oregon, Rhode Island, and Washington, allow partner benefits in varying degree, with the most extensive provisions in California, New Jersey, Hawaii, and Maine (Gavin 2004, 483; American Bar Association Section Family Law Working Group on Same Sex Marriages and Non-Marital Unions 2004, 22; Human Rights Campaign 2005c).[54]

CIVIL UNIONS AND PARTNER BENEFITS

In April 2005, Connecticut joined Vermont in establishing civil unions for same-sex couples. At the time, it was the only state to create civil unions without a mandate from the courts. The law extended state and local benefits, including tax provisions, to same-sex partners. At the same time, however, the lower house added an amendment that defined marriage as a union between a man and a woman (*Washington Post* April 13, 2005; April 14, 2005). When the law took effect on October 1, 2005, Connecticut same-sex couples became eligible for all benefits of marriage under state law, but their union will not be recognized under federal law, nor is it likely be acknowledged in most states (*Connecticut Post* September 29, 2005; *New York Times* October 1, 2005).[55]

California became the first state to allow same-sex marriage without a court order when the legislature narrowly approved the Civil Marriage and Religious Freedom Protection Act, on September 6, 2005. The next day, Republican Governor Arnold Schwarzenegger promised to veto it "out of respect for the will of the people" (Peterson 2005b; *Los Angeles Times* September 8, 2005). Citing Proposition 22, the governor said that the people had spoken, and the matter should now be resolved by either the courts or another vote of the people (*Daily News of Los Angeles* September 8, 2005). A few weeks later, on September 29, 2005, Schwarzenegger made good on his promise to veto the bill, insisting in his veto message that he still believed in "full protection under the law" for gay couples. The author of the bill, Assemblyman Mark Leno, Democrat from San Francisco, charged the governor with "hiding behind the fig leaf of Proposition 22," adding that "he cannot claim to support fair and equal legal protections for same-sex couples and veto the very bill that would have provided it for them" (*Los Angeles Times* September 30, 2005; *San Francisco Chronicle* September 30, 2005).

DEBATE OVER SUPPORT FOR CIVIL UNIONS

Gay rights advocates are split about the wisdom of pursuing (or accepting) civil unions. On hearing of the decision by the Vermont Supreme Court, the plaintiffs said they were very pleased that the court had ruled in their favor, but were nevertheless "disappointed" with the ruling. One characterized it as being allowed "on the bus, but . . . still being made to ride at the back of the bus" (quoted in Eskridge 2002, 55). Similarly, continuing the "separate but equal" analogy, as the civil union option was being debated in Massachusetts, Dianne Wilkerson, Democratic state senator from Boston, stated she could not support a position in which people were not being treated equally (Evans 2004, 16). And a participant in one of the New Paltz, New York, weddings said "civil unions alone—without marriage denote a 'second class citizenship' [that] she and her spouse would not accept" (*Poughkeepsie Journal* February 28, 2004).

On the other hand, as one of the *Baker* plaintiffs noted in speaking of the ruling, the gay and lesbian community must remember that it "is so much more than anyone else has had in the United States before" (quoted in Eskridge 2002, 55). And after Dean signed the bill, a gay member of the Vermont House of Representatives declared, "I couldn't be happier with the results"; the term has "a significance and symbolism that is very appropriate" (quoted in Eskridge 2002, 79).

Some take a pragmatic view, arguing that given the substantial opposition to same-sex marriage, it is more strategic to support civil unions in the hope that society will become more tolerant and eventually accept the idea of marriage. Acclimating society to the image of same-sex couples in civil unions, they contend, will facilitate challenges to opposite-sex marriage laws (see Kubasek, Frondorf, and Minnick 2004).

THE PUBLIC'S VIEW

The wisdom of accepting civil unions, in the short run at least, is validated by examining public opinion data, which show that the public appears more receptive to same-sex civil unions than to same-sex marriage. Questions about same-sex marriage and civil unions have become standard on most public opinion polls for a decade. Analysis of poll results conducted from 1996 to 2006 by a variety of organizations, including Harris, Gallup, ABC News, CBS News/*New York Times*, *USA Today*, CNN, and the Pew Research Center, shows continued opposition to same-sex marriage by a majority of Americans, but after a spike in 2004, there has been a decline in opposition in the last two years.

National surveys conducted by the Pew Research Center (2006) have tracked views on same-sex marriage since 1996. When Pew first began asking questions about legalizing same-sex marriage in June 1996, 65 percent were opposed. In March 2001, 57 percent expressed opposition, and in July 2003, immediately after the Court's decision in *Lawrence*, 53 percent of the respondents declared themselves against same-sex marriage. But, according to the Pew survey, once the public became more familiar with *Lawrence* and *Goodridge*, and the issue began to play an increasingly important role in the 2004 election campaign with the talk of a constitutional amendment to make it illegal, opposition mounted and reached a high in February 2004, when 63 percent of the respondents were against legalizing same-sex marriage.

The Pew data also showed that opposition decreased somewhat in 2005 and 2006, with 53 percent opposed in a July 2005 poll and 51 percent opposed in a March 2006 survey. Similarly, when focusing specifically on those who say they are "strongly opposed" to same-sex marriage, in July 2003, 30 percent were in this category; a high point of 42 percent was reached in February 2004, which then dropped to a low of 28 percent in March 2006.

The backlash against same-sex marriage that arose in the middle of 2003 and continued through 2004 has been attributable largely to *Lawrence* and the attention focused on it during the 2004 election campaign. Even though a majority of Americans remain opposed to same-sex marriage, perhaps because less attention has been focused on it, the public has become more accepting of it (Egan, Persily, and Wallsten 2006).

National polls conducted by the *Boston Globe*, the Pew Research Center, and CBS News/*New York Times* in 2005 report trends of declining opposition to same-sex marriage since 2003 (PollingReport.com 2006a). Similarly, a CNN/*USA Today*/Gallup poll conducted from April 29 to May 1, 2005, showed that opposition to same-sex marriage, which had been up to 68 percent in March 2005, dropped to 56 percent in the more recent poll (*USA Today* May 17, 2005). And an even more recent survey conducted by Gallup from May 8 to 11, 2006, also confirms that, although there is still a majority against it, the public's aversion to same-sex marriages has generally declined over the last two to three years (PollingReport.com 2006a).

The attitudes of Massachusetts citizens, where the debate crystallized as a result of the successful litigation, took a dramatic positive turn according to a *Boston Globe* poll conducted in March 2005. In February 2004 (after the decision, but before the weddings had begun to be performed), Massachusetts voters were against the proposed change in marriage policy by a margin of 53 to 35 percent. In the March 2005 poll, 56 percent were reported to be in favor of same-sex marriage, with 37 percent opposed (*USA Today* May 17, 2005).

Although much of the opposition to same-sex marriage focused on the fear that it would harm opposite-sex marriages, in another survey of Massachusetts registered voters, 65 percent believed it has not "weakened the institution of marriage," with only 13 percent saying same-sex marriage "has had a negative effect on married heterosexuals"; 71 percent of the respondents anticipated that the state would "become more and more accepting of same-sex marriage" (*USA Today* May 17, 2005).

A majority of Americans were also opposed to civil unions, but they have become more accepting of such arrangements. A CBS News/*New York Times* poll conducted in July 2003 found that 54 percent of the respondents expressed opposition to civil unions, and 39 percent approved (*New York Times* December 21, 2003).

When Gallup first began asking respondents about "civil unions, giving them some of the legal rights of married couples," in October 2000, it reported that 54 percent were opposed, with 42 percent in favor. Over the next two years, there were slight shifts, and by May 2002, only a bare majority of 51 percent were opposed, with 46 percent in favor (Gallup 2002). In May 2003, Gallup (2003b) reported that opposition to civil unions had further diminished to 49 percent (with 49 percent in favor).[56] A nationwide survey by the *Boston Globe* poll conducted from May 4 to May 9, 2005, asked, "What about civil unions between gay or lesbian couples that would give them some, but not all, of the legal rights of married couples? Should same-sex couples be allowed to form civil unions but not legally marry in your state?" Forty-one percent said "no," while 46 percent said "yes" (PollingReport.com 2006a). And a more recent ABC News poll, conducted from May 31 to June 4, 2006, reported similar results. Respondents were asked, "Do you think homosexual couples should or should not be allowed to form legally recognized civil unions, giving them the legal rights of married couples in areas such as health insurance, inheritance and pension coverage?" Forty-eight percent said they "should not be," and 45 percent agreed they "should" be (PollingReport.com 2006a). Thus, although Americans are still uncertain of their views on civil unions, they view these relationships more favorably than marriage relationships.

A nationwide Harris Interactive (2000) poll compared responses from surveys conducted in 1996 and 2000 to the question "How do you feel about so-called single sex marriages, between two men or two women?" Although the rate of disapproval decreased in the four years, a majority of American adults were against same-sex marriage in 1996 and were still against it in 2000. When the focus of the question was on marriage between two men, 64 percent of the respondents disapproved in 1996, and 57 percent disapproved in 2000. When the question referred to two women, 63 percent of the respondents disapproved in 1996, and 55 percent in 2000.

Gallup (2006a) also first asked about the legality of gay marriages in 1996, and the trend in these surveys is similar to the Harris data. When respondents were asked in March 1996 if they thought "marriages between homosexuals should or should not be recognized by the law as valid, with the same rights as traditional marriages," 68 percent said they should not be, and only 27 percent said they should. In a poll conducted in August 2005, 59 percent of the respondents said they should not be valid, and 37 percent said they should.[57] Almost a year later, the ABC News poll, conducted from May 31 to June 4, 2006, found little change in support for same-sex marriage. Respondents were asked, "Do you think it should be legal or illegal for homosexual couples to get married?" A solid majority of 58 percent said it should be "illegal," and only 36 percent said it should be "legal."

Not surprisingly, given the opposition to same-sex marriage, surveys show that a majority of respondents also supported a constitutional amendment to ban gay marriage. A nationwide poll conducted from December 10 to 13, 2003, by CBS News/*New York Times* that asked whether respondents "would favor or oppose an amendment to the Constitution that would allow marriage only between a man and a woman," 55 percent of the respondents said they would favor it, and 40 were opposed (*New York Times* December 21, 2003; *Congressional Quarterly Weekly* January 10, 2004).[58]

Gallup began asking about attitudes toward a proposed constitutional amendment in 2003. When asked whether they "favor or oppose a constitutional amendment that would define marriage as being between a man and a woman, thus barring marriages between gay or lesbian couples," in the survey conducted in July 2003, 50 percent were in favor, and 45 percent were opposed (Gallup 2005a). In a survey conducted in late April–early May 2005, Gallup (2005c) reported that 53 percent favored it, and 44 percent were opposed. Support for the amendment is dropping. The more recent ABC News poll, conducted from May 31 to June 4—after the president had called attention to the issue—reported that only 42 percent said they would "support amending the U.S. Constitution to make it against the law for homosexual couples to get married anywhere in the U.S." (PollingReport.com 2006a).

Perhaps as the 2004 campaign rhetoric has receded over time and Congress has taken no action on the FMA, the American people saw less need for it.

Although there are some variations over time, and the results are affected to some degree by the wording of the questions and the order in which they are asked, the polls show that most Americans disapprove of same-sex marriage; they are more willing to accept civil unions and believe that couples in civil unions should have many of the same rights as married couples. The data show that while support for same-sex marriage has increased over the last decade, the nation is far from approving of it. The data also suggest, however, that despite disapproval of same-sex marriage, there is not widespread approval of a constitutional amendment against it.

NOTES

1. The federal courts play only a minor role in marriage policymaking; and until 1996, the president and Congress played virtually no role. Congress's involvement in marriage laws, a policy area traditionally left to the states, raises questions about interfering with state autonomy and undermining the vitality of the United States federalist system. Ironically, both critics and advocates of same-sex marriage, as well as those who fear its impact on the federal system, voice these concerns (see, for example, Bash 2004).

2. Perhaps the justices in these states were more inclined to oppose public opinion and support litigants challenging same-sex marriage restrictions because, like federal court judges, they are appointed to the bench, most for lengthy terms.

3. The Lovings violated two provisions of the Virginia Code: marrying outside Virginia and returning to it and marrying a person of another race.

4. From 1967 to 1990, numerous opinions cited *Loving*, frequently for its intolerance toward racial classifications, but many times as well as for its strong endorsement of the right to marry as a fundamental right (Wardle 1998, 308–9).

5. Almost a decade later, the Supreme Court reaffirmed the importance of marriage in *Safley v. Turner* (1987), a case in which prison marriage and mail regulations were challenged. The Missouri Division of Corrections prevented inmates from marrying other inmates or civilians without permission from the prison superintendent, who will grant it only if a compelling reason (such as pregnancy or the birth of a child) exists. Citing *Zablocki*, the Court held that the regulation infringes on the constitutional right of prisoners to marry, rejecting the state's argument that the rule was justified by the special security concerns arising in prisons. Predating the arguments of same-sex marriage proponents, the Court portrayed marriages as "expressions of emotional support and public commitment" (95).

6. The United States Supreme Court summarily dismissed Baker's appeal "for want of a substantial federal question" (*Nelson* 1972). A significant number of courts, although not all, have interpreted this to be mean there is no fundamental right to marry a person of the same sex (see W. Duncan 2004; Bossin 2005).

7. The California Supreme Court declared sex a suspect category in *Sail'er Inn*, and four justices agreed to elevate sex-based classifications to strict scrutiny in *Frontiero*.

8. The Supreme Court denied certiorari in *Howerton* (1982b).

9. Article 1, §5 of the Hawaii Constitution states, "No person shall be deprived of life, liberty or property without due process of law, nor be denied the equal protection of the laws, nor be denied the enjoyment of the person's civil rights or be discriminated against in the exercise thereof because of race, religion, sex or ancestry." Article I, §6 states, "The right of the people to privacy is recognized and shall not be infringed without the showing of a compelling state interest."

10. Hawaii judges are appointed by the governor and approved by the senate for an initial term of ten years. The governor selects from among names submitted by

the Judicial Selection Commission; justices may be retained by the commission but must retire when they reach 70 (Hawaii State Judiciary 2006).

11. Article 1, §3 of the Hawaii Constitution states, "Equality of rights under the law shall not be denied or abridged by the State on account of sex."

12. *Loving* played a crucial role in the Hawaii Supreme Court's opinion in *Baehr*. Indeed, as Coolidge (1998, 204–5) notes, the "*Loving* Analogy" was the primary impetus for the court's ruling in *Baehr*. "As *Loving* [was] about broadening marriage to include interracial couples, so *Baehr* [was] about broadening marriage to include same sex couples."

13. In spring 1997, the legislature proposed the following constitutional amendment to be put on the ballot in the November election: "The legislature shall have the power to reserve marriage to opposite-sex couples." It was approved by the voters on November 3, 1998, to become Article 1, §23 of the Hawaii Constitution.

14. Article I, §25 of the Alaska Constitution states, "To be valid or recognized in this State, a marriage may exist only between one man and one woman."

15. Alaska judges are appointed by the governor, who selects from among a list of names submitted by the Alaska Judicial Council. Once appointed, judges on the supreme court and court of appeals must run on a retention ballot in the first general election held more than three years after their appointment. Thereafter, they must run every ten years (Alaska Judicial Appointment Process 2006).

16. Article I, §22 of the Alaska Constitution states, "The right of the people to privacy is recognized and shall not be infringed."

17. The plaintiffs' complaint was based on three counts. The first two, claiming that the state's refusal to grant them a marriage license violated the Alaska Constitution, were mooted by the adoption of the constitutional amendment against same-sex marriage. Count 3 challenged the Alaska marriage law on state and federal constitutional grounds. The superior court ruled that the complaint did not sufficiently allege that the plaintiffs were denied any specific benefits but merely claimed that the Alaska marriage law violated the state and federal constitutions; it dismissed this count on the grounds that the matter was not ripe for controversy, and the Alaska Supreme Court affirmed (*Brause v. Department of Health & Social Services* 2001).

18. Gay rights supporters attempted to amend DOMA by adding an employment discrimination provision; although a compromise was reached in the Senate to allow a separate vote on it, it failed (see chapter 5).

19. The Full Faith and Credit clause provides that "Full Faith and Credit shall be given in each State to the public Acts, Records, and judicial Proceedings of every other State. And the Congress may by general Laws prescribe the Manner in which such Acts, Records and Proceedings shall be proved, and the Effect thereof."

20. Section 2 of DOMA, codified at 28 U.S.C. §1738C, states, "No State, territory, or possession of the United States, or Indian tribe, shall be required to give effect to any public act, record, or judicial proceeding of any other State, territory, possession, or tribe respecting a relationship between persons of the same sex that is treated

as a marriage under the laws of such other State, territory, possession, or tribe, or a right or claim arising from such relationship." It did not prevent states from recognizing same-sex marriages.

21. Section 3 of DOMA, codified at 1 U.S.C. §7, states, "In determining the meaning of any Act of Congress, or of any ruling, regulation, or interpretation of the various administrative bureaus and agencies of the United States, the word 'marriage' means only a legal union between one man and one woman as husband and wife, and the word 'spouse' refers only to a person of the opposite sex who is a husband or a wife."

22. There are numerous financial and legal benefits that accrue from being legally wed. A 1997 GAO study found 1,049 "federal rights, responsibilities, and privileges" adhering to marriage. These included taxation, survivor benefits, family law, health care, real estate, and bankruptcy. In 2004, the number had risen to 1,138 (American Bar Association Section Family Law Working Group on Same Sex Marriages and Non-Marital Unions 2004, 16).

23. Holland (1998, 395) also believes DOMA is unconstitutional. Like Tribe, he thinks it exceeds congressional authority under the FF&C clause and also violates the equal protection component of the Fifth Amendment's due process clause.

24. The *Wilson* court also held that there is no fundamental right to marry a person of the same sex, and heightened scrutiny is inappropriate for equal protection analysis. It applied rational basis review and found DOMA rationally related to the government's interest in procreation and the welfare of children in families. The court also found no justification in the plaintiffs' other claims.

25. According to §§32–35 of the Vermont Constitution, supreme court justices and superior and district judges in Vermont are appointed by the governor, who selects from among a list submitted by the judicial nominating board. When their six-year term expires, they must run for retention (Vermont Statutes Online 2006).

26. Chapter I, Article 7 of the Vermont Constitution, known as the common benefits clause, states, "That government is, or ought to be, instituted for the common benefit, protection, and security of the people, nation, or community."

27. The United States Supreme Court held in *Michigan v. Long* (1983) that a state court decision is insulated from high court review when the state court unambiguously declares that it is based exclusively on state constitutional grounds.

28. The principle by which state courts interpret their state constitutions more expansively than the United States Constitution, known as judicial federalism, has been in evidence for a number of decades. Brennan, one of the foremost proponents of judicial federalism on the Supreme Court, urged state courts to be more protective of civil liberties and civil rights in the face of retrenchment by the high court (Brennan 1986; see Fitzpatrick 2004).

29. The legislature authorized same-sex couples to adopt after the Vermont Supreme Court held that the statute barring such adoptions was unconstitutional in *In re B.L.V.B.* (1993).

30. The Massachusetts marriage licensing law was silent on the legality of same-sex marriage. The question was whether the legislature intended to prevent same-sex couples from marrying.

31. Justices of the Massachusetts Supreme Judicial Court are appointed by the governor with the consent of the Executive Council; justices remain in office until they must retire at 70 (Massachusetts Court System 2006).

32. Among other things, the plaintiffs claimed their rights under Articles 1, 6, 7, and 10 of the Massachusetts Declaration of Rights were violated.

Article 1 states, "All people are born free and equal and have certain natural, essential and unalienable rights; among which may be reckoned the right of enjoying and defending their lives and liberties; that of acquiring, possessing and protecting property; in fine, that of seeking and obtaining their safety and happiness. Equality under the law shall not be denied or abridged because of sex, race, color, creed or national origin."

Article 6 states, "No man, nor corporation, or association of men, have any other title to obtain advantages, or particular and exclusive privileges, distinct from those of the community, than what arises from the consideration of services rendered to the public."

Article 7 states, "Government is instituted for the common good; for the protection, safety, prosperity, and happiness of the people; and not for the profit, honor, or private interest of any one man, family or class of men: Therefore the people alone have an incontestable, unalienable, and indefeasible right to institute government; and to reform, alter, or totally change the same, when their protection, safety, prosperity and happiness require it."

Article 10 states, "Each individual of the society has a right to be protected by it in the enjoyment of his life, liberty and property, according to standing laws."

33. Before *Goodridge* was decided in November 2003, same-sex marriages were permitted in Belgium, the Netherlands, and a few Canadian provinces (W. Duncan 2005, 114).

34. The United States Supreme Court denied certiorari in *Largess* (2004c).

35. At the time of the decision, three other jurisdictions also did not bar same-sex marriage: New Jersey, New Mexico, and the District of Columbia (*New York Times* March 31, 2006). On September 28, 2006, Massachusetts superior court judge Connolly ruled that gay couples are permitted to wed in Rhode Island, but not New York, clearing the way for same-sex couples from Rhode Island to marry in Massachusetts (*Cote-Witacre* 2006b).

36. On July 10, 2006, in *Schulman v. Attorney General* (2006), the Massachusetts Supreme Judicial Court ruled that an initiative petition that sought to overrule *Goodridge* and redefine marriage as between a man and a woman could be considered by the legislature. However, at the state constitutional convention on July 12, 2006, the legislature postponed a vote on the measure by adjourning before it was considered, thereby destroying the chances for placing it on the ballot in November 2008.

37. The California First District Court of Appeal heard arguments in July 2006, and several months later, it reversed the lower court and upheld the Family Code statutes defining marriage as the union of a man and a woman (*In re Marriage Cases* 2006).

38. Article I, §20 of the Oregon Constitution states, "No law shall be passed granting to any citizen or class of citizens privileges, or immunities, which, upon the same terms, shall not equally belong to all citizens."

39. Another attempt to limit same-sex marriage, of questionable constitutional validity, came from Representative John Hostettler, Republican from Indiana, who, with forty-eight cosponsors, introduced the Marriage Protection Act, H.R. 3313, on October 16, 2003. The bill proposed to deny jurisdiction to the federal courts, including the Supreme Court, in challenges to DOMA's nonrecognition provision that affords states the right not to recognize same-sex marriages legal in other states. Hostettler said the law was "necessary to prevent a handful of lifetime-appointed Federal judges from overturning the considered judgment of state citizens and their elected legislatures" (United States House Committee on the Judiciary 2004, 2–3). As the Marriage Protection Act of 2004, H.R. 3313 was approved in the House in a 233–194 vote (United States House of Representatives 2004). But although it was sent to the Senate and referred to the Judiciary Committee on September 7, 2004, no further action was taken on it.

40. The original language stated, "Marriage in the United States shall consist only of the union between a man and a woman. Neither this constitution nor the constitution of any state, nor state or federal law, shall be construed to require that marital status or the legal incidents thereof be conferred upon unmarried couples or groups." Subsequently it was altered by striking the phrase "nor state or federal law" so that the new version read "Marriage in the United States shall consist only of the union of a man and a woman. Neither this Constitution, nor the Constitution of any State, shall be construed to require that marriage or the legal incidents thereof be conferred upon any union other than the union of a man and a woman." Presumably, the latter version was intended to allow states to legalize civil unions (*Congressional Quarterly Weekly* March 27, 2004).

41. The Senate version was Senate Joint Resolution 40; the House version was House Joint Resolution 106.

42. The Marriage Protection Amendment, S.J. Res. 1, states, "Marriage in the United States shall consist only of the union of a man and a woman. Neither this Constitution, nor the Constitution of any State, shall be construed to require that marriage or the legal incidents thereof be conferred upon any union other than the union of a man and a woman."

43. Although the event had been scheduled to take place in the Rose Garden, the venue was changed in an attempt to downplay the significance of the president's statement (*Washington Post* June 6, 2006).

44. Article I, §29 of the Nebraska Constitution states, "Only marriage between a man and a woman shall be valid or recognized in Nebraska. The uniting of two

persons of the same sex in a civil union, domestic partnership, or other similar same-sex relationship shall not be valid or recognized in Nebraska."

45. The district court had found in favor of the plaintiffs. When the defendants appealed, the court of appeal transferred the case to the state supreme court (*Forum for Equality PAC v. McKeithen* 2004).

46. The "single subject rule" is a Georgia constitutional principle that "prohibits the inclusion in one legislative enactment multiple subjects having no common objective" (at 1).

47. On July 6, 2006, in *Perdue v. O'Kelley* (2006), the Georgia Supreme Court reinstated the amendment in the state constitution, overturning the trial court's ruling that it violated the "single subject rule" for ballot measures.

48. See CNN (2004a) for the results of the referenda in the eleven states as well as the text of the amendments.

49. There was overwhelming support for the Alabama amendment in the June 6, 2006 election. And in *American Civil Liberties Union of Tennessee v. Darnell* (2006), the Tennessee Supreme Court allowed the proposed constitutional amendment to remain on the ballot for the November election, dismissing the suit brought by the ACLU on the grounds that it lacked standing. In the 2006 election, eight states had amendments banning same-sex marriage on the ballot; they succeeded in all but Arizona (*Los Angeles Times* November 9, 2006; see CNN 2006 for results of state votes).

50. On July 6, 2006, in *Hernandez v. Robles* (2006), the New York Court of Appeals affirmed the lower court and upheld the New York Domestic Relations law restricting marriage to a man and a woman as rational. Speaking for a 4–2 majority, Judge Smith wrote, "We hold that the New York Constitution does not compel recognition of marriages between members of the same sex. Whether such marriages should be recognized is a question to be addressed by the Legislature" (at 1). The ruling was based on four separate lawsuits filed by forty-four gay and lesbian couples in New York. On October 25, 2006, in *Lewis v. Harris* (2006), the New Jersey Supreme Court ruled that the state must provide the same rights and benefits to same-sex couples that it grants opposite-sex couples; the court gave the legislature six months to comply with its decision, leaving it to the legislature to decide whether to allow "marriages" or "civil unions." It opted for the latter.

51. Same-sex marriage opponents had placed Measure 36 on the November 2004 ballot after the lower court ruled in favor of the gay rights advocates in Multnomah County (*The Oregonian* November 5, 2005).

52. In *Andersen v. King County* (2006), the Washington Supreme Court reversed both lower court rulings in a consolidated opinion, holding that the state's 1998 DOMA was constitutional.

53. The plaintiffs in *Kandu*, who were married in British Columbia in 2003, filed for joint bankruptcy in Tacoma, Washington, a few months later. The government opposed the joint petition, contending that the bankruptcy law restricted joint filings to spouses only and that DOMA allows only a man and a woman to be con-

sidered spouses. The plaintiff responded by arguing that DOMA was unconstitutional under the Fourth, Fifth, and Tenth Amendments as well as principles of comity. According to the bankruptcy judge, no other court had decided this issue. The court held that *Lawrence* did not guarantee a fundamental right to same-sex marriage and minimal scrutiny was appropriate. He found DOMA rationally related to the government's interest in advancing the welfare of children in an opposite-sex marriage. Snyder added that his

> personal view that children raised by same-sex couples enjoy benefits possibly different, but equal, to those raised by opposite-sex couples, is not relevant to the Court's ultimate decision. It is within the province of Congress, not the courts, to weigh the evidence and legislate on such issues, unless it can be established that the legislation is not rationally related to a legitimate governmental end. Thus, although this Court may not personally agree with the positions asserted by the UST [United States Trustee] in support of DOMA, applying the rational basis test as set forth by the Supreme Court, this Court cannot say that DOMA's limitation of marriage to one man and one woman is not wholly irrelevant to the achievement of the government's interest. (146)

54. See Bowman (2004) for discussion of the variations of cohabitation laws in the United States.

55. When Connecticut created civil unions, it barred same-sex marriage. By 2006, the only remaining states that did not explicitly bar same-sex marriage were New Jersey, New Mexico, New York, Rhode Island, and the District of Columbia (*New York Times* March 31, 2006).

56. Gallup (2004a) reports that support for civil unions is higher on surveys in which respondents are first asked about same-sex marriage than when they are questioned about civil unions first.

57. Support for same-sex marriage is slightly higher when respondents are not asked about "homosexual rights and relations" first (Gallup 2006a).

58. Another survey conducted by the University of Pennsylvania's Annenberg Center that asked respondents whether they "favor or oppose the federal government adopting an amendment banning gay marriage" produced a positive response of only 40 percent, with 52 percent opposed. According to David Moore, editor at the Gallup Poll, people are going to respond more favorably to questions that contain the word *allow* than to those that contain the word *ban*; moreover using *federal government* is likely to make people opposed (*Congressional Quarterly Weekly* January 10, 2004).

CHAPTER 4

Contesting Inequality in the Military

A S the nation's "largest single employer," the military has been called "the last bastion of institutionalized homophobia" (Dyer 1990, xviii). The country's attention was sharply drawn to the issue of military policy toward gays and lesbians in 1993 when the newly elected president and Congress crafted the policy popularly known as "Don't Ask, Don't Tell."[1] More than a decade later, the intent and application of this policy are still much debated.

The intense publicity engendered by the debate over gays in the military often obscured the fact that the armed services have had a long-standing policy against recruiting and retaining gay members.[2] Coexisting with the policy of exclusion, however, is also a long history of homosexuals serving in the armed forces, dating back to 1778, when Baron Frederich Wilhelm Ludolph Gerhard Augustin von Steuben arrived at Valley Forge to offer his services to the commander, General George Washington. Despite Washington's publicly stated gratitude to von Steuben—well known as a homosexual on both sides of the Atlantic—a few days after the Baron arrived, Lieutenant Gotthold Frederick Enslin was "drummed out" of the Continental Army. Enslin's expulsion was the first known incident of separation from the service for homosexuality (Shilts 1993, chap. 1; see Fotopoulos 1994).

The justifications for excluding gay military personnel have ranged from mental illness to security risk to, more recently, concern for maintaining morale, good order, and discipline (subsumed under the term "unit cohesion"). Based on these, the policy toward homosexuals has alternated between mandatory and discretionary discharge, but paradoxically, during times of war, when the military's concern for maintaining good order and discipline should purportedly be at its peak, gays have been allowed to serve openly (Lehring 2003; see Osburn 1995).

Many of the arguments opposing the inclusion of gays in the military echo those raised in opposition to the integration of African Americans in 1948 and women in the 1970s (see Bianco 1996; Benecke and Dodge 1996).[3] Historian Roger Wilkins, assistant attorney general in the 1960s, compared the arguments. "They said we [African Americans] were too promiscuous, were cowardly and lazy. Some of the same things are being said about gays. There are all kinds of soldiers who are lazy, cowardly and promiscuous, and it has nothing to do with race or sexual orientation" (*New York Times* June 28, 1993).

In the post–World War II era, the frenzy of removing homosexuals from the federal government resulted in numerous discharges from the military as well. In the immediate postwar period, about 1,000 people a year were discharged; within a few years, the number doubled to 2,000 a year and increased by another 50 percent by the early 1960s (D'Emilio 1983, 44–5; see Haggerty 2003).

The Defense Department's (DoD) policy on homosexuality appears in the Uniform Code of Military Justice (UCMJ) and DoD directives specifying procedures for dismissal for committing sodomy (including consensual sodomy), assault, and indecent acts.[4] Additionally, each service has individual regulations. But despite the myriad regulations and policies, the laxity in wartime demonstrates that the military's position on gays in service is often governed by expediency. When the needs of the service require particular individuals or increased numbers, antigay policies are put aside, and discharges and other disciplinary actions slow to a trickle or disappear entirely (Shilts 1993).[5] As Haggerty (2003, 10) explains, over time, policies toward homosexuals "have been selectively enacted, enforced, rationalized, ignored, and repealed." Indeed, after the horrific events of September 11, 2001, the Pentagon halted all discharges of members of the armed services through a "stop loss" order—even of known lesbians and gays; a decade earlier, during the first Gulf War, it had also done so (Lehring 2003, 1–2; D. Miller 1998).

DEVELOPMENT OF MILITARY POLICY

In the 1940s, military policy reflected the prevailing view of homosexuality as a mental disorder, and although there were some efforts to exclude homosexuals from service, the need for personnel was a significant countervailing factor. World War II marked a turning point in the nation's treatment of homosexuals in service; after the war, with the need for manpower diminished, the policies were enforced more vigorously, resulting in numerous involuntary separations from the service. The change in attitude was accompanied by a shift in focus. Prior to the 1940s, dismissal was based on conduct, that is, the commission of an act of sodomy; in the postwar era, the attention shifted to status or identity, that is, to sexual orientation. A 1949 DoD directive declared that homosexuals were not permitted to serve and known homosexuals should be immediately removed. Despite the stern language, however, homosexuals were allowed into combat during the Korean War (Pizzutillo 1997, 129).

Beginning in the 1950s, the DoD commissioned a number of studies to bolster its contention that homosexuals were unfit for military duty and merited automatic discharge. Although none of the studies agreed with these conclusions, the military continued to cling to the policies of exclusion; nor did the commendable records of the discharged individuals preclude it from arguing that homosexuals were unsuitable for military service. In each case, because the results were not to its liking, the military either delayed publication or attempted to alter the findings of these studies.

The first inquiry, conducted in 1957, resulted in a 639-page analysis entitled *Report of the Board Appointed to Prepare and Submit Recommendations to the Secretary of the Navy for the Revision of Policies, Procedures and Directives Dealing with Homosexuals.* It was known as the Crittenden Report, after its author, Captain S. H. Crittenden, Jr., chair of the five-member commission.

The primary impetus behind this investigation was to ascertain if homosexuals in the military constituted a national security threat through their vulnerability to blackmail under threat of exposure. The study found no factual evidence of a linkage between homosexuality and ability and negated inferences that gays constituted risks to national security or were more likely to be sexual predators. Among its findings were that numerous homosexuals had served in all branches of the service and "the concept that homosexuals necessarily pose a security threat is unsupported by adequate factual data" (quoted in M. Lewis 1990, 144; Haggerty 2003). Yet, although arguing for greater tolerance of "Class III homosexuals," the report cautioned against wholesale abandonment of the military policy of dismissing gay servicemen and women. Displeased with the findings, the navy suppressed the report for twenty years and released it only when forced in response to a Freedom of Information Act request (Shilts 1993; Haggerty 2003).[6]

No further empirical studies of the effect of homosexuality on military service were conducted for thirty years until a report entitled *Nonconforming Sexual Orientations and Military Suitability* came out in December 1988 (Dyer 1990, xvi–ii). It stated "unequivocally that gay men and lesbians pose no special security threat and, more importantly, are every bit as suitable for service as heterosexuals." The DoD was also dissatisfied with these findings and attempted to order the authors to alter their conclusions as well as those in a subsequent 1989 report (Dyer 1990, xvi–ii). And in August 1993, the Rand Corporation released the results of its $1.3 million study, but only after Senate Democrats threatened to hold up a defense appropriations bill. This study, echoing the findings of the earlier reports that the military would not be adversely affected, was ready to be released in the spring but was held up by the Pentagon until the Senate hearings on "Don't Ask, Don't Tell" were almost concluded and its impact would be minimized (Osburn and Benecke 1996, 273).

In 1981, in an attempt to clarify military policy toward gays, the DoD issued Directive 1332.14, to take effect on January 28, 1982, to create uniform policies for the discharge of enlisted personnel across the branches of the armed forces, including separation procedures and potential defenses.[7] According to a General Accounting Office (GAO) report entitled *DOD's Policy on Homosexuality*, under the new policy, gay enlisted personnel would be specifically discharged for homosexuality (United States General Accounting Office 1992).[8]

Directive 1332.14 explicitly stated that "homosexuality is incompatible with military service. The presence in the military environment of persons who engage in homosexual conduct or who, by their statements, demonstrate a propensity to engage in homosexual conduct, seriously impairs the accomplishment of the military mission . . . [and] adversely affects the ability of the Military Services to maintain discipline, good order and morale." A homosexual was defined as "a person, regardless of sex, who engages in, desires to engage in, or intends to engage in homosexual acts," and "a homosexual act means bodily contact, actively undertaken or passively permitted, between members of the same sex for the purpose of satisfying sexual desires."[9]

Over time, the military's official policy toward gays has shifted. Prior to 1981, homosexuality had been considered only "a possible disqualification for military service," allowing exceptions at the military's discretion. After 1981, discharge was mandatory, with the regulations specifying that "retention of an admitted homosexual is not permitted absent an express finding that the soldier in question is in fact not homosexual" (*Watkins v. United States Army* 1983, 689). The policy of excluding all homosexuals was justified because, by definition, a person with a homosexual orientation was presumed to belong to a class that engaged in conduct that impaired the military mission. And there was no opportunity to refute the presumption other than to prove oneself not a homosexual (Wells-Petry 1995). Thus, the distinction between status (having a homosexual orientation) and conduct (engaging in homosexual acts) was obliterated, and identification as lesbian or gay was enough to justify separation from the service (Jacobson 1996; Herek 1996). For the most part, the courts acquiesced in this policy, and their treatment of the distinction between status and conduct in sexual minority cases has been characterized as "convoluted and unprincipled" (Valdes 1994, 386).

The GAO's 1992 report also indicated that from FY 1980 through FY 1990, the armed forces dismissed 16,919 servicewomen and servicemen for homosexuality, an average of 1,500 a year. The data also show that servicewomen are much more likely to be discharged for homosexuality then servicemen. The high point of the dismissals was in 1982, when just under 2,000 individuals were released in one year. Although the Defense Department did not keep records of investigations or court costs, the GAO (1992) estimated that the cost of the policy in replacing the discharged personnel was $28,226 for each enlisted servicemember and $120,772 for each officer. It estimated these costs at $27 million in 1990 alone.

LITIGATING THE BAN ON HOMOSEXUALITY

As gay men and lesbians began to litigate the military's policy toward homosexuals, they often met with defeat, extraordinarily hampered by the judiciary's reluctance to override the military's judgment about the unsuitability of homosexuals in the armed forces.

One of the earliest examples of judicial deference to an argument of military necessity is *Korematsu v. United States* (1944), in which the Supreme Court retroactively upheld the relocation and internment of Japanese Americans during World War II. Although *Korematsu* has long been appropriately rejected for its racism, more recent cases such as *Parker v. Levy* (1974), *Brown v. Glines* (1980), *Rostker v. Goldberg* (1981), and *Goldman v. Weinberger* (1986) are continually cited by lower courts to justify their rulings that depart from civilian standards of privacy, equal protection, and freedom of expression.[10]

In *Parker*, the Court rejected a First Amendment challenge to the conviction of an army doctor court-martialed for urging enlisted men to refuse to obey orders that might lead them into combat. It emphasized that it "has long recognized that the military is, by necessity, a specialized society separate from civilian society" (743). Similarly, in *Brown*, the Court upheld a regulation requiring members of the air force to obtain approval from their commanding officers before circulating petitions on base. More broadly, the Court stated that "to ensure that they always are capable of performing their mission promptly and reliably, the military services 'must insist upon a respect for duty and a discipline without counterpart in civilian life'" (354, quoting *Schlesinger v. Councilman* 1975, 757).

Another First Amendment challenge was defeated in *Goldman*, in which the Court denied the claim of an ordained rabbi that the regulation prohibiting members of the air force from wearing headgear while indoors prevented him from wearing his yarmulke (skullcap) and infringed on his free exercise of religion. Here, the Court stressed the need to defer to the "considered professional judgment" of the military in determining regulations to advance "the overall group mission" (508). And in *Rostker*, the Court rejected an equal protection challenge to the Military Selective Service Act establishing a male-only registration policy, declaring that "judicial deference to such congressional exercise of authority is at its apogee when legislative action under the congressional authority to raise and support armies and make rules and regulations for their governance is challenged" (70).

In the years preceding 1982, before DoD Directive 1233.14 had made the discharge of gays mandatory, the military had left the decision to discharge a gay member of the armed services to the discretion of the commanding officer, without, however, providing any standards to govern the decision to dismiss. Despite the required deference to the military, Judge Gesell of the District of Columbia District Court expressed concern that the military's failure to specify the criteria for dismissal offended the due process clause. Gesell reviewed the air force's discharge of Sergeant Leonard Matlovich for homosexual activity in *Matlovich v. Secretary of the Air Force* (1976), announcing his decision shortly after the Supreme Court affirmed the three-judge district court ruling for the state in *Commonwealth's Attorney* (1976).

Gesell cited *Commonwealth's Attorney* in rejecting Matlovich's constitutional privacy claim. Recognizing the plaintiff's heroism and valor, the judge seemed distressed about his obligation to defer to the military in this case, stressing that his task was limited only to determining whether the air force regulation against gays was rational. He acknowledged the military's legitimate need for discipline and combat readiness and declined to consider the regulation "so irrational that it may be branded arbitrary."[11] It was evident that he reached this conclusion reluctantly, saying that attitudes toward homosexuality were changing and calling upon the air force to reappraise its policy, characterizing it a "knee-jerk reaction" (*Matlovich* 1976, at 3).

In *Berg v. Claytor* (1977), Ensign Vernon "Copy" Berg was dismissed from the navy for homosexual conduct. He filed suit against the secretary of the navy in federal court, arguing that he was deprived of his First Amendment right of association as well of his rights to privacy and due process. Gesell easily dismissed the First Amendment claim, but expressed concern that Berg's right to privacy may have been compromised. Balancing the precedents of *Griswold* and *Roe* against *Commonwealth's Attorney*, however, he held that there was no right to engage in homosexual conduct.

Gesell found Berg's due process argument equally unavailing. Because there was no fundamental right to engage in homosexual sodomy, the navy had to satisfy only minimal scrutiny and show that its policy was rationally related to a legitimate governmental interest. By this time, the navy had abandoned both morality and fear of security risk as justifications for its policy. Instead it defended it on the grounds "that given the special tasks performed by the Navy, homosexuals present an obstruction to efficient operations" by destroying their credibility and causing their men to lose respect for them (*Berg* 1977, 80). Rejecting Berg's contention that the navy had no evidence to support this assertion, Gesell ruled that because it was not irrational, it met the due process standard.

The cases were consolidated on appeal in the District of Columbia Circuit Court. Speaking for the circuit panel, Court of Claims judge Davis (sitting by designation) appeared most struck by the fact that there was no explanation of the criteria used to decide whether to retain or remove gay personnel (*Berg* 1978; *Matlovich* 1978).[12] Moreover, in Matlovich's case, Davis intimated that although there was no specific evidence, Matlovich's decision to openly challenge the air force's policy toward homosexuals and the widespread media attention surrounding the case might have prompted his removal. The appellate court thus vacated and remanded both rulings, holding that both services had violated due process by insufficiently articulating its standards for discharge.[13]

Not all litigants fared as well as Matlovich and Berg. Indeed, their victories proved to be unique in the long line of cases challenging the military's policy of excluding gays. A frequently cited case in the Ninth Circuit, *Beller v. Middendorf* (1980), which was a consolidation of three lower court rulings, was an important win for the government.

One of the three lower court rulings reviewed in *Beller* was *Saal v. Middendorf* (1977), which arose when Mary Roseann Saal sued the secretary of the navy, claiming a violation of her Fifth Amendment right to due process.[14] She had enlisted in 1971, signing up for a three-year hitch in 1972. Before that term was up, the navy initiated an investigation into her homosexuality, as a result of which she signed a statement that she had engaged in homosexual sex. When it began discharge proceedings against her, she filed suit. After lengthy legal wrangling, during which her record was marked ineligible for reenlistment under the navy policy mandating automatic separation of homosexuals, she was finally discharged in 1975. Following her discharge, she amended her complaint, claiming that the navy had deprived her of due process in removing her and blocking her reenlistment.

Recognizing the obligation to defer to military judgment as well as to apply the correct standard of constitutional review, California district court judge Schwarzer emphasized that individuals are not entirely stripped of their constitutional rights upon entering the service. He noted that under navy policy, discharge is mandatory only in cases of drug sales or trafficking, homosexuality, and sexual perversion. In other instances of alleged misconduct, the navy determines whether discharge is appropriate and often offers counseling and rehabilitation. Because there was no evidence of her unfitness save for her homosexuality, Schwarzer ordered the navy to judge her fitness, ruling "that due process requires plaintiff's [Saal's] fitness to serve to be evaluated in light of *all relevant factors* and free of any policy of mandatory exclusion" (203; the emphasis is in the original).

In *Beller v. Middendorf* (1980), the Ninth Circuit ruled on Saal's appeal together with appeals from James Miller and Dennis Beller, two defendants who, unlike her, lost in the courts below. Although the facts of the three cases differed somewhat, there was enough similarity in them to allow the court to decide them jointly; despite commendable service records, all three had been separated from the navy on the basis of their homosexuality.

Announcing the opinion of the three-judge panel, Judge (now Justice) Kennedy began by reviewing the navy policy toward homosexuals: "Members involved in homosexuality are military liabilities who cannot be tolerated in a military organization. . . . Their prompt separation is essential" (802). The court interpreted the policy as requiring mandatory discharge, although allowing the secretary some discretion to retain individuals based on unknown idiosyncratic factors unrelated to fitness.[15]

Kennedy noted that the appeals did not raise equal protection issues, thus obviating the need to determine whether homosexuals constituted a suspect or semisuspect class. Instead, the court looked to the fundamental rights cases, but without deciding whether there was a fundamental right to engage in homosexual sodomy, it held that even assuming "some kinds of government regulation of private consensual homosexual behavior may face substantial constitutional challenge," the facts of these cases present different circumstances (810). Here, Kennedy noted, the court was being asked to judge a military regulation that prohibits persons from engaging in homosexual conduct while in service. It held that the individual's right to homosexual conduct (whatever its precise boundaries) was outweighed by the importance of the government interest involved and the practical difficulty of determining harm in each case. The navy was not an ordinary employer, Kennedy continued, for the courts have long held that constitutional rights are not accorded ordinary force in the military.

The navy had justified its policy by emphasizing its need to maintain discipline and effectiveness and avoid the "tensions and hostilities" accompanying the presence of homosexuals (811). Kennedy reiterated the familiar paean to judicial deference, saying "constitutional rights must be viewed in the light of the special circumstances and needs of the armed forces" (810). He ended by saying that the navy could rationally conclude that the regulations served its military needs and that a more lenient policy might signal "tacit approval" of homosexual conduct (811). Although Kennedy implied that the rules might cut too wide a swath, the court nonetheless found them reasonable.[16] It affirmed the lower court rulings in Beller and Miller's cases and reversed the judgment in Saal's.[17]

In *Dronenberg v. Zech* (1982), another case arising out of the District of Columbia District Court, the navy had discharged James Dronenburg for misconduct for engaging in homosexual acts in a navy barracks.[18] Suing to prevent his discharge, Dronenburg argued that discharging homosexuals on the sole grounds of their sexual orientation violated their rights of privacy and equal protection. Relying on the Ninth Circuit's decision in *Beller*, district court judge Easch awarded the navy summary judgment.

On appeal, the District of Columbia Circuit Court rejected Dronenburg's claim that homosexual activity is constitutionally protected under the due process clause, characterizing the Supreme Court's summary affirmance of the three-judge district court opinion in *Commonwealth's Attorney* as a ruling on the merits. Speaking for the panel, Judge Bork reasoned that if a law criminalizing homosexuality is constitutional under civilian standards, it is surely so in a military setting. But even if *Commonwealth's Attorney* did not permit a ban on homosexual sodomy, he said, *Griswold* and its progeny should not be interpreted to extend the right of privacy to homosexual conduct.

With no constitutionally protected right at issue, Bork merely asked whether the navy policy is rationally related to a legitimate goal. Without requiring the navy to substantiate its position, the court held that it can rationally conclude that homosexual conduct has a harmful effect on "morale and discipline," adding that "the Navy is not required to produce social science data or the results of controlled experiments to prove what common sense and common experience demonstrate" (*Dronenberg v. Zech* 1984, 1398).

Another significant Ninth Circuit case that was litigated for almost ten years revolved around the military career of Staff Sergeant Perry Watkins, who had acknowledged he had "homosexual tendencies" when he was drafted in 1967. This case illustrates the resources expended by the military to expel one soldier from the army, a soldier who, by all accounts, was an exemplary company clerk who excelled at his job.

Watkins's sexual orientation, about which he was very open, was noted on his preinduction medical form as well as on other official documents.[19] Subsequently, in a 1968 affidavit to an Army Criminal Investigation Division agent, he stated that he had been gay since he was thirteen and that he engaged in homosexual conduct with two servicemen. When his first enlistment expired in 1970, he was given an honorable discharge; a year later, he reenlisted for a second three-year term. In 1974, he reenlisted for a six-year term, but in 1975, the army began discharge proceedings against him for "unsuitability due to homosexuality" (*Watkins v. United States Army* 1982a, 252). He again admitted his homosexuality at an administrative discharge board hearing; his commander testified at the hearing, calling Watkins "the best clerk" in his experience, adding that his "homosexuality did not affect the company." Another member of his company testified that "everyone in the company knew that plaintiff [Watkins] was a homosexual and that . . . [it] had not caused any problems or elicited any complaints" (253). The board unanimously determined that the army should retain him.

In 1977, Watkins applied for a position in the Nuclear Surety Personnel Reliability Program and was initially denied a security clearance and rejected from the program because of his homosexuality; he appealed and was admitted in 1978. A year later, he reenlisted for another three years. His security clearance was revoked in 1980 following another investigation prompted by his homosexuality. In 1981, on the basis of the new army regulations mandating the discharge of homosexuals without regard to performance, the army began new discharge proceedings against him. He filed suit in August 1981, challenging the revocation of his security clearance and the threatened discharge.[20]

In May 1982, after the army board voted to discharge him, but before the discharge was carried out, Washington district court judge Rothstein of the Washington District Court issued an injunction preventing the army from discharging him on the basis of statements admitting his homosexuality. She ruled that the army's double jeopardy regulation barred it from discharging him at this time because, based on the same evidence, it had decided to retain him in 1975 (*Watkins v. United States Army* 1982a).

In response, the army sought to block his reenlistment, citing a regulation that homosexuality constituted an absolute bar to reenlistment. Rothstein subsequently enjoined the army from refusing to allow him to reenlist on the basis of his homosexuality (*Watkins v. United States Army* 1982b). The army permitted Watkins to reenlist for a six-year term on November 1, 1982, as long as the injunction remained in place.

On appeal, the Ninth Circuit reversed. Speaking for the circuit panel, Judge Choy held that a federal court cannot order the army to disregard its regulations absent a finding of unconstitutionality or violation of statutory authority (*Watkins v. United States Army* 1983).

Judge Norris concurred with the panel, declaring himself obligated to "to follow *Beller*."[21] He added, however, that in *Beller*, "our court abdicated one of its primary duties: to safeguard individual rights against intrusions engendered by governmental insensitivity or bigotry. To me," he added, "the Army's current bias against homosexuals is no less repugnant to fundamental constitutional principles than was its long-standing prejudice against minority servicemen" (*Watkins v. United States Army* 1983, 691).

With the case back in her court on remand, Rothstein upheld the regulation and granted the army's motion for summary judgment. Watkins appealed, raising a number of constitutional and statutory claims, and a divided panel of the Ninth Circuit reversed (*Watkins v. United States Army* 1988). Announcing the opinion for the panel, Norris rejected most of Watkins's arguments, although he seemed to struggle in dismissing the First Amendment claim. Applying equal protection analysis, Norris assessed the army's discharge and reenlistment regulations and found that both were aimed at sexual orientation, not homosexual conduct. He rejected the army's argument that *Bowers* foreclosed this discussion because *Bowers*, he said, was based on the due process clause, not on an equal protection analysis.

Moreover, he said, *Bowers* does not imply "that the state may penalize gays for their sexual orientation" (*Watkins v. United States Army* 1988, 1439). After a lengthy analysis, Norris concluded that gays met the criteria for a suspect class and applied strict scrutiny to the army regulations. Aware that judicial deference was called for, he nevertheless found that the army failed to show the regulations had a compelling justification and ordered Watkins reinstated in the army.

Judge Reinhardt dissented. Saying that he vigorously disapproved of *Bowers* and predicted it would be overruled, he argued that it supported the army policy.[22]

On rehearing en banc, the circuit court refrained from addressing the equal protection analysis and, in a fractured opinion, ruled in Watkins's favor (*Watkins v. United States Army* 1989). The decision, announced by Judge Pregerson, held that by continually allowing Watkins to reenlist, the army had disregarded its own regulations about barring homosexuals from reenlisting and was now "estopped" (barred) from refusing to reinstate him (704).[23] The Ninth Circuit expressly withdrew the panel's ruling, thereby nullifying Norris's analysis of homosexuality and equal protection and eliminating an important precedent for future gay rights litigants.

In a lengthy concurring opinion to the en banc ruling, Norris applied the equal protection analysis the en banc court avoided.[24] Echoing his opinion for the three-judge panel, he rejected the army's contention that *Bowers* precluded Watkins from succeeding in making an equal protection claim, reiterating that *Bowers* was decided on due process grounds and did not provide a basis for discriminating against homosexuals. Moreover, he added, *Bowers* allows the state to punish persons for committing sexual conduct, but not for their sexual orientation. Noting that no other circuit had addressed the issue of whether persons of homosexual orientation should be considered a suspect class, Norris reviewed the criteria for determining whether the law merits a higher form of scrutiny: There must be a history of invidious intentional discrimination stemming from prejudice or stereotype that is based on immutable characteristics that bear no relationship to ability, and the individuals complaining of discrimination must lack the political power to seek redress from the government.[25]

Based on these measures, he believed that homosexuals constituted a suspect class when defined by status or orientation, entitling them to strict scrutiny. Norris acknowledged that reviewing courts show greater deference to military regulations, but found the army's justifications lacking because they were based on prejudice rather than on legitimate policy concerns.

Comparing the army's current treatment of gays to its past treatment of racial minorities, he concluded that the regulations unconstitutionally discriminated against gays.

Norris cited the high court's recent decision in *City of Cleburne* (1985), for although the Court had denied the class in that case suspect or semisuspect status, it held that the Cleburne zoning ordinance seemed to reflect the city's "irrational prejudice" against people with mental disabilities (438). Similarly, in *Palmore v. Sidoti* (1984), the Court had held that a state court ruling granting custody to a child's father because her white mother married an African American man rested on societal prejudice; it cautioned that "private biases may be outside the reach of the law, but the law cannot, directly or indirectly, give them effect" (433).[26]

Also concurring in Pregerson's majority opinion, Canby stressed that he believed Watkins had been denied equal protection. With the majority, he agreed that the case should be decided under the principle of equitable estoppel, but felt that because "the constitutional issue is a recurring one," the court should address it (*Watkins v. United States Army* 1989, 731).

At roughly the same time *Watkins* was being decided in the Ninth Circuit, Miriam benShalom's case against the army reserves was being considered by the Seventh Circuit. benShalom had been honorably discharged for unsuitability on the basis of her homosexuality, despite the absence of any evidence that she engaged in homosexual acts. When she sued, Wisconsin district court judge Evans awarded her summary judgment and ordered her reinstated, finding that the army had violated her rights of free speech, association, and privacy *(benShalom v. Secretary of the Army* 1980). Instead the army changed her records to reflect the honorable discharge when her enlistment had expired and offered her back pay. In 1983, after years of unsuccessful settlement negotiations, she moved to have the army declared in contempt for not obeying the court's order to have her reinstated. Her motion was denied, but the court ordered the army to award her back pay of almost $1,000.

On appeal, the Seventh Circuit upheld the district court on the contempt issue, but vacated the monetary award (*benShalom v. Secretary of the Army* 1985). The case was remanded to the lower court, which again ordered the army to reinstate her for the remainder of her enlistment period.

The appeals court affirmed, cautioning the army not to retaliate against her for successfully winning reinstatement (*benShalom v. Secretary of the Army* 1987). Circuit court judge Cummings explicitly warned that "her assignments and orders must not be tainted in any way by her professed off-base lesbianism. Put more simply," he said, "the Army may not make benShalom's life in the Army more difficult or burdensome because of her sexual preference" (724). She was finally reinstated in September 1987, almost eleven years after she had been dismissed by the army reserve.

The litigation began anew when benShalom sought to reenlist for another six-year term in 1988. The army refused, citing a new army regulation that declared homosexuality "a nonwaivable moral and administrative disqualification" and pointing to her original statements about her homosexuality that had caused her discharge in 1976 (benShalom v. Marsh 1989a, 1374). She obtained a court order directing the army to consider her reenlistment without regard to her sexual orientation, but the army instead extended her earlier enlistment. After being found in contempt, the army finally allowed her to reenlist, pending the outcome of the case.

District court judge Gordon noted that, as in the first benShalom case, the army still refused to distinguish between status and conduct, viewing persons with homosexual orientations unfit for military service because their statements revealed a propensity to engage in homosexual acts. Quoting extensively from the district court's 1980 ruling, Gordon questioned whether the army policy infringed on speech by sweeping more broadly than necessary to protect its interest in discipline. Because it assumed that persons with homosexual orientations will necessarily engage in homosexual conduct, he believed the army violated her right to freedom of expression.

Turning to the equal protection challenge, Gordon agreed with benShalom that laws affecting persons of homosexual orientation, absent evidence of conduct, require heightened scrutiny. Previous cases, he said, failed to distinguish between laws based on status and laws based on conduct. Acknowledging Bowers, Gordon recognized that homosexuals, defined by their conduct, do not constitute a suspect or semisuspect class. But because benShalom's conduct was not involved here—only her orientation—the court held that homosexuals were a suspect class and laws affecting them must be reviewed with strict scrutiny.

As it turned out, the level of scrutiny was irrelevant to the outcome of the case. Gordon found that although the government's interest was compelling, there was no rational relationship between it and the regulation under review. He concluded, "The challenged regulation can survive deferential scrutiny only if the Secretary is correct in the assertion that the status-conduct distinction is bogus. The Secretary insists that the regulation is aimed at conduct and that we must presume a correlation between orientation and conduct. I disagree" (benShalom v. Marsh 1989a, 1380).

On appeal, the Seventh Circuit disagreed with the lower court's finding of a First Amendment violation, holding that the army can better determine its needs than a court. "We do not believe," said Judge Wood, speaking for the three-judge panel, "that the Army must assume the risk that the presence of homosexuals within the service will not compromise the admittedly significant government interests [of morale, discipline, and fighting effectiveness]" (*benShalom v. Marsh* 1989b, 461). Moreover, he said, the regulation does not impair expression because it freely allows discussion of homosexuality, including criticism of the army policy; it reaches only individuals who desire to commit homosexual acts or have committed them. Rejecting the district court's analysis, the Seventh Circuit found it reasonable to assume benShalom's declaration of her homosexuality may be construed as a likelihood that she will engage in homosexual conduct.

Wood concluded that although the Constitution protects her right to discuss homosexuality, it does not protect her right to proclaim herself to be one because the army has concluded that homosexuals are unacceptable for service. He admitted that the regulation might discourage her or others from declaring their homosexuality and might be unconstitutional in a civilian world but believed that the army should not be judged according to the First Amendment standards of civilian life.

The appellate court also rejected the lower court judge's analysis of the equal protection violation, again because it was insufficiently sensitive to the military context. Wood declared that the district court had erred in declaring homosexual orientation a suspect classification and in distinguishing between conduct and status. Although he acknowledged that there was no evidence of her homosexual conduct, he found that her declaration of lesbianism may rightly be construed as an admission that she had engaged, and will again engage, in homosexual conduct.

By permitting the army to conflate status with conduct, the Seventh Circuit appeared to avoid the effect of *Robinson v. California* (1962), in which the Supreme Court overturned a California law making narcotics addiction unlawful. Holding that the Constitution bars punishment for status (that is, orientation), the high court ruled that the state may not punish addiction absent proof of criminal conduct. Subsequently, in *Powell v. Texas* (1968), in a fractured ruling on a statute that criminalized public intoxication, the Court maintained the distinction between status and conduct; the disagreement among the justices arose from their inability to agree on the boundaries of each. However, in *benShalom*, "the Seventh Circuit allowed the Army to do precisely what *Robinson* and *Powell* prohibited: rely on evidence of status to

presume unproven criminal conduct, and then rely on the presumed conduct to justify the punishment of status" (Valdes 1994, 406).

Finally, ruling on *benShalom*'s equal protection claim, Wood cited
Bowers, reasoning that if homosexual conduct may be criminalized, then
homosexuality cannot be a suspect or semisuspect class for equal protection
purposes, and minimal scrutiny is appropriate. Again, he stressed that the
courts should not second-guess the army's reasonable determination that
homosexuals are inappropriate for military service. Reflecting his belief
that homosexuals are not an oppressed minority, Wood ended by saying that
gays should apply their increasing political power to lobby Congress to
change the policy.[27]

Another case demonstrating the effect of *Bowers* on the lower courts,
Woodward v. United States (1989), began in 1974 when naval officer James
Woodward was seen in the officer's club with an enlisted man who was being
separated from the navy for homosexual conduct. When questioned,
Woodward acknowledged he had "homosexual tendencies" (a fact that he
had revealed when he enlisted in the naval reserve two years earlier); he was
removed from active duty, and, after he refused to resign, he was placed in
the naval reserves (1069).

After a protracted legal battle in the courts, primarily because of jurisdictional disputes, his discharge was upheld on the grounds that he was
released because of his performance, not because of his arguably constitutionally protected homosexuality. Speaking for a panel of the U.S. Court of
Appeals for the Federal Circuit, Judge Archer rejected the navy's contention
that its decisions were immune from judicial review. He cited the recent
Supreme Court ruling in *Webster v. Doe* (1988) that constitutional claims
may be adjudicated despite the power entrusted to the defense secretary to
remove officers from active duty.[28] However, because *Bowers* had established
that homosexual conduct is not a fundamental right, Archer rejected
Woodward's claim that the navy abridged his right to privacy, ignoring the
fact that the government had produced no evidence of homosexual conduct.

Assessing Woodward's equal protection argument, Archer pointed out
that homosexuals had none of the indicia of a suspect or semisuspect class;
moreover, he added, *Bowers* negated their ability to claim discrimination.
Applying minimal scrutiny, the court affirmed that the navy's policy was
rationally related to a legitimate goal of maintaining order. Archer concluded
by reiterating that courts must defer to the military "when adjudicating matters involving their decisions on discipline, morale, composition and the
like" (*Woodward* 1989, 1077).[29]

Shortly after *benShalom* was decided in the Seventh Circuit, the Ninth Circuit ruled in the case of Captain (Reverend) Dusty Pruitt, a lesbian who served in the army between 1971 and 1975. When her term was up, she joined the army reserves and was promoted to major. After the *Los Angeles Times* published an interview with her about her multiple roles as minister, lesbian, and officer in 1983, her security clearance was revoked, and she was recommended for discharge, which was finalized in 1986. There was no evidence that she had engaged in homosexual conduct.

She filed suit for reinstatement, contending that because she was punished on the basis of her declaration of homosexuality, the army had infringed on her First Amendment right as well as her right to privacy. District court judge Gray said it was irrelevant that she had not engaged in homosexual conduct because her discharge was based on the principle that "homosexuality is incompatible with military service . . . [and] seriously impairs the accomplishment of the military mission" (*Pruitt v. Weinberger* 1987, 627). And, he continued, she was unsuitable even if she merely wanted to, or intended to, commit homosexual acts. Without discussing her privacy claim, the court granted the army's motion to dismiss.

On appeal, the Ninth Circuit addressed Pruitt's argument that the newspaper article, in which she discussed her homosexuality, was political speech protected by the First Amendment. However, speaking for a unanimous panel, Canby cited *benShalom v. Marsh* (1989b) and found that "Pruitt was discharged not for the content of her speech, but for being a homosexual" (*Pruitt v. Cheney* 1992, 1163).

Turning to the equal protection issue, Canby noted that although Pruitt had not raised it, the lower court should not have dismissed her complaint because she had alleged sufficient facts to show that she was discriminated against on the basis of her homosexuality.[30] Although the army cited *Beller*, the court ruled that it was not applicable because the plaintiffs there had been discharged for homosexual conduct. Additionally, *Beller* was inapposite because it was decided on due process grounds only and had not addressed the issue of discrimination on equal protection grounds. Finally, because it had been decided before *Palmore* and *City of Cleburne* had clearly established that societal prejudice cannot justify discrimination, Canby believed that it was time to reexamine *Beller's* conclusions.

In the end, although the appeals court rejected heightened scrutiny for classifications based on sexual orientation, it applied a more rigorous basis of review than the traditional minimal scrutiny approach (see Delchin 1996). Citing an earlier Ninth Circuit ruling on the military's policy of enhancing the investigation of gays for security clearances, Canby said, "We required the government to establish on the record that its policy had a rational basis" and refused to accept the military's argument that the discriminatory treatment of "homosexuals should be held to be rational as a matter of law, without any justification in the record at all" (*Pruitt v. Cheney* 1992, 1166).[31]

The circuit court reversed and remanded the case. Because the lower court had granted the government's motion to dismiss Pruitt's claim before any evidence had been presented, the panel held that, on remand, she would have an opportunity to show that her complaint stated a valid claim and to present evidence to support it; the government would have to show its policy is rational.[32] Canby ended by expressing confidence that the lower court would be mindful of its duty to defer to the military's judgment and expertise.[33]

A later district court case in the Ninth Circuit came to the opposite conclusion about the appropriate level of scrutiny. In *Dahl v. Secretary of the United States Navy* (1993), Mel Dahl, who had been honorably discharged from the navy in 1982 for disclosing he was gay, sued for reinstatement. He denied he had been involved in any homosexual activity after enlisting in the navy. The lower court granted the government's motion to dismiss, and the Ninth Circuit reversed and remanded in light of *Pruitt v. Cheney* (1992). Before the lower court ruled in the matter again, Dahl dropped all claims except those based on the First Amendment and equal protection. He contended that gays met the criteria for treatment as a suspect class for two reasons: First, a 1988 study by the Defense Personnel Security Research and Education Center concluded that homosexuality is determined at birth; second, Congress's refusal to lift the ban on gays in the military shows they lack political power.

California district court judge Schwartz was not persuaded that Dahl had shown that gays satisfied the standards for applying strict scrutiny in the Ninth Circuit. Moreover, he disagreed that the government has to prove it has a rational basis for treating gays differently. In his view, *Pruitt*'s holding that the government show that its policy is rational was likely overruled by *Heller v. Doe* (1993), and he would place the burden on the plaintiff to "negate every conceivable rational basis for the policy" (*Dahl* 1993, 1326).[34] Concluding that, in this case, the plaintiff met his burden in showing the navy had no rational basis for its policy, Schwartz granted Dahl's motion for summary judgment on the equal protection claim and ordered him reinstated.

One of the last cases decided on the basis of the 1981 directives began in 1980 when seventeen-year-old Volker Keith Meinhold enlisted in the navy. He served with distinction for twelve years and was never officially questioned about his sexual orientation but often spoke of it publicly. On May 19, 1992, he was interviewed on an ABC national news show and declared, "Yes, I am in fact gay" (*Meinhold v. United States Department of Defense* 1994, 1472).[35] The navy began proceedings against him and honorably discharged him three months later without any evidence that he had engaged in any prohibited homosexual acts. He filed suit in district court, seeking reinstatement.

District court judge Hatter cited numerous irregularities in the conduct of his discharge proceedings, such as allowing improper evidence and failing to indicate the standard for the decision to expel him (*Meinhold v. United States Department of Defense* 1992). As in *Watkins*, the court based its decision on the principle of equitable estoppel because Meinhold had been told that he would not be discharged for homosexuality as long as he conformed to the rules of conduct. Finally, Hatter held that the navy violated Meinhold's right of equal protection because the link between the regulation and the desired goal was irrational. Given these facts, the court granted Meinhold the preliminary injunction he sought.

Following the subsequent hearing on Meinhold's request for a permanent injunction, Hatter issued his ruling in *Meinhold v. United States Department of Defense* (1993). Addressing the equal protection claim, he cited *Pruitt* and ordered the military to provide factual evidence that its policy was rational as applied to individuals with a homosexual orientation, such as Meinhold. Quoting from Defense Secretary Richard Cheney's statement, made on national television in December 1992, that the military no longer considered gays a security risk, Hatter assessed the remaining arguments to justify the ban: "maintaining discipline, good order and morale; fostering mutual trust and confidence among servicemembers; the need to recruit and retain servicemembers; and maintaining public acceptability by the Navy" (*Meinhold v. United States Department of Defense* 1993, 1457).

The only piece of evidence the navy produced to substantiate its policy was the 1992 GAO report on the DoD's policy on homosexuality, which, ironically, as the court pointed out, contained an admission by the DoD that there was no scientific evidence to support its policy toward homosexuals. On the contrary, Hatter stressed, there were a number of empirical studies commissioned by the navy that concluded there were no negative effects associated with homosexuals serving in the military; indeed, these studies indicated the opposite was true. Further, the judge cited the experience of other nations that had rescinded their bans on gays in the military as well as a statement by a former assistant secretary of defense, Lawrence Korb. Korb, who was one of the witnesses in the "Don't Ask, Don't Tell" hearings and had been a key figure in formulating the military's exclusionary policy during the Reagan administration, was no longer convinced the ban on gays was justified.

Concluding that the navy's policy was based on "cultural myths and false stereotypes," the district court granted Meinhold a permanent injunction, rescinded his discharge, and barred the DoD "from discharging or denying enlistment to any person based on sexual orientation in the absence of sexual conduct which interferes with the military mission of the armed forces of the United States" (1458).[36]

On appeal, the Ninth Circuit acceded to the navy's judgment that persons who engage in homosexual acts or have a "propensity" to do so are unsuitable for military life. But discharges cannot be based on a declaration of homosexuality alone, unless "the statement itself manifests a concrete, expressed desire or intent to engage in homosexual acts" (*Meinhold v. United States Department of Defense* 1994, 1472).[37] Speaking for the circuit panel, Judge Rymer found that the navy had improperly applied the regulations to Meinhold and affirmed the lower court order reinstating him but struck that part of the ruling ordering a nationwide injunction as overly broad.[38]

Likely the last case decided on the basis of the policy before "Don't Ask, Don't Tell" went into effect arose in a District of Columbia District Court. It began in 1987, when, despite his exemplary record, Joseph Steffan had been compelled to resign from the Naval Academy six weeks before his graduation, forgoing his degree as well as his commission. He had confided to two classmates that he was gay, and when questioned by an academy official (the Commandant of Midshipmen), he acknowledged it.[39] To avoid an involuntary discharge and have his homosexuality noted on his record, he resigned.[40] About a year and a half later, he asked to withdraw his resignation, and when his request was denied, he filed suit in the District of Columbia District Court, claiming a violation of his equal protection rights.[41]

Steffan raised the familiar argument that laws affecting sexual orientation merit heightened scrutiny, distinguishing earlier cases in which homosexuals had been removed from the armed forces on the grounds of conduct rather than status as in his case.[42] Judge Gasch of the District of Columbia District Court acknowledged the difficulty in determining whether his disciplinary action resulted from homosexual conduct, but concluded that it was based primarily on his orientation.[43] Noting that in *benShalom v. Marsh* (1989b), the Seventh Circuit had rejected strict scrutiny for classifications based on sexual orientation, Gasch reviewed the criteria for determining whether the plaintiff should be considered a member of a suspect class. He based his analysis on *Bowen v. Gilliard* (1987), in which the Supreme Court determined that heightened scrutiny was inappropriate for a certain type of welfare law, and *Lyng v. Castillo* (1986), another entitlement case. "Under Bowen," Gasch said, "the plaintiff must: 1) have suffered a history of discrimination, 2) exhibit obvious, immutable, or distinguishing characteristics that define him as a member of a discrete group; and 3) show that the group is a minority or politically powerless, or alternatively show that the statutory classification at issue burdens a fundamental right" (*Steffan v. Cheney* 1991, 5, citing *Bowen* 1987, 602–3). Applying the test, he concluded, as the Seventh Circuit had, that these characteristics do not apply to homosexuals, and therefore heightened scrutiny is unwarranted.[44]

In applying minimal scrutiny, Gasch concurred with the government that it "has a legitimate interest in good order and morale, the system of rank and command, and discipline in the Military Services" (*Steffan v. Cheney* 1991, 12). He believed that *Dronenburg* controlled even though homosexual conduct was involved there, and echoing *Dronenburg*, he found that the regulation was motivated by morality, not prejudice as Steffan had claimed. As an afterthought, although neither side raised the issue, Gasch took judicial notice of the fact that concern about AIDS provided further justification for the navy policy.

On appeal, the three-judge circuit panel adopted a more sympathetic tone, stressing Steffan's excellent record in the academy and revealing the manner in which he was treated by the academy administration. Speaking for the panel, Judge Mikva began with the traditional bow of judicial deference to the military's judgment and expertise, but noted that the court's duty to defer is not unlimited. "A court," he said, "need not close its eyes to the dictates of the Constitution whenever the military is involved—not even when it professes a national security interest in its conduct. There is no 'military exception' to the Constitution. Indeed," he added, "even when the Supreme Court has deferred to a military judgment, it has been careful to do so only within the confines of ordinary constitutional analysis . . . [and] this is particularly true for equal protection cases" (*Stefan v. Aspin* 1993, 62). Mikva concluded that even in cases involving the military, courts are not required to absolve themselves entirely from the process of judicial review, especially when plaintiffs raise equal protection challenges, an area in which judges have great expertise.

Reiterating that Steffan was discharged solely on the basis of his status as a homosexual, Mikva noted that this issue had not yet been decided in the District of Columbia circuit, at the same time conceding that the courts have ruled out heightened scrutiny in cases involving homosexual conduct. Declining to decide whether laws affecting homosexual orientation are entitled to a higher form of scrutiny, he applied minimal scrutiny to the regulations, merely asking if they had a rational basis.

The government argued that by stating he was a homosexual, Steffan was admitting to a desire or intention "to engage in homosexual conduct" (64). However, Mikva emphasized that the navy acted solely on the basis of Steffan's statement; he did not acknowledge, nor was he asked about, homosexual conduct. Therefore, his discharge stemmed entirely from his homosexual orientation, that is, on a desire to engage in a homosexual act, not on the act itself. Brushing aside the navy's rather fanciful attempt to distinguish between a person who was merely attracted to members of the same sex, a "celibate homosexual," and one who desired to engage in homosexual conduct, Mikva parsed the language of the 1981 directives. In doing so, he was skeptical of the navy's insistence that its only concern was with homosexual acts, because in his view, "the Directives as a whole are far more concerned with status—with thoughts and desires—than with conduct" (64).

The court held that the navy policy preemptively dismissed individuals who simply desired to engage in homosexual acts or had a propensity to do. But, Mikva said, the navy cannot rationally assume that a person who simply thinks about committing an illegal act will do so. "Many of us 'desire' in the abstract to do things and yet refrain from doing them simply because they are against the rules" (65). He also took the navy to task for its judgment that the mere presence of homosexuals will harm morale and invade the privacy of heterosexuals, apparently because of their inability to control their lechery. Even presuming the navy's "fears are well-founded," he said, they "are patently insufficient to justify discriminatory policy, even under rationality review, because each depends solely upon the prejudice of third parties" (67). Citing *Palmore* and *City of Cleburne*, Mikva stressed that such thinking merely fosters bigotry. And finally, he dismissed the lower court's reference to AIDS, saying homosexual orientation does not cause or spread the disease.

Because it found no rational relationship between the directives and a legitimate government interest, the court upheld Steffan's equal protection claim and ordered the navy to award him his diploma and reinstate him as a commissioned officer.[45]

The government moved for reconsideration of the court's order to commission him, and the appellate court decided on its own to rehear the case en banc; in the process, it vacated the panel's ruling (*Steffan v. Aspin* 1994).

Speaking for a divided court, District of Columbia circuit court judge Silberman announced the decision. Because it was unclear whether the DoD directives or the Naval Academy regulations had been applied in Steffan's case, the court examined both.[46] Beginning with the Naval Academy regulations, Silberman stressed the duty to defer to the government, reiterating the Supreme Court's oft-stated refrain that in reviewing military regulations and procedures "courts owe even more special deference to the 'considered professional judgment' of appropriate military officials" (*Steffan v. Perry* 1994, 685, quoting *Goldman* 1986, 509).

Applying rationality-based review to the Naval Academy regulations, the court stressed that Steffan himself had conceded that the government had a legitimate reason to discharge personnel who engage in homosexual conduct as well as those who indicate an intention to do so. The issue therefore was whether the policy of discharging midshipmen who merely declare their homosexuality (without evidence that they have engaged in homosexual acts or intend to) reasonably furthers the goal of removing those who engage in homosexual conduct.

Taking the opposite position from Mikva, Silberman found that the military may reasonably assume that a declaration of homosexuality constitutes an admission that one has engaged in homosexual conduct or is likely to do so. And, he stated, removing such individuals from the service advances a legitimate government purpose. Given the serious consequences that the navy believes homosexuals have on morale and discipline, Silberman emphasized, the court must not second-guess its judgment about the relationship between those who admit to homosexuality and those who commit homosexual acts.

Addressing Steffan's argument that the law must acknowledge a distinction between status and conduct, the court conceded that although persons cannot be punished under criminal law for their status, they can be judged on the basis of their status in an employment context such as this. Additionally, Silberman said, it was entirely proper for the government to conflate status with conduct, reasoning that sexual orientation is inextricably related to sexual conduct.

Turning to the DoD directives, Silberman noted that Steffan's primary challenge was that it was inappropriate to consider an individual "who desires to engage in" a homosexual act as a homosexual because that infringes on constitutionally protected private thoughts.[47] The court rejected his argument on the grounds that Steffan never contended that his declaration of homosexuality was limited only to desires and excluded conduct or intentions.[48] In short, the court concluded that there was no evidence that the navy based Steffan's discharge on the "desires" clause.

THE ORIGINS OF "DON'T ASK, DON'T TELL"

In June 1992, House Armed Services Committee member Patricia Schroeder, Democrat from Colorado, attempted to end discrimination against gays in the armed services by adding an amendment making it illegal for the military to discriminate on the basis of sexual orientation to a defense reauthorization bill. She rejected the Pentagon's claim that its policy protected heterosexuals against sexual pressure from gays, saying "Women have been subjected to leers forever and we've been told to get a life, that that's how it is" (*Congressional Quarterly Weekly* November 21, 1992, 3678).

In a letter to Schroeder in May 1992, General Colin Powell, an African American and Chairman of the Joint Chiefs of Staff, took great pains to differentiate between race and sexual orientation. He wrote, "I can assure you I need no reminders concerning the history of African Americans in the defense of their nation. . . . Skin color is a benign, non-behavioral characteristic. Sexual orientation is perhaps the most profound of human behavioral characteristics. Comparison of the two is a convenient but invalid argument" (*Seattle Times* June 7, 1992).[49] Reflecting the debate among gay rights advocates, Barney Frank and Gerry Studds, both gay and both Democrats from Massachusetts, warned against putting the measure to a vote because it would almost certainly lose; the vote was not taken (McFeeley 2000).

As the first major presidential candidate to seek gay votes, Clinton promised to repeal the long-standing ban on gays in the military, a position that in large part earned him almost three-quarters of the gay vote and millions of dollars in campaign funds.[50] Gay rights organizations were reported to have donated hundreds of thousands of dollars, and it was widely known that Clinton was influenced by his longtime friend David Mixner, who played an active role in his campaign and served as his liaison to the gay community. On the other side, speakers at the Republican Convention, such as Patrick Buchanan, denounced gays, making it clear to most that they were unwelcome in the party. Ironically, the Republicans did not take on Clinton over the issue of exclusion of gays from the military during the 1992 campaign, in part because they were already viewed as intolerant because of their convention's focus on the culture war, code language in part for the dispute over gay rights.

The debate over the status of gays in the military became intensified almost immediately after Clinton was elected president. Shortly after his inauguration, on January 25, 1993, Clinton ordered Defense Secretary Les Aspin to prepare a draft executive order by July 15, 1993, to end the military's discrimination against homosexuals.[51]

The president proposed that the military refrain from questioning potential recruits about their sexual orientation and cease taking actions against suspected homosexuals during the six-month interim before the ban would be lifted.[52] Meanwhile, Senate Republicans threatened to seek legislation to continue the ban in force. Opposition from Capitol Hill and veterans groups mounted, and on January 29 after negotiations with Sam Nunn, Democrat from Georgia and chair of the Senate Armed Services Committee, and the Joint Chiefs of Staff, Clinton announced a six-month moratorium on lifting the ban, having secured Nunn's agreement to hold hearings. The agreement specified a cessation on questioning recruits about their sexual orientation, but a continuation of punishment meted out for acts of homosexuality. Additionally, the attorney general was empowered to block dismissals solely on the basis of homosexuality, but such service members would be removed from active duty and placed on "standby reserve," during which time they would receive no pay or benefits; commanding officers would have the authority to reassign accused or acknowledged homosexuals.

Clinton acknowledged that the "compromise is not everything I would have hoped for or everything that I have stood for, but it is plainly a substantial step in the right direction." Despite the moratorium, however, Republicans indicated their intention to go ahead with legislation to codify the ban into law by attaching it as an amendment to the proposed Family and Medical Leave Act (Clinton 1993a; *Congressional Quarterly Weekly* January 30, 1993, 226).

The Senate Armed Services Committee held hearings on March 29 and 31, 1993.[53] Nunn led off by stressing the need to move slowly on the issue, linking it to national security because of its potential effect on troop morale and cohesion. He intimated that the compromise reached in January might be the final solution, terming the policy "Don't Ask, Don't Tell."

Although the hearings were purportedly balanced, the testimony was carefully orchestrated. Prejudices were stated as facts, with heterosexual members of the military supporting the existing exclusionary policy. They cited their discomfort with having to serve with gays and lesbians and spoke of the deleterious effects of openly gay service members on unit cohesion. No heterosexual currently in the military spoke in favor of lifting the ban, and the gay witnesses, almost all ex-military, were far outnumbered by proponents of the ban (D. Miller 1998, chap. 3).

Former Assistant Secretary of Defense Korb, who had designed the existing policy during the Reagan administration, testified in favor of lifting the ban, comparing it to Truman's executive order integrating the military; in his view, any problems that arose could be overcome just as they had been in 1948.

The hearings aired disagreements over the definition of status and conduct, with proponents of ending the ban saying it was crucial to distinguish between the two, and opponents denying that the distinction could be made because the act of describing oneself as a homosexual involved conduct. An important unanswered question was whether a private statement of one's sexual orientation would constitute "telling" under the new provisions (*Congressional Quarterly Weekly* April 3, 1993, 851).

On May 4 and 5, 1993, the House Armed Services Committee held hearings during which most testifying, including retired army general Norman Schwarzkopf—famous for his role in the first Gulf War—expressed intense opposition to lifting the ban.[54]

Clinton sought to maintain the distinction between status and conduct, making only the latter punishable by dismissal, and wanting to allow gays to be able to acknowledge their homosexuality. Nunn, however, insisted that merely imparting information about one's homosexuality would have a negative effect on cohesion and morale.[55]

Meanwhile, Frank proposed another compromise, termed "Don't Ask, Don't Tell, Don't Investigate." His proposal, in which restrictions would apply only when individuals were in uniform, on duty, and on the base, resulted from his belief that the president did not have the votes to repeal the ban; it also was an attempt to derail the Nunn proposal. Although Clinton was pleased with his support, gay rights activists attacked Frank for abandoning the effort to eliminate the ban outright (see Rayside 1996).

With most Republicans firmly opposed to lifting the ban, the key players in the debate were the conservative members of Clinton's own party led by Nunn. Around the end of May, it began to appear that a coalition was beginning to form around Nunn's proposed "Don't Ask, Don't Tell," an arrangement similar to the compromise embodied in Clinton's January policy that proved to be only a modest departure from the existing policy: New recruits would not be questioned about their sexual orientation and would be dismissed only for homosexual conduct; but although a homosexual orientation alone would not be grounds for discharge, troops would likely be dismissed if they declared their orientations (*Congressional Quarterly Weekly* May 15, 1993, 1240).

It became clear that as the July 15 deadline approached, the effort to rescind the ban was no longer a viable option, with opposition mounted from Republicans and conservative Democrats in Congress, veterans groups, anti-gay forces within the military, and the religious right. Gay rights activists also seemed to misjudge the intensity of the opposition and overestimate the political capital Clinton was willing to commit to rescind the ban. For the most part, gay rights groups sought to convince Clinton to proceed with the executive order, despite the fact that it would almost certainly be overturned by congressional legislation (see Rimmerman 1996; Rayside 1996).

Throughout this process, Aspin had been meeting with the Joint Chiefs to arrive at a policy they could accept; their support was crucial in persuading the conservatives in Clinton's party to vote for it. The Chiefs, with Powell as their spokesperson, made it known that they would accept only a policy in which gay men and lesbians kept their sexual orientation secret (*Congressional Quarterly Weekly* July 17, 1993, 1889). Early in the controversy, Powell was quoted as saying that "homosexual behavior 'is inconsistent with maintaining good order and discipline. It's difficult in a military setting where there is no privacy to introduce a group of individuals—proud, brave, loyal good Americans, but who favor a homosexual lifestyle—and put them in with heterosexuals who would prefer not to have somebody of the same sex find them sexually attractive.'" (*Houston Chronicle* February 6, 1992).

Ultimately the Chiefs endorsed the proposed plan, characterizing it as a slightly revised version of the policy that had been in effect since early 1980, with Powell calling it "an honorable compromise" (*Congressional Quarterly Weekly* July 24, 1993, 1966).

On July 19, 1993, at Fort McNair's National Defense University in Washington, Clinton announced the formulation of a compromise policy: "Don't Ask, Don't Tell, Don't Pursue."[56] He described the new approach as "a real step forward," a policy that is "the right thing to do and the best way to do it." During his talk at Fort McNair, he explained that his view to end the ban had evolved from a speech made at Harvard University's Kennedy School of Government during the 1992 campaign. In that speech, he now explained, he had been asked about reports that it cost approximately $500 million to remove 17,000 homosexuals from the military during the 1980s and his views on lifting the ban. Up until that time, he said, "this question had never before been presented to me, and I had never had the opportunity to discuss it with anyone. I stated then what I still believe, that I thought there ought to be a presumption that people who wish to do so should be able to serve their country if they are willing to conform to the high standards of the military and that the emphasis should be always on people's conduct, not their status" (Clinton 1993c).

As often happens with a compromise, neither side was satisfied with the outcome: Clinton was skewered by the right for his attempt to secure what they called "special treatment" for gays.[57] Moreover, the mere fact that he attempted to change the policy also hurt him politically with the mainstream for it gave the impression that he was consumed by the issue at a time when his primary focus should have been on more important issues such as the economy (*Washington Post* July 20, 1993). The gay community itself was divided over the wisdom of undertaking to repeal the ban, believing there were more significant issues to which he should devote resources such as fighting AIDS or employment discrimination (see Rimmerman 1996; Osburn and Benecke 1996). They also criticized Clinton for reneging on his pledge to end the ban and not confronting Congress and the military head-on; many blamed him for what they considered his half-hearted efforts to fulfill his campaign pledge.

IMPLEMENTING "DON'T ASK, DON'T TELL"

Despite the rhetoric accompanying the new policy, it was strikingly similar to the one it replaced (see Wells-Petry 1995; Woodruff 1995). No longer declaring that "homosexuality is incompatible with military service," the policy now states that "a person's sexual orientation is considered a personal and private matter and is not a bar to service unless manifested by homosexual conduct."[58] However, by broadly defining conduct to include a declaration of a homosexual orientation as well as a homosexual act, it continued to blur the distinction between status and conduct, thus extending the accommodation only to silenced homosexuals.

Both old and new policies essentially treat declarations of homosexuality as grounds for discharge. Under the old policy, because a homosexual orientation was grounds for discharge, a declaration of homosexuality was viewed as evidence of the orientation. Under the new policy, although a homosexual orientation (that is, status) alone is not grounds for discharge, a declaration of homosexuality is considered conduct and thereby becomes grounds for discharge (D. Miller 1998). To put it simply, speech became conduct. To some, it seemed as if "Don't Ask, Don't Tell" "offer[ed] nothing more than a newly phrased warning for lesbians and gays to return to the closet" (Pacelle 1996, 216).

Eager to exercise its control, Congress insisted on codifying the policy, thus ensuring that it would have a role in future revisions.[59] To emphasize its supremacy over military policy, the law explicitly cited Congress's authority to "establish qualifications or and conditions of service in the armed forces."[60] The statute reinforced the long-standing rule against homosexuals in the military, adopting Nunn's language that "the presence in the armed forces of persons who demonstrate a propensity or intent to engage in homosexual acts would create an unacceptable risk to the high standards of morale, good order and discipline, and unit cohesion that are the essence of military capability."[61] In July, the Senate and House Armed Services Committees approved the Nunn language as §571 of the 1994 Defense Authorization Act, codified at 10 U.S.C. §654.[62]

A few months later, on September 29, 1993, in a vote of 301–134, the House passed H.R. 2401, codifying the language of the gay ban approved by the Senate and House committees earlier in July.[63] An unsuccessful attempt was made to order the Pentagon to resume questioning recruits about their sexual orientations; the law gave the Pentagon the discretion to decide whether to return to this policy. The House also defeated a proposal to omit references to gays in military defense bills, leaving the matter up to the president (*Congressional Quarterly Weekly* October 2, 1993, 2668). The Senate approved the final measure on October 6, 1993.[64]

On November 30, 1993, Clinton signed the National Defense Authorization Act of 1994, with "Don't Ask, Don't Tell" codified at 10 U.S.C. §654.[65] Purportedly differentiating between status and conduct, the act spelled out three forbidden areas of homosexual activity that would justify dismissal from the service: (1) §654(b)(1) "The [service] member has engaged in, attempted to engage in, or solicited another to engage in a homosexual act or acts" (the acts provision); (2) §654(b)(2) "the member has stated that he or she is a homosexual or bisexual, or words to that effect" (the statements provision); (3) §654(b)(3) "the member has married or attempted to marry a person known to be of the same biological sex" (the marriage provision).[66] New DoD directives, promulgated in 1993, took effect on February 28, 1994.[67]

In 1993, while "Don't Ask, Don't Tell" was being laboriously crafted, the military suffered two reversals in the courts. First, in September, the California district court judge issued his sweeping nationwide injunction in *Meinhold*, ordering the Pentagon not to discriminate against homosexuals.[68] The second setback occurred in November when the three-judge panel of the District of Columbia Court of Appeals unanimously ruled against the military in the *Steffan* case. Both victories turned out to be short-lived, how-ever, as the decisions were reversed in later rulings.

CHALLENGING "DON'T ASK, DON'T TELL"

Gay rights advocates lost little time in challenging the new policy, primarily on First Amendment (claiming that by being disciplined for "telling," they were punished for their speech) and equal protection grounds (arguing that the policy discriminated against them because of their status as homosexu-als, which was irrationally based on prejudice). The advantage of claiming a First Amendment violation was clear in that courts would be more likely to apply strict scrutiny to the policy. However, because the Supreme Court has made exceptions to this practice in First Amendment cases involving military matters (see *United States v. O'Brien* 1968), the outcome was uncer-tain. And with the high court's decision in *Bowers*, the success of the privacy and due process arguments was problematic.

The first challenge to the new policy arose in a Brooklyn courtroom. It was brought by six gay and lesbian members of the armed services who claimed that §571 of the National Defense Authorization Act of 1994 violated their First and Fifth Amendment rights.[69] Judge Nickerson of the federal dis-trict court expressed skepticism of the government's position that it was con-cerned only with conduct (*Able v. United States* 1994). To characterize a declaration of homosexuality as conduct, he said, "is to call into question the Act's assurance that it deals only with homosexual acts" (1041). After giv-ing the requisite nod toward judicial deference to the military, Nickerson found the law unnecessarily broad in furthering the government's interest.

Using minimal scrutiny to evaluate the plaintiffs' equal protection chal-lenge, the court reviewed a number of earlier cases in which the old military policy banning homosexuality had been challenged and found that courts were split, some finding it irrational to distinguish between homosexuals and heterosexuals, some not. Applying the standards for a preliminary injunction, the court ruled in the plaintiffs' favor.

When the case reached the Second Circuit, in a per curiam opinion, the court held that Nickerson had failed to apply the proper standard for issu-ing the injunction and remanded the case with instructions to join the pre-liminary injunction hearing with the trial on the merits for a permanent injunction (*Able* 1995a).

When the case was remanded to his court, following a four-day trial on the merits, Nickerson reassessed his ruling on the First and Fifth Amendment claims, focusing on §654(b)(2), the "statements provision." As he explained, according to the law and regulations, although sexual orientation is no longer grounds for separation from the service, homosexual conduct is. To avoid dismissal, according to §654(b)(2), a declaration of homosexuality must be rebutted by showing that the service member "is not a person who engages in, attempts to engage in, has a propensity to engage in, or intends to engage in homosexual acts."[70] He noted that although "the Directives purport to distinguish homosexual 'orientation' from homosexual 'propensity,' defining homosexual 'orientation' as 'an abstract sexual preference for persons of a particular sex,' and homosexual 'propensity' as evidencing 'a likelihood that a person engages in or will engage in' homosexual acts," they do not explain how an orientation becomes a propensity merely by being articulated (*Able* 1995c, 972). He accused the government of trying to "avoid the First Amendment by defining 'conduct' to include statements revealing one's homosexual status" (975).

Nickerson traced the evolution of the military's antigay policy from the 1920s, when homosexuality was viewed as a mental disorder, to the 1980s, when homosexuals were considered a threat to national security, and to the 1990s, when they were regarded as responsible for the spread of diseases such as hepatitis or syphilis. This law, however, was not based on any of these premises, he said; indeed, its legislative history shows that many high military officials testified to the exemplary status of gays as members of the armed services. Yet, despite this recognition, Nickerson noted, the government believed it necessary that homosexuals remain mute about their status, with the rationale that by revealing it, they were evidencing a likelihood to engage in the forbidden conduct. And to avoid the First Amendment violation, the government defined a declaration of homosexuality as evidence of a propensity for conduct, not as speech.

The judge criticized the law for not clearly distinguishing between a homosexual orientation and a homosexual propensity, characterizing this as a crucial difference since the former is permissible, while the latter results in disciplinary action. Moreover, he said, the law places the burden on the service members to rebut the presumption by proving they do not engage in, nor have the propensity to engage, in homosexual acts, a virtually impossible task.[71] Thus, according to the court, because revealing a homosexual orientation is almost a certain guarantee of separation from the service, the punishment is based purely on speech in violation of the First Amendment.

Characterizing the policy as "Byzantine," Nickerson accused the government of hiding its real purpose: placating heterosexual prejudices by ensuring that they remain unaware of the homosexuals serving among them. But knowing that it would not survive judicial review, he said, the government "pretend[ed] that the concern was over, not the mere presence of homosexuals in the Services, but their potential acts" (977). Finally, he made short shrift of the government's equal protection argument, holding that it failed to show why it differentiated between heterosexuals and homosexuals in the exercise of free speech, thus violating the Fifth Amendment.

The government appealed the district court's finding that §654(b)(2) was unconstitutional, while the plaintiffs challenged one of the lower court's earlier rulings dismissing their claim against §654(b)(1) on grounds of standing (*Able* 1995b).

The Second Circuit panel, with Judge Walker announcing the opinion, agreed with the plaintiffs that their claim should not have been dismissed for lack of standing and remanded the case to the lower court for a determination of the constitutionality of §654(b)(1) (*Able* 1996). However, at the same time, the court rejected the district court's reasoning for finding §654(b)(1) unconstitutional and vacated that part of the ruling.

The government had argued that it placed no burden on speech because the speech involved was merely evidence of conduct; but if there were an incidental burden on speech, it was justifiable under the more relaxed scrutiny accorded to military regulations. The appellate court agreed that "given the rational connection between the statement 'I am a homosexual' and the likelihood that the declarant will commit homosexual acts, §654(b)(2) is no more restrictive than necessary" and furthers the government's important interest in preventing homosexual acts (1296). The court added that as the government had conceded, if, on remand, the district court determines that the restrictions in §654(b)(1) are unconstitutional, the speech restrictions in §654(b)(2) would also be unconstitutional.

Returning to his court for his third ruling in the case in three years, Nickerson considered whether §654(b)(1) violated equal protection. He cited *Romer*, saying it "established that government discrimination against homosexuals in and of itself violates the constitutional guarantee of equal protection. Implicit in this holding," he added, "is a determination that such discrimination, without more, is either inherently irrational or invidious" (*Able* 1997, 852).

The judge framed the issue as whether equal protection mandated similar treatment of homosexuals and heterosexuals. Again, the answer seemed clear when he launched into a critique of the history of discrimination against homosexuals, graphically portraying the pink triangles forced on them during the Holocaust. Quoting from such high-ranking military officials as Powell and Schwarzkopf that gays are as capable, honorable, and law-abiding as heterosexuals, the judge stressed that the government no longer justifies the differential treatment of gays on their inherent deficiencies, and the Code of Military Justice already punishes sexual misconduct with no distinction between heterosexuals and homosexuals. He questioned why there must be a law to punish "innocuous" behavior such as handholding or kissing directed against gays, sarcastically pointing out that "it is hard to imagine why the mere holding of hands off base and in private is dangerous to the mission of the Armed Forces if done by a homosexual but not if done by a heterosexual" (857). Surely, he said, it cannot be that the government believes it will thwart more serious acts of sexual misbehavior by gays because it has already admitted that gays are no more likely to commit serious acts of misconduct. It must therefore be, he reasoned, that the government is anxious to avoid any displays of homosexuality.

The government asserted three reasons to justify its policy: unit cohesion, reducing sexual tension, and protecting the privacy of heterosexuals. Insisting it was aware of the deference owed Congress, the court nevertheless found all three wanting. The real reason for the policy, Nickerson believed, was to "cater to the prejudices" and fears of heterosexuals who disapprove of homosexuals in their midst (862). Citing *City of Cleburne, Palmore,* and *Romer,* he ruled that such prejudices cannot justify differential treatment by the government. Although he suggested that because of the history of discrimination against homosexuals, it would be appropriate to use a higher form of scrutiny, Nickerson conceded that precedent required him to apply minimal scrutiny. But even under minimal scrutiny, largely because the policy was based on societal prejudice against gays, he held that §654(b)(1) violated equal protection and thus §654(b)(2) was unconstitutional as well.

On appeal again, Walker accepted the government's argument that Nickerson had not appropriately deferred to its authority over military affairs (*Able* 1998). Nickerson had erred, Walker said, by relying on *City of Cleburne, Palmore,* and *Romer*; because none of those cases involved the military, the Court had been able to scrutinize the government's asserted reasons more carefully. In this case, however, judicial deference prevented the court from requiring the government to justify its reasons for the restrictions on homosexuals. As long as the military believed its policy furthered the legitimate goals of unit cohesion and personal privacy and reduced sexual tensions, the court should inquire no further. In response to the plaintiffs' argument that these reasons are not rationally related to the ban on homosexual conduct, the court found that expert testimony from numerous sources during committee hearings gave Congress ample reason to believe "that those who engage in homosexual acts would compromise the effectiveness of the military" (*Able* 1998, 635).[72]

While *Able* was making its slow progress through the Second Circuit, gay service members were raising challenges to "Don't Ask, Don't Tell" in other circuits; there were two cases in the Fourth Circuit and one each in the Eighth and Ninth Circuits. The cases differed somewhat: Three involved the navy and one the air force; three of the plaintiffs in these cases faced discharge merely because they declared they were gay, and one admitted to homosexual conduct. Yet, despite their differences, the analyses and results of the cases were strikingly similar. In all, the plaintiffs challenged their separation from the service on essentially two grounds: First, they argued that "Don't Ask, Don't Tell" violated their First Amendment rights by punishing them for their speech; second, they claimed it violated their right to equal protection by discriminating against them on the basis of their sexual orientation without a legitimate justification.

The Fourth Circuit case arose in a Virginia district court when Paul Thomasson sued to prevent his discharge from the navy. Two days after the new directives went into effect, Thomasson, a lieutenant with an excellent service record, delivered a letter to the navy high command declaring his homosexuality. There was no evidence that he committed homosexual acts, but he refused to rebut the presumption of homosexuality that arose from his statement. His discharge was approved but held in abeyance while his lawsuit was in progress.

Citing the First Amendment, Thomasson argued to the district court that he was being punished for the content of his speech. But district court judge Hilton disagreed, saying that under the "Don't Ask, Don't Tell" policy, as the navy had contended, his discharge was not based on his speech, but rather on the fact that his "statement gave rise to a presumption that he engages in, or has a propensity or intent to engage in, homosexual acts" (*Thomasson v. Perry* 1995, 823). Hilton emphasized that Thomasson's discharge did not arise from his words alone, as Thomasson argued, but from the fact that the navy may rationally believe that his declaration of homosexuality is inextricably linked to the commission of a homosexual act. Furthermore, he said, all circuits that had evaluated this First Amendment claim under the old directives had come to the same conclusion.

Thomasson also contended that he was discriminated against on the basis of his sexual orientation and that such a classification merits strict scrutiny. Citing the prevailing view in the circuits that rationality review is the proper standard for claims affecting homosexuality, Hilton emphasized that although there is not an automatic exception for laws involving the military, a reviewing court must accord proper deference to its judgment and expertise. In light of the voluminous testimony, the extensive legislative findings, and the congressional floor debates, it was evident that Congress had carefully considered and articulated a legitimate purpose for excluding those who engage in homosexual conduct or have a propensity to do so.

Because of the importance of maintaining an effective fighting force, the court believed the military had a legitimate concern for maintaining unit cohesion and a reasonable belief that known homosexuals undermine unit cohesion by diminishing privacy and enhancing sexual tensions. Rather than prejudice, as the plaintiff charged, the court found that the policy stemmed from the government's realistic fear of the consequences of placing homosexuals in the barracks.

Similarly, the judge found it reasonable for Congress to assume that declarations of homosexuality are linked to a propensity to engage in homosexual conduct. Although he conceded that some declared homosexuals may not in fact engage in the forbidden conduct, when using minimal scrutiny, he explained, the court must defer to the military's assumption of the linkage between word and action.[73]

Following a rehearing, the Fourth Circuit sitting en banc delivered a 9–4 opinion, with Judge Wilkinson announcing the opinion (*Thomasson* 1996a). He devoted most of the ruling to reviewing the legislative history of the policy, focusing on the extensive hearings and congressional and executive branch consultations that accompanied passage of the law.[74]

The outcome of the case was clear when Wilkinson characterized the law as "a statute that embodies the exhaustive efforts of the democratically accountable branches of American government and an enactment that reflects month after month of political negotiation and deliberation. Such products of the democratic process are seldom completely tidy or universally satisfactory, but it is precisely on that account that they deserve judicial respect" (*Thomasson* 1996a, 923).

Wilkinson summarily rejected Thomasson's plea that the court substitute its judgment for the other two branches, especially in an area constitutionally committed to the governance of Congress and the president, and by extension, the military. Acknowledging that courts have a constitutional duty to review congressional actions, the judge stressed the impropriety of second-guessing the government's judgment about the harm caused by homosexuals in the service.

Citing the District of Columbia circuit court's ruling in *Steffan v. Perry* (1994), the Fourth Circuit swiftly disposed of Thomasson's equal protection claim, first by underscoring the propriety of using minimal scrutiny and then by agreeing with the lower court that the ends of the policy (removing homosexuals from military service) were legitimate and the link between the means (removing declared homosexuals) and the end is reasonable. Based on testimony from experts such as Powell and Schwarzkopf, the judge concluded that Congress could reasonably decide that "sexual tensions and attractions could play havoc with a military unit's discipline and solidarity" (*Thomasson* 1996a, 929).

Turning his attention to §654(b)(2), the "statements provision," Wilkinson reasoned that if Congress can legitimately prevent the commission of homosexual acts, it can surely discharge those with a "propensity or intent" to engage in such conduct, thereby rejecting Thomasson's argument that Congress should not be allowed to assume that declared homosexuals will engage in the forbidden conduct.[75]

Before the Fourth Circuit had handed down its decision in *Thomasson*, a second Virginia district court ruled on another challenge to "Don't Ask, Don't Tell," devoting its entire opinion to the First Amendment issue (*Thorne v. United States Department of Defense* 1996a). In this case, Lieutenant Tracy Thorne was discharged from the navy in March 1995 some time after he disclosed he was gay. The review board recommended his discharge on finding that his statement gave rise to a presumption that he had a "propensity" for homosexual conduct, which he failed to rebut. The government's by-now familiar argument was that his declaration was not speech but was evidence of conduct because it gave rise to a rebuttable presumption.

Thorne illustrates that when deference to military judgment is constrained and the court engages in a close textual analysis of the law and regulations, rather than merely accepting the government's assertions, the government's victory is not assured. District court judge Ellis framed the question in the case as turning on whether the presumption was indeed rebuttable. Citing several dictionary definitions of "propensity," he concluded that the presumption can be rebutted only by the individual denying his or her homosexuality. According to Ellis, "the statute says, tautologically, nothing more than this: a service member who declares his or her homosexuality will be severed from the service unless the member convinces the fact finder that he or she is not a homosexual" (1365). The impossibility of rebutting the presumption is illustrated by the fact that, as Ellis pointed out, the law defines a homosexual as a person who "has a propensity to engage in, or intends to engage in homosexual acts." Based on this interpretation, he believed the law is aimed at speech, not conduct.

Ellis explained that the regulations define "propensity" differently from the statute so that while a statement of one's homosexuality also creates a presumption under the regulations, it can presumably be rebutted by a declaration that he or she is not likely to engage in homosexual conduct. However, because there was insufficient information to determine whether the regulations actually allowed for a meaningful rebuttable of the presumption in practice, the court asked for supplemental information upon which to base this judgment.

Turning to Thorne's claim that the policy was unconstitutional as it applied to him, the judge assessed the government's claim that even if "Don't Ask, Don't Tell" restricted speech, it was justified. Because the words "I am a homosexual" (as opposed to "I am a heterosexual") were at issue, the court ruled that the restriction was based on content, which would ordinarily merit strict scrutiny. However, as the case involved military policy, the judge applied what he called "a moderated version of strict scrutiny," borrowing from the language of intermediate scrutiny that required the government to show that policy "substantially further an important governmental interest" (1370).

Agreeing that the three interests typically asserted by the government—privacy, reducing sexual tension, and unit polarization—are important, the judge addressed the many inconsistencies in the government's argument. He conceded that it may be true, as the government contended, that the privacy of nonhomosexuals is invaded when they are forced to sleep near, and shower with, individuals who might find them sexually attractive. It was unclear, however, how simply refraining from speaking the forbidden words protects their privacy. The problem could have been resolved, he said, if all homosexuals had simply been banned from the military, but the government had rejected this approach; instead, it had simply decided to order homosexuals to keep their homosexuality a secret.

Similarly, Ellis found the government did not adequately explain how dismissing a vocal homosexual while allowing a silent homosexual to serve minimizes sexual tensions. Indeed, the judge believed the opposite was more likely true because vocal homosexuals would be carefully watched and therefore less likely to act on their homosexuality. Finally, he was not persuaded by the government's contention that units become polarized when gays serve openly. Although he agreed that the topic may be divisive, he believed that removing openly gay members would not ensure unity. The regulations permit members of the armed services to read gay literature, march in gay pride parades, and even advocate that gays be allowed to serve in the military, any of which, he felt, could trigger heated debate. He concluded that allowing gays to serve but preventing them from revealing their sexual orientation does not substantially further the military's stated goals.

Several months later, Ellis addressed the issue left open in his first opinion, that is, whether the presumption was actually rebuttable under the regulations (*Thorne v. United States Department of Defense* 1996b). He also ruled on whether, as the government argued, the circuit's decision in *Thomasson* (1996a) required him to dismiss Thorne's action. Ultimately, he decided that although *Thomasson* may not have conclusively decided that the presumption was rebuttable, the supplemental record revealed that eight individuals on the verge of discharge had succeeded in rebutting the presumption: four by promising to remain celibate, two by declaring themselves confused and disavowing their statements of homosexuality, and one by showing that he revealed his homosexuality in a confidential counseling session.[76] Based on this, Ellis found that the presumption was rebuttable and ruled against Thorne's First Amendment claim.[77]

Indicating that he was somewhat uncomfortable with this second ruling, Ellis emphasized that he had addressed only Thorne's First Amendment challenge, and "nothing in the opinion or the result reached should be construed as reflecting the Court's views, irrelevant here, on the Plan's morality or its wisdom as public policy" (*Thorne v. United States Department of Defense* 1996b, 930).

The Eighth Circuit case was brought in a Nebraska district court by Captain Richard Richenberg when he challenged his dismissal from the air force following his declaration of homosexuality (*Richenberg v. Perry* 1995). Richenberg had entered the air force in 1985 and served with distinction, including a stint in the first Gulf War. When he was about to be sent to Saudi Arabia in April 1993, he asked to be relieved of duty, and when his request was denied, he told his commanding officer, as well as friends and fellow officers, that he was gay.

After a review board inquiry, he was recommended for dismissal and filed suit in federal court to challenge the constitutionality of the military policy toward gays. An initial order for his discharge was suspended until "Don't Ask, Don't Tell" was put into effect; he was again recommended for dismissal after another set of hearings. In granting summary judgment to the government, district court judge Strom emphasized the court's limited role in judging the constitutionality of congressional policy, especially in matters concerning military authority.

Richenberg argued that even though neither the Eighth Circuit nor the Supreme Court had ever applied heightened scrutiny to homosexuals, it was appropriate to do so because they shared the traits of other suspect classes. Alternatively, he argued the court should use heightened scrutiny because he was discriminated against on the basis of gender. Strom summarily rejected both arguments and applied rational basis review. He also declined to accept Richenberg's argument that the government's policy stemmed from prejudice against gays, holding that, as Congress had determined, the military's legitimate interest in combat readiness was enhanced by good order and discipline, two elements that would be jeopardized by the presence of gays in uniform. He further found that discharging homosexuals for declaring their homosexuality was rationally related to this goal because the military could infer that persons making such declarations had a propensity to engage in homosexual acts.

Addressing Richenberg's due process claim, Strom found that he was given an opportunity to rebut the presumption arising from his statement and chose not to do so. And finally, he determined that there was no violation of Richenberg's right to privacy. Noting that no other court has accepted a homosexual's privacy claim under the old directives, he believed "that even if the ['Don't Ask, Don't Tell'] policy does implicate plaintiff's privacy interests, they are outweighed by the military's legitimate interests" (1313–4).

On appeal, the Eighth Circuit followed the lead of the other circuits and easily rejected Richenberg's equal protection claim, denying his request to use heightened scrutiny (*Richenberg v. Perry* 1996). Speaking for a divided panel, circuit court judge Loken declined to use heightened scrutiny, explaining that five other circuits, as well as the Supreme Court in *Romer*, had similarly rejected heightened scrutiny when reviewing laws affecting homosexuals.[78]

In applying rationality review, the court reiterated the familiar theme about its obligation to defer to the military judgment. It rejected Richenberg's argument that the government's policy is motivated entirely by an irrational prejudice of, and hatred toward, those with a homosexual orientation. Indeed, it held, Congress had defined homosexuals only as those who commit, intend to commit, or have a propensity to commit homosexual acts, and the DoD directives explicitly exclude punishment of individuals "for their homosexual thoughts, opinions, fantasies, or orientation" (*Richenberg v. Perry* 1996, 261). Because it is rational to believe that homosexuals will engage in homosexual acts, Congress could believe that excluding homosexuals will reduce the sexual tensions emanating from their presence that impair the military mission.

Richenberg fared no better on his First Amendment claim; indeed, the court devoted little more than a single paragraph to it. Citing *Thomasson*, the court stated that the law does not target speech as such; the speech that is involved—the declaration of homosexuality—is merely evidence of a propensity to engage in the forbidden conduct that is proper grounds for dismissal from the service.[79]

Unlike the other cases, Mark Philips's challenge to "Don't Ask, Don't Tell" in the Ninth Circuit involved an admission of homosexual conduct. In 1992, after four years in the service, Philips announced that he was a homosexual, had engaged in homosexual acts, and would continue to do so. Although he was scheduled for discharge under the 1981 DoD directives in place at the time, the order was not carried out because of uncertainty over the upcoming policy changes. After a new hearing, the review board found that he had engaged in homosexual acts and recommended him for honorable discharge on the basis of the new law.

Philips, a machinist's mate with an excellent service record, filed suit to prevent his discharge. Judge Dwyer of the Washington district court cited the Ninth Circuit's refusal to use heightened scrutiny in classifications involving sexual orientation and applied minimal scrutiny *(Philips v. Perry* 1995). With both parties stipulating to the government's legitimate interest in an effective military, the only issue for the court to decide was whether the law rationally furthered this goal. Philips argued that the policy was motivated by prejudice and dislike toward gays, unacceptable rationales even under minimal scrutiny. Acknowledging that homosexuals have served well and honorably, Dwyer declared himself bound by *Meinhold* (1994), in which the Ninth Circuit expressly drew a distinction between status and conduct and held that persons engaging in homosexual acts can be excluded from the military. Although *Meinhold* was decided before the current policy was in effect, Dwyer believed the cases were sufficiently alike that *Meinhold* controlled. Also dismissing Philips's privacy and First Amendment claims on the basis of past Ninth Circuit decisions, the court awarded summary judgment to the government.[80]

Ending with a personal note suggesting his discomfort with the decision, Dwyer stated that although the new policies appear to recognize a difference between homosexual conduct and status, "they still result . . . in a loss to the nation of soldiers and sailors who serve with honor" (*Philips* 1995, 548).

Speaking for the Ninth Circuit panel on appeal, Judge Rymer took pains to refute Philips's claim that the policies stemmed from prejudice and were unconstitutional under *Palmore* and *City of Cleburne* (*Philips* 1997). Those cases were distinguishable, she said, because the prejudice against the plaintiffs there depended entirely on their status, not on their conduct. Moreover, they were inapposite because they did not involve military regulations. She further rejected Philips's contention that the navy's asserted justifications for its policy—maintaining good order and discipline, alleviating sexual tension, and enhancing privacy—were mere subterfuges for prejudice against homosexuals and concluded "that the relationship between the Navy's mission and its policy on homosexual acts is not so attenuated as to render the distinction arbitrary and irrational" (1429).

After quickly dismissing Philips's First Amendment claim, Rymer cited *Pruitt* and held that Philips was discharged on the basis of his conduct, not his statements. The appellate court affirmed the court below.

Judge Fletcher, dissenting, argued that by differentiating between the private sexual activities of heterosexuals and homosexuals, the military policy did not rationally further a legitimate government end. Although the government's interest in a cohesive unit was legitimate, because, as the government conceded, there was no relationship between sexual orientation and ability to perform, the policy did not advance this aim. In her view, the policy was based on prejudice.

A more recent challenge to "Don't Ask, Don't Tell" was presented in *Rumsfeld v. Forum for Academic and Institutional Rights, Inc.* (2006). The case arose from a law, known as the Solomon Amendment, enacted in 1994 in the annual appropriation defense bill.[81] Under this law, federal research funds were withheld from colleges and universities that barred recruiters from their campuses because of the military's discriminatory policy toward gays. The policy threatened to cut funding to the entire institution; the government also expanded the federal agencies from which funds would be withheld. The ban on the military was typically part of a larger university effort to restrict access to all employers that discriminated on the basis of sexual orientation. In 2004, Congress amended the law to require law schools and their parent institutions to treat military recruiters equally with other recruiters. An association of law schools, the Forum for Academic and Institutional Rights (FAIR), and a number of organizations and individual plaintiffs filed suit.[82] Citing *Dale*, they argued that like the Boy Scouts, they were expressive associations and that their First Amendment right to convey their message against discrimination was harmed by being forced to include military recruiters. The plaintiffs also claimed that the Solomon Amendment infringed on the "unconstitutional conditions doctrine" by attaching the receipt of federal funds to restrictions on speech. A third issue was whether the government violated the "compelled speech" doctrine by forcing the schools to agree with the government's "Don't Ask, Don't Tell" policy.

The district court ruled in favor of the government, and in a 2–1 opinion in *Forum for Academic and Institutional Rights, Inc. v. Rumsfeld* (2004), the Third Circuit reversed.[83] The circuit court panel agreed that under *Dale*, the law schools had a First Amendment right to prevent discriminatory employers from recruiting on campus. The irony of course is that *Dale* endorsed the Boy Scouts' right to discriminate against the gay scoutmaster, while this case, based on the same principle, allowed the law schools to deliver a message of nondiscrimination. It also held that the law violated the compelled speech doctrine by requiring the schools to convey the discriminatory message of "Don't Ask, Don't Tell."

In *Rumsfeld v. Forum for Academic and Institutional Rights, Inc.* (2006), the Supreme Court reversed and unanimously upheld the Solomon Amendment. The Court held that Congress's authority "'to raise and support Armies' and 'to provide and maintain a Navy' . . . includes the authority to require campus access for military recruiters" (1306). And because Congress could impose this condition directly, the Solomon Amendment "does not place an unconstitutional condition on the receipt of federal funds" (1307). The Court further held that the law abridged neither the "compelled speech" principle articulated in *Hurley* nor the right of "expressive association" found in *Dale*.

Assessing "Don't Ask, Don't Tell"

On February 28, 1995, the one-year anniversary of "Don't Ask, Don't Tell," the watchdog group Servicemembers Legal Defense Network (SLDN) released a report that identified four types of violations of the law: questioning members of the armed forces about their sexuality, increasing the circumstances in which revealing their sexual orientation has negative consequences, hunting down individuals believed to be homosexual, and excusing harassment of gay servicemen and servicewomen (Osburn and Benecke 1996, 250).

In the first five years that "Don't Ask, Don't Tell" was in effect, over 4,000 gays and lesbians were dismissed from the armed services, and ironically, the rate of discharge increased over time. As under the 1981 regulations, women continue to be overrepresented among the discharges (D'Amico 2000).[84]

The story of navy senior chief Timothy McVeigh, a seventeen-year veteran, illustrates how the navy (mis)interpreted "Don't Ask, Don't Tell." McVeigh's homosexuality was discovered through a search of a purportedly confidential America Online (AOL) profile in which he had listed his marital status as gay. When this was reported, the navy launched an illegal investigation (without the requisite warrant or court order) and began discharge proceedings against him, informing him it was on the basis of "homosexual conduct, as evidenced by your statement that you are a homosexual" (*McVeigh v. Cohen* 1998, 217). At his hearing, McVeigh tried to rebut the presumption established by his statement, in part by citing past relationships with women, but the board found he had engaged in homosexual conduct and recommended dismissal.

McVeigh filed suit to halt the discharge, claiming the navy violated "Don't Ask, Don't Tell" as well as the Electronic Communications Privacy Act (ECPA). As district court judge Sporkin characterized his claim, although McVeigh complied with the policy in not revealing his status, "the Navy impermissibly 'asked' and zealously 'pursued'" without the credible information needed to undertake an investigation (218). Moreover, the means by which it secured the information from AOL failed to follow the correct procedures of the ECPA. Explaining that this was the first case to interpret the application of "Don't Ask, Don't Tell," Sporkin issued the injunction barring McVeigh's dismissal.

Adding what appeared to be a personal note, Sporkin characterized McVeigh as a victim of employment discrimination because it was clear that his sexual orientation had not affected his work. He believed the navy had contravened the purpose of the policy, which was to allow individuals like McVeigh to serve their country honorably. He ended by commenting "that the defenses mounted against gays in the military have been tried before in our nation's history—against blacks and women" (221).

In its report entitled *Ten Years of Don't Ask, Don't Tell. A Disservice to the Nation*, the Servicemembers Legal Defense Network (2004) documented abuses in the implementation of "Don't Ask, Don't Tell," indicating that McVeigh's story is not unique. His case illustrates that the military has not abided by its part of the agreement not to ask and not to pursue. Additionally, despite the specific limitations on the circumstances under which investigations may be commenced under "Don't Ask, Don't Tell," its stated concern for privacy, and explicit prohibition on "witchhunts," it appears that "the most objectionable enforcement tactics, those that were criticized most during the 1993 congressional hearings, are still being used" (Marcosson 1995, 86; see Seamon 1999; Lehring 2003).

Looking more broadly at the first ten years "Don't Ask, Don't Tell" was in effect, a United States General Accounting Office (2005) report entitled *Military Personnel: Financial Costs and Loss of Critical Skills Due to DOD's Homosexual Conduct Policy Cannot Be Completely Estimated* demonstrates that gays have continued to be discharged in large numbers. The data indicate that from FY 1994 through FY 2003, 9,488 service members (on active or active reserve duty) were dismissed, some of whom had critical occupational or language skills, including Arabic, Farsi, and Korean.[85] Aside from the loss of such key personnel, the study estimated the cost of recruiting potential replacements at about $95 million, not including expenditures for investigations, out-processing, counseling, and court expenses for which the Defense Department does not collect data (see also Servicemembers Legal Defense Network 2005).

Another challenge to "Don't Ask, Don't Tell" arose in December 2004 when the SLDN filed *Cook v. Rumsfeld* (2004) in a Massachusetts federal district court on behalf of twelve discharged servicemembers representing all branches of the military. The suit alleged the government violated their equal protection, privacy, and First Amendment rights.[86] Shortly thereafter, on March 2, 2005, Representative Martin Meehan, Democrat from Massachusetts, introduced a bill entitled the Military Readiness Enhancement Act of 2005 (H.R. 1059). Its purpose was to replace "Don't Ask, Don't Tell" "with a policy of non-discrimination on the basis of sexual orientation." It would have banned discrimination against current members of the armed services and allowed qualified men and women who were separated for homosexuality or bisexuality to be reinstated; it was sent to the House Committee on Armed Services, from which it has not emerged.

Less than two months after *Romer* was decided, litigants began to cite it to support their claims against "Don't Ask, Don't Tell" (R. Dodson 1999, 293). Indeed, the plaintiffs might have benefited from *Romer*, had the courts been willing to apply it to military circumstances. Pizzutillo (1997, 1327) argues that the "heightened rational basis standard" applied in *Romer* should have been a potent weapon in attacking dismissals under "Don't Ask, Don't Tell," requiring courts to recognize that a policy based on prejudice cannot be a legitimate government interest. However, although it is true that *Thomasson* was decided prior to *Romer*, both *Richenberg* and *Philips* were decided after *Romer*, and they barely mentioned it.

Writing in the wake of *Lawrence,* Mazur (2004, 424) believes that the plaintiffs erred by not sufficiently challenging the government's litigating posture in "Don't Ask, Don't Tell" cases. In her view, the justifications offered by the government do not reflect "informed and thoughtful judgment" and are not offered "in good faith for the purpose of maintaining military readiness." She believes instead that "the policy, in fact, has absolutely nothing to do with military readiness." The cases show that, thus far, the courts disagree.

THE PUBLIC'S VIEW

Ironically, despite the military's intense opposition, surveys show that the public is strongly in favor of allowing gays to serve in the military. Yang's (1997, 481–2) analysis of attitudes toward gays in the military, based on surveys by Gallup, CBS, the National Election Studies, Harris Interactive, and CBS/*New York Times,* shows that from the late 1970s to the early 1990s, the public has generally approved of gays serving in the armed services. He notes that there was a slight drop in late 1992 and early 1993 when the issue received a great deal of media attention, but approval had risen again by 1994. As Yang's study suggests, when "Don't Ask, Don't Tell" was constantly in the media, the largely negative publicity surrounding it may have accelerated the public's opposition. Gallup (2004b) reported on an NBC/*Wall Street Journal* poll conducted in late July 1993 that asked respondents whether "they favor or oppose allowing openly gay men and lesbian women to serve in the military," only 40 percent responded favorably, and 52 percent were opposed. By November 2004, however, when a CNN/*USA Today*/ Gallup poll asked the same question, 63 percent were in favor, and only 32 percent were opposed.[87]

Polls conducted by Gallup over a period of thirteen years also show the public's steadily rising agreement with the idea that "homosexuals should be hired for" the armed services. In a June 1992 survey, 57 percent said they should, and in May 2005, 76 percent agreed they should (Gallup 2005b).

These Gallup data are consistent with data from other polls and surveys.[88] When a Fox News poll asked registered voters in January 2000 whether they "think gay men and lesbians should be allowed to serve openly in the military," 57 percent said "yes," and 30 percent said "no" (see PollingReport.com 2006b).

Worded slightly differently, a December 2003 Gallup (2003c) poll reported that 79 percent of the respondents believed that "people who are openly gay or homosexual" should be permitted to serve in the military, and only 18 percent were opposed. One of the latest surveys on attitudes toward a number of social policies, including gays in the military, released by the Pew Research Center (2006), found that 60 percent of the respondents favored "allowing gays and lesbians to serve openly in the military," with only 32 percent opposed; in 1994, 52 percent had been in favor, and 45 percent were opposed.

Americans appear most supportive when the questions ask whether homosexuals should be "hired" for the military. But although they still approve, when the questions explicitly raise views on "Don't Ask, Don't Tell" by asking whether gays should be permitted to "serve openly," the support seems to drop somewhat. Despite these differences, however, the surveys consistently show that the majority of the American people have little difficulty with gays serving in the military and that the courts are simply failing to recognize that the military's arguments about gays destroying morale and unit cohesion do not resonate with the public.

NOTES

1. When the policy was first introduced, it was officially known as "Don't Ask, Don't Tell, Don't Pursue." In February 2000, following the brutal murder of Private First Class Barry Winchell, the Pentagon added "Don't Harass" to the title of the policy.

2. The policy toward gays applies to service in the army, navy, air force, Marines, coast guard, and college ROTC units.

3. Executive Order No. 9981, issued by Truman on July 26, 1948, ordered the integration of African Americans into the armed forces. In the same year, Congress passed the Women's Armed Services Integration Act to enhance career opportunities for women in the military.

4. Article 125 (10 U.S.C. §925) contains a gender-neutral prohibition of sodomy; Article 134 (10 U.S.C. §934), known as "the "General Article," is a catch-all criminal code forbidding "all disorders and neglects to the prejudice of good order and discipline in the armed forces, [and] all conduct of a nature to bring discredit upon the armed forces." Conviction under §934 requires the military to allege the commission of a specific offense that meets both criteria.

5. Shilts (1993, chap. 6) discusses men who attempted to avoid service in Vietnam by pretending to be gay, the so-called gay deceivers, as well as men who were actually gay and the military's reluctance to enforce regulations against both during wartime in the face of personnel shortages. He also notes that turning a blind eye to the regulations was not unique to the Vietnam War.

6. Class III homosexuals were defined as individuals who "only exhibit, profess, or admit homosexual tendencies and wherein there are no specific provable acts or offenses, or court-martial jurisdiction does not exist" (Haggerty 2003, 24).

7. The directive was again revised on December 21, 1993.

8. Directive 1332.30 provided for separation procedures for officers; it was revised in 1986 (United States General Accounting Office 1992).

9. At that time, Congress's only regulation of consensual sexual activity in the military was found in 10 U.S.C. §925, which specifies both heterosexual and homosexual sodomy as court-martial offenses.

10. In 1987, as part of the National Defense Authorization Act, Congress enacted 10 U.S.C. §774, which states, "A member of the armed forces may wear an item of religious apparel while wearing the uniform of the member's armed force [except] . . . (1) in circumstances with respect to which the Secretary determines that the wearing of the item would interfere with the performance of the member's military duties; or (2) if the Secretary determines . . . that the item of apparel is not neat and conservative."

11. In *City of Cleburne* (1985, 446), the Court stated, "The State may not rely on a classification whose relationship to an asserted goal is so attenuated as to render the distinction arbitrary or irrational" (citing *Zobel v. Williams* 1982, 61–3, and *United States Department of Agriculture v. Moreno* 1973, 535).

12. In part as a result of *Matlovich*, the 1981 directive removed the commander's discretion, thus making dismissal for homosexuality mandatory (Jacobson 1996, 58 n4).

13. On remand, Gesell ordered the air force to reinstate Matlovich with back pay and other benefits (*Matlovich* 1980). Although he was permitted to reenlist, Matlovich eventually reached a settlement with the air force (Haggerty 2003, 33).

14. The lower court opinions in the other two cases are not reported.

15. There were more lenient navy policies in place at the time of the decision, but the navy determined that these did not apply to the litigants.

16. In *Rich v. Secretary of the Army* (1984), the Tenth Circuit followed *Beller* in supporting the military against the claims of two discharged servicemen despite the fact that no illegal act was proven.

17. The panel denied rehearing, and the entire circuit denied the motion to hear the case en banc in *Miller v. Rumsfeld* (1981). Judge Norris dissented from the court's refusal to rehear the case en banc. The Supreme Court subsequently denied certiorari in *Miller v. Weinberger* (1981) and *Beller v. Lehman* (1981).

18. There are some narrowly defined exceptions to the mandatory discharge; Dronenburg did not fit into any of these.

19. The military doctors apparently did not believe his declaration of "homosexual tendencies" and considered him qualified for admission (*Watkins* 1989, 709).

20. Watkins had originally filed suit in August 1981 asking the court to order his security clearance reinstated, but when he received notice that the army was proceeding with a discharge hearing against him, he amended his complaint in October to seek an injunction against his discharge; the district court did not address the issue of the revoked security clearance.

21. Norris noted that in *Miller v. Rumsfeld* (1981), he had dissented from the circuit's refusal to grant *Beller* a rehearing en banc.

22. Sunstein (1988) disagrees, contending that the majority correctly rejected *Bowers* as controlling in *Watkins*. In Sunstein's view, although *Bowers's* due process analysis held that sodomy could be criminalized, the two constitutional clauses derive from different principles and operate independently of each other. Thus, "it is always immaterial to an equal protection challenge that members of the victimized group are engaging in conduct that could be prohibited on a general basis" (1167).

23. Rothstein had also based her ruling on the estoppel doctrine.

24. In *Bolling v. Sharpe* (1954), the Supreme Court held that unlike the Fourteenth Amendment, the Fifth Amendment does not guarantee equal protection of the laws. But because "discrimination may be so unjustifiable as to be violative of due process," the Court held that the due process clause of the Fifth Amendment contains an equal protection component (499). Therefore, equal protection claims against the federal government are based on the Fifth Amendment's due process clause.

25. The courts use strict scrutiny, however, when a racial classification is involved, no matter what the race of the persons complaining of discrimination (see Gerstmann 2003).

26. The Supreme Court denied certiorari in *United States Army v. Watkins* (1990).

27. The Supreme Court denied certiorari in *benShalom v. Stone* (1990).

28. This case is discussed in chapter 5.

29. The Supreme Court denied certiorari in *Woodward* (1990).

30. The panel deciding *Pruitt* had delayed its decision until the full circuit court decided *Watkins* (1989). But because the en banc ruling in *Watkins* did not address the equal protection claim, it offered no guidance to the panel on *Pruitt's* equal protection argument.

31. Canby cited *High Tech Gays v. Defense Industry Security Clearance Office* (1990a), discussed in chapter 5.

32. A complaint must contain allegations that state a claim upon which relief can be granted. Before any evidence is presented, a defendant may move to dismiss the complaint for "failure to state a claim upon which relief can be granted" under Federal Rules of Evidence 12(b)(6). Complaints must be viewed liberally, and, as the Supreme Court stated in *Conley v. Gibson* (1957, 45–6), "a complaint should not be dismissed for failure to state a claim unless it appears beyond doubt that the plaintiff can prove no set of facts in support of his claim which would entitle him to relief." In Pruitt's case, her claim had been dismissed on the basis of her complaint in the early stages of the litigation, with neither side presenting evidence on the merits. By refusing to uphold the lower court's ruling, the court was giving her an opportunity to argue the merits of her case before the court.

33. The Supreme Court denied certiorari in *Cheney v. Pruitt* (1992).

34. Schwartz explained that

> if the evidence, construed in the light most favorable to defendants, shows that there is no reasonably conceivable rational basis for the homosexual exclusion policy, and the court cannot conceive of a rational basis (i.e., because it is based solely on illegitimate prejudice), then plaintiff is entitled to summary judgment. Alternatively, if the evidence, construed in the light most favorable to plaintiff, shows that there is any reasonably conceivable rational basis for the policy, then defendants are entitled to summary judgment. Finally, if the evidence creates a disputed issue of material fact as to the policy's rationality, then neither party is entitled to summary judgment." (*Dahl* 1993, 1327)

35. Mazur (1999, 228) believes cases such as these leave the erroneous impression that the military would ignore sexual orientation if the issue were not thrust into the public eye.

36. In *Cammermeyer v. Aspin* (1994), Colonel Margarethe Cammermeyer, a greatly admired and much-decorated officer in the Washington State National Guard, fell under the military's exclusion policy. In response to a question on her application to the Army War College, she indicated she was a lesbian, but denied sexual activity. Although she continued to serve after this revelation, she was eventually released from the Guard over the protests of the governor of the state, among others. She was said to be the highest ranking officer discharged for homosexuality. Decided under the 1981 directives, the case revolved around the distinction between orientation and conduct and whether a homosexual orientation indicates a propensity for the latter. Citing Ninth Circuit cases, Judge Zilly found that her declaration of her homosexuality "itself is not reliable evidence of her desire or propensity to engage on homosexual conduct" (920). Speaking for the three-judge panel of the Ninth Circuit, Judge Kozinski upheld that portion of the lower court ruling in *Cammermeyer v. Perry* (1996).

37. Because the provisions relating to homosexuality in the DoD regulations and the *Naval Military Personnel Manual* were virtually identical, the court treated them as one.

38. The court announced *Meinhold* in August 1994. Although "Don't Ask, Don't Tell" had taken effect on February 28, 1994, and the regulations under which Meinhold was discharged were no longer valid, the case was decided under the old DoD and navy regulations.

39. The commandant asked, "Are you willing to state at this time that you are a homosexual?" He replied, "Yes, sir" (*Stefan v. Aspin* 1993, 60).

40. As the court explained in *Steffan v. Cheney* (1989a, 116), "Navy regulations provide that homosexuality 'severely limit[s] a midshipman's aptitude and potential for commissioned service' [and] . . . homosexual midshipmen are considered for separation from the Naval Academy on the basis of their insufficient aptitude."

41. Steffan originally claimed the navy infringed on his constitutional rights of freedom of speech and association, due process, and equal protection. The district court denied the government's motion to dismiss in *Steffan v. Cheney* (1989a).

42. This argument stemmed from the principle that homosexual status was not inextricably linked to conduct and that under criminal law, he should be judged only by his actions, not by who he is (see Wells-Petry 1995).

43. Although Steffan claimed a Fifth Amendment privilege against self-incrimination, the lower court dismissed his complaint because he refused to answer deposition questions about whether he had engaged in homosexual activities during and after his time at the academy (*Steffan v. Cheney* 1989b). The court held that the information was relevant because the navy could refuse to reinstate him if he had engaged in such conduct. The lower court's dismissal of Steffan's complaint was reversed by the District of Columbia circuit court in a per curiam opinion in *Steffan v. Cheney* (1990). The appellate court found the information irrelevant because he had been separated on the basis of his homosexual status, not for homosexual conduct.

44. After the Supreme Court's ruling in *Bowers* (1986), the circuit courts refused to apply heightened scrutiny to homosexual status, reasoning that it would be inappropriate to treat sexual orientation as a suspect or semisuspect classification under the equal protection analysis if the behavior upon which the classification was based could be outlawed. Also by holding that the military may reasonably assume that a declaration of homosexuality is an indication of homosexual conduct, the courts negated the "status-conduct distinction" that had seemingly left open by *Bowers* (Aguiar 1996).

45. In *Cammermeyer v. Aspin* (1994, 926), the district court also found that the reasons offered by the military to exclude gays were "grounded solely in prejudice."

46. The court did not decide this case under the newly implemented "Don't Ask, Don't Tell" policy.

47. According to the DoD directives, "homosexual means a person, regardless of sex, who engages in, desires to engage in, or intends to engage in homosexual acts."

48. Steffan's facial challenge failed when he conceded the regulations could be constitutionally applied to others, and his "as-applied" challenge failed because he never proved that the regulations were unconstitutional as applied to him.

49. A few weeks after Powell's letter to Schroeder, Seattle mayor Norm Rice wrote to Secretary of Defense Cheney, comparing the ban on gays with racial segregation. Assailing the decision to discharge Margarethe Cammermeyer from the Washington National Guard, Rice charged, "Fifty years ago, the armed services of this country were segregated by race for many of the same reasons now offered to support the military's ban on service by lesbians and gay men" (*Seattle Times* June 7, 1992).

50. In addition to their efforts in the national campaign, gays organized to support candidates at state and municipal levels (*Congressional Quarterly Weekly* July 10, 1993, 1814–5; July 24, 1993, 1975–6).

51. Clinton's memorandum to the secretary of defense stated,

I hereby direct you to submit to me prior to July 15, 1993, a draft of an Executive order ending discrimination on the basis of sexual orientation in determining who may serve in the Armed Forces of the United States. The draft of the Executive order should be accompanied by the results of a study to be conducted over the next six months on how this revision in policy would be carried out in a manner that is practical, realistic, and consistent with the high standards of combat effectiveness and unit cohesion our Armed Forces must maintain. In preparing the draft, I direct you to consult fully with the Joint Chiefs of Staff and the military services, with other Departments affected by the order, with the Congress, and with concerned individuals and organizations outside the executive branch. (Clinton 1993b)

52. The procedure to remove suspected homosexuals at the time involved either an expedited administrative hearing on the basis of suspected homosexual activities, including the service member's own statement about his or her sexual orientation, or a court-martial (or other disciplinary procedure) for homosexual acts specifically prohibited in the UCMJ (*Congressional Quarterly Weekly* January 30, 1993, 226).

53. The Senate committee also held hearings on April 29, May 7, 10, and 11, and July 20 to July 22, 1993.

54. The House committee also held hearings from July 21 to July 23, 1993.

55. MacCoun's (1996) research on factors related to group cohesion in the military suggests there would be little negative effect on cohesion or morale from lifting the ban. His study shows that while allowing gays to openly serve in the military might have some effect on social cohesion (friendship or closeness among the members of the group), it was unlikely to affect task cohesion (a shared commitment to achieving a goal). Osburn (1995, 213–4) discusses other studies that indicate that unit cohesion depends on factors related to the job performance.

56. Coincidentally, this occurred the same day the Colorado Supreme Court upheld the injunction against Amendment 2 in *Evans v. Romer* (1993b).

57. Data reported by Wilcox and Wolpert (1996) indicate that Clinton lost support most heavily among those who were extremely opposed to lifting the ban, but that his (and others') support for repeal ultimately persuaded many people.

58. Woodruff (1995) notes that the new law equates having a homosexual orientation to being a homosexual, which, by definition, means that one is presumed to engage in the forbidden conduct. The DoD directives apparently contradict the law by distinguishing between orientation and conduct. The courts have not adequately addressed (or resolved) this matter.

59. Racial segregation in the military was a product of DoD regulations that were supplanted by Truman's executive order in 1948.

60. 10 U.S.C. §654(a)(3).

61. 10 U.S.C. §654(a)(15).

62. Section 571 made extensive findings about the character of life within the military, emphasizing the need for restrictions on homosexuals in the military environment.

63. The ban on gays in the military was formerly a DoD policy; it is now codified into law.

64. Because the pertinent sections of the bills were identical, the Senate-House conference did not affect §654. The House agreed to the conference report on November 10, 1993, and the Senate on November 17, 1993.

65. November 1993 is in FY 1994.

66. The first two provisions specified the evidence that could be presented to rebut the presumption of homosexuality.

67. The 1993 DoD directives appeared in 32 C.F.R. pt. 41, app. A.

68. In response to the Clinton's administration's request, the Supreme Court granted an emergency stay of the order in *United States Department of Defense v. Meinhold* (1993).

69. The lead plaintiff, Lieutenant Colonel Jane Able, was a pseudonym (Mazur 1999, 227).

70. Although the statute itself does not define "propensity," the regulations define it as "more than an abstract preference or desire to engage in homosexual acts; it indicates a likelihood that a person engages in or will engage in homosexual conduct."

71. The court noted the dictionary definition of propensity as "an innate or inherent tendency" or a "natural inclination" (*Able* 1995c, 975).

72. Gay rights advocates decided not to file a petition for certiorari in *Abel*, believing the Court would not grant it since it had denied certiorari in all such military cases (Cain 2000, 201).

73. Osburn (1995) argues that in cases based on equal protection claims, the courts should ask whether it is rational to differentiate between heterosexuals and gays who both declare their sexual orientation privately, rather than questioning whether it is rational for the government to link declarations of homosexuality with homosexual conduct.

74. After hearing oral argument, the circuit voted on its own to rehear the case en banc.

75. The Supreme Court denied certiorari in *Thomasson* (1996b).

76. The record did not indicate how the eighth member rebutted the presumption.

77. The Fourth Circuit affirmed the lower court's ruling in *Thorne* (1998a), and the Supreme Court denied certiorari in *Thorne* (1998b).

78. The circuits cited by the *Richenberg* court were the Seventh (*benShalom*), Tenth (*Rich*), District of Columbia (*Steffan*), Ninth (*Meinhold*), and the Federal Circuit (*Woodward*). Nguyen (2001), however, argues that the Supreme Court used a higher standard, the so-called heightened rationality review, in *Romer*, and the reasons for using it there apply equally to challenges to the military's policy toward gays and should be employed by the courts in "Don't Ask, Don't Tell" cases.

79. The Supreme Court denied certiorari in *Richenberg v. Cohen* (1997).

80. The court admitted that the plaintiff might have a legitimate constitutional challenge to §654(b)(2) but was not deciding that issue since his discharge was permissible under §654(b)(1).

81. The Solomon Amendment, 10 U.S.C. §983, was proposed by Representative Gerald Solomon, Republican from New York, in 1994 in response to the actions of the State University of New York that prohibited the military from recruiting on campus (*Congressional Quarterly Weekly* September 17, 1994, 2588).

82. Although the Solomon Amendment applied to all institutions of higher education, the law schools were at the heart of the controversy because the military actively recruits their graduates for the Judge Advocate General's Corps, and the law schools as a group have been more concerned about discriminatory recruitment on the basis of sexual orientation.

83. The appellate court issued a preliminary injunction and then stayed its order pending appeal to the Supreme Court.

84. See D'Amico (2000) for an assessment of the Defense Department's explanation for the discharges.

85. These figures do not include the Coast Guard, the Army National Guard, the Air National Guard, or reservists not on active duty (United States General Accounting Office 2005).

86. In *Cook v. Rumsfeld* (2006), the district court dismissed the complaint.

87. Wilcox and Wolpert (1996, 128) report the results of an analysis by the Center for Media and Politics that 73 percent of the stories about the issue of gays in the military during the controversy were critical, that is, were opposed to the "Don't Ask, Don't Tell" policy.

88. The American National Election Studies conducted in the presidential election years from 1992 through 2004 also showed that most agreed that gays should be allowed to serve in the military (Haeberle 1999; American National Election Studies 2000; 2004).

CHAPTER 5

Challenging Employment Discrimination

HOMOSEXUALITY has long been considered adequate grounds for adverse employment actions, and discrimination is still widely felt in the gay community (Ekeberg and Tumber 2004, 387). A study of surveys conducted between 1980 and 1997 shows that almost 50 percent of gays and lesbians had experienced discrimination on the job at least once (Association of the Bar of the City of New York, Committee on Sex and Law 1997, 736–7). A poll released in September 2002 by Harris Interactive/Witeck-Combs Communication (2002) reported that most GLBT respondents answered affirmatively to the question "Have you ever faced any of these forms of discrimination in the workplace because of your sexual orientation or gender identity?" Twenty-three percent of the respondents reported being "harassed on the job by co-workers"; 12 percent claimed they had been "denied a promotion or job advancement." The results also showed that 9 percent of the GLBT respondents believed they were "fired or dismissed unfairly," and 8 percent reported being "pressured to quit my job because of harassment or hostility."[1]

In the same survey, all respondents said that GLBTs "often" (29 percent) or "sometimes" (47 percent) experience discrimination in the workplace, the second highest group after adults 65 and older.

The next year, Harris Interactive/Witeck-Combs Communications (2003) reported similar results: 41 percent of GLBT adults said they confronted some kind of discrimination on the job because of their sexual orientation. Moreover, heterosexuals who reported that they have ever heard someone at their current or most recent job tell jokes about people who are

189

gay, lesbian, bisexual, or transgender increased from 45 percent in 2002 to 52 percent in 2003.

LOCAL ANTIDISCRIMINATION ORDINANCES

In the 1970s, cities and counties around the nation began to enact civil rights laws and ordinances barring discrimination in public and private employment on the basis of sexual orientation (see Eskridge 1999; Lewis and Edelson 2000).[2] By 1999, about 165 cities and counties around the nation had banned job discrimination against gays (Barnard and Downing 1999, 558; see Wood 2003).[3] Some, such as San Francisco, require its contractors and subcontractors to have policies against discrimination. It also has become increasingly common for private employers to prohibit discrimination on the basis of sexual orientation; more than half of the Fortune Five Hundred companies as well as many universities have included such bans in their personnel policies (Alexander 2002, 271; see www.hrc.org).

Additionally, thousands of employers around the nation, including over two hundred Fortune Five Hundred companies, state and local governments, and colleges and universities provide health or medical benefits to the domestic partners of their gay employees (see www.hrc.org).[4] In October 2005, the Alaska Supreme Court ordered the state and the City of Anchorage to provide spousal benefits, including health insurance, to their employees' same-sex partners, as they do to the spouses of their employees. Basing its ruling on the state constitution's equal protection clause, the court noted that, unlike the case for opposite-sex couples, Alaska does not permit same-sex couples to marry. Holding that it did not have to determine the appropriate level of scrutiny because the policy failed to pass even minimum scrutiny, the court recognized the state's legitimate interest in costs and administrative convenience as well as in promoting marriage but ruled that these did not justify the absolute deprivation of benefits to same-sex partners (*Alaska Civil Liberties Union v. Alaska* 2005).

For almost a decade, the City of San Francisco has had a policy prohibiting it from entering into contracts with businesses that discriminate between domestic partners and spouses in the distribution of benefits. However, although the City of New York itself provides the same benefits to the domestic partners of its employees as it does to employees' spouses, in February 2006, the New York State Court of Appeals ruled that a law mandating that the city do business only with contractors who provide the same benefits for the domestic partners of employees that they provide for the spouses of employees was invalid; the court held that it conflicted with a state law requiring competitive bids for contracts. The Equal Benefits Law had been passed by the city council despite Mayor Michael Bloomberg's opposition and over his veto (*Council of City of New York v. Bloomberg* (2006).

Despite these gains, discrimination and harassment remain facts of life for many gays, especially in public school and local law enforcement settings (see, for example, *Childers v. Dallas Police Department* 1981, *National Gay Task Force v. Board of Education* 1984, *Rowland v. Mad River Local School District* 1984, *Jantz v. Muci* 1991, *Weaver v. Nebo School District* 1998, *Glover v. Williamsburg Local School District Board of Education* 1998, *Quinn v. Nassau County Police Department* 1999, and *Schroeder v. Hamilton School District* 2002). A much-publicized case in the Georgia attorney general's office, *Sharar v. Bowers* (1997), demonstrates that the courts are still unsympathetic to gay plaintiffs in employment discrimination cases.[5]

The litigants in such cases, with mixed results, claimed their rights were variously violated under the First and Fourteenth Amendments as well as state constitutional or statutory guarantees. In deciding these disputes, the courts were often required to determine whether there was a legal distinction between homosexual conduct and a homosexual orientation (the conduct-status distinction) and whether the employers had sufficient grounds to justify their employment decisions.

STATE ANTIDISCRIMINATION LAWS

At the state level, Wisconsin was the first state to pass an antidiscrimination law in 1982. More than twenty years later, Democratic governor Christine Gregoire signed an antidiscrimination bill into law in the state of Washington after the state senate voted 25–23 to approve an amendment to its civil rights law. The measure added discrimination on the basis of sexual orientation, gender expression, and gender identity to the state law banning discrimination in housing, employment, insurance, public accommodations, and lending. A bill outlawing discrimination on the basis of sexual orientation had first been unsuccessfully introduced in the legislature in 1976.

Signed by Gregoire on January 31, 2006, the law took effect on June 8, 2006. There was an unsuccessful attempt to nullify the law by placing it on the ballot in the 2006 election. The Christian Coalition of Washington had supported this effort to invalidate the law; Equal Rights Washington had urged voters to retain it (Human Rights Campaign 2006b; *Seattle Times*

January 31, 2006; *Seattle Post-Intelligencer* January 31, 2006; *Washington Employment Law Letter* October 2006).

Events in Maine demonstrate that the repeal of antidiscrimination laws is a real possibility. In November 2005, Maine voters finally approved a law enacted earlier in the year that amended the Maine Human Rights Act making discrimination in employment, housing, credit, public accommodations, and education illegal. In Maine, voters are permitted to repeal legislation through a "people's veto" provision in the state constitution. They had succeeded in doing so twice before—in 1998 and 2000. This time, a group called Maine Won't Discriminate was able to convince the voters to retain the law (*Portland Press Herald* November 9, 2005).

As a result of the passage of the Washington bill, seventeen states plus the District of Columbia have antidiscrimination laws; seven states include discrimination on the basis of gender identity as a prohibited act (Human Rights Campaign 2006a).[6] Additionally, a number of states bar sexual orientation discrimination in public employment through executive order (see Barnard and Downing 1999).

FEDERAL ANTIDISCRIMINATION LAW

An overwhelming majority of Americans (82 percent) believe, at least in principle, "that the federal government should treat homosexuals and heterosexuals equally," according to a CNN/*Time* poll conducted in 1998 (PollingReport.com 2006b).[7] Yet there is little support from the federal government for equal rights. Litigants have long argued that federal law prohibits employment discrimination against gays because the ban on sex discrimination in Title VII of the 1964 Civil Rights Act applies to sexual orientation as well as sex (see Gehman and Gray 2005; Putignano 1997). They have had a difficult time, however, in convincing the courts that Congress intended Title VII to encompass discrimination based on sexual orientation, and most courts have interpreted the federal law quite narrowly (see Ekeberg and Tumber 2004; Leonard 2004/2005). Moreover, Congress has consistently refused to enact federal legislation against discrimination on the basis of sexual orientation.

Transgender plaintiffs have been somewhat more successful in arguing that Title VII bars discrimination on the basis of gender identity. They typically cite *Price Waterhouse v. Hopkins* (1989), in which the Court found that the employer's refusal to promote Ann Hopkins to partner in the accounting firm because she did not conform to stereotypical gender norms of femininity violated Title VII. Under *Hopkins*, discrimination stemming from sex stereotyping became a violation of Title VII.[8] Although the Supreme Court made it clear in *Hopkins* that Title VII applies to both sex and gender, however, many lower courts do not interpret the law that way, applying it to sex discrimination only (King 2002).[9]

The courts have been more receptive to complaints of harassment on the basis of sexual orientation under Title VII. In *Oncale v. Sundowner Offshore Services Inc.* (1998), the Supreme Court reversed a Fifth Circuit ruling and held that Title VII applies to male-on-male harassment as long as the plaintiff alleges harassing behavior of a sexual nature. But a few years later, a suit was brought by a gay employee against a Las Vegas hotel, the plaintiff charging that he was sexually harassed by his co-workers and supervisor. Despite *Oncale*, the district court ruled against him, holding that he was harassed because of his sexual orientation and not because of his sex.[10] The court awarded the employer summary judgment because Title VII's prohibition against sex discrimination was not applicable to discrimination based on sexual orientation.

A divided panel of the Ninth Circuit agreed, affirming the lower court decision (*Rene v. MGM Grand Hotel* 2001). The Ninth Circuit, sitting en banc, reversed, finding that Rene, who was gay, had stated a claim for sex discrimination under Title VII. Speaking for a plurality of the court, Fletcher said this was clearly a case of a hostile environment because of sex, and, citing *Oncale*, she said that it did not defeat Rene's claim that he was harassed because of his sexual orientation (*Rene v. MGM Grand Hotel* 2002).[11]

Most circuits, however, reject claims of discrimination on the basis of sexual orientation unless, as in *Hopkins* and *Oncale*, the plaintiffs allege they were subject to discrimination because they did not conform to stereotypical notions of masculinity and femininity. Gay and lesbian plaintiffs seeking relief under Title VII for harassment or discrimination may be able to survive motions to dismiss or for summary judgment only if they include such words in their complaints (Greenberg 2002).

FEDERAL WORKERS

The first litigation efforts challenging discriminatory employment actions were brought on behalf of federal civil service workers. As in the military, homosexuality was considered grounds for dismissal from the federal civilian workforce as far back as the 1880s, when the civil service system was created (Cain 1993). Although these cases generally did not receive the attention devoted to those arising in the military, discrimination in the federal civilian workforce was widespread, with consequences that followed employees for their entire lives. In the 1950s, as part of its efforts to rout homosexuals out of the government, the Federal Bureau of Investigation (FBI) provided the Civil Service Commission (CSC), the agency in charge of personnel management, with the names of individuals arrested for homosexuality by local police departments around the country (Murdoch and Price 2001, 36–7).

In bringing lawsuits against the CSC (its name later changed to the Office of Personnel Management [OPM]), plaintiffs asked the courts to reverse CSC decisions to discharge (or refuse to hire) gay employees. In such cases, the CSC echoed the military's claims that homosexuality negatively affected unit cohesion, declaring that it is detrimental to job performance because it detracts from the "efficiency of the service." When security clearances were at issue, the government's arguments reflected the stereotypical view of gays as threats to national security.

Federal employees are protected by constitutional due process guarantees, but not surprisingly, given the climate of opinion about homosexuality in the 1960s and the courts' sensitivity about intruding on the prerogatives of the executive branch, judges were often reluctant to overturn CSC decisions. Evidence of a single homosexual act, even committed well before the onset of employment, was often enough for a court to uphold a dismissal. In *Dew v. Halaby* (1963), for example, William Dew was discharged for allegedly committing homosexual acts when he was a teen and for smoking marijuana while in the air force.

Dew, an air force veteran, was working for the Central Intelligence Agency (CIA) when he was compelled to take a lie detector test for a security clearance. When the evidence of his past emerged, he was allowed to resign, and he succeeded in obtaining a position as an air traffic controller. He was discharged from that post as well when the results of the lie detector test became known. Despite a psychiatric evaluation that concluded that he did not have a "homosexual personality disorder" (583), his internal appeals were denied. The district court granted summary judgment to the government, and he appealed.

Speaking for the District of Columbia circuit court panel, Judge Washington explained that the primary issue in the case was whether the CSC's action in discharging Dew on the basis of his preemployment homosexual acts was "arbitrary and capricious." No, said Washington, "common sense" indicates that the regulations must encompass preemployment behavior because the grounds for removal also applied to initial hiring decisions (586). This view, the judge added, was consistent with past judicial decisions. Washington agreed with the CSC "that such acts 'may have, and can be determined to have, an adverse impact upon the efficiency of the service'" (587). Therefore, because the CSC could reasonably believe that Dew's past behavior would resurface, the court held it was not arbitrary or capricious to remove him from the job.

Judge Wright sharply dissented, charging that this was the first instance in the fifty-year history of the Civil Service Act that a court upheld a CSC decision to fire a permanent employee with a veteran's preference for conduct occurring before his employment began. He warned that based on this ruling, all civil service employees are vulnerable to any past misbehavior that can be used as an excuse to remove them from their jobs. He pointed out that there was no evidence in the record to show that Dew's role as an air traffic controller was affected by his earlier homosexual acts; on the contrary, the judge noted, his supervisor had testified to his satisfactory work performance.[12]

A few years later, another District of Columbia circuit court decision weighed the legality of the government's decision to refuse to hire an applicant for a civil service job because of his homosexuality (*Scott v. Macy* 1965). When interviewing for a job in 1962, Bruce Scott was asked about two encounters with the police—a 1947 arrest for loitering and another arrest in 1951—as well as undisclosed information that he was a homosexual. He explained the arrests and refused to answer the question about his sexual orientation, saying it was irrelevant.

Scott was rejected for the position on the basis of "immoral conduct," and when he asked for clarification, he was told only that there was "convincing evidence" that he had "engaged in homosexual conduct, which is considered contrary to generally-recognized and accepted standards of morality" (183). Following an unsuccessful internal appeal, he filed suit in federal court and lost.

Speaking for the three-judge circuit panel, chief judge Bazelon acknowledged that Scott was not an employee but insisted that he was still entitled to fair treatment, free from discrimination. In charging Scott with "immoral conduct," the CSC had not only denied him a government job but threatened his ability to find others (184). Because of the seriousness of these consequences, Bazelon said the CSC cannot simply accuse him of homosexuality without providing specific evidence of immoral conduct and explaining how it related to his job performance. The appellate court remanded the case, instructing the lower court to enter summary judgment in Scott's favor.[13]

Judge Burger, soon to become Chief Justice Burger of the United States Supreme Court, dissented, arguing that the majority failed to address Scott's principle claim that sexual orientation is irrelevant in a civil service job. Burger said he believed it is relevant and that gays should be barred from these positions.

The turning point in establishing constitutional protection for civil service employees was *Norton v. Macy* (1969). Beginning as a typical police stop, it resulted in a ruling that began to afford gays protection from arbitrary dismissals. The case arose when Clifford Norton was fired from his job as a budget analyst at the National Aeronautics and Space Administration (NASA), following an incident on October 22, 1962.

Norton's dismissal resulted from an encounter with two Morals Squad officers in Washington, D.C., who observed him driving around Lafayette Square, stop and pick a man up, drive him around the square, and drop him off at his own car. When the police stopped and questioned the men, the passenger said that Norton had touched his leg during the trip around the square. Both men were arrested and brought to the police station, where Norton was interrogated by the police for several hours and then by the head of NASA (who had been summoned to the police station to observe part of the interrogation and review Norton's ostensibly confidential arrest record). Norton admitted to engaging in homosexual acts in the past but denied that he had made advances to the man in the car. The agency determined otherwise, concluding "that this act amounted to 'immoral, indecent, and disgraceful conduct'" and that he "possesses 'traits of character and personality which render [him] . . . unsuitable for further Government employment'" (1163).

When Norton sued to be reinstated, the district court granted the agency's motion for summary judgment. On appeal, speaking for a divided panel, Bazelon found that although the CSC had wide latitude in determining an employee's fitness, it is constrained by constitutional guarantees imposed by the due process clause, especially when an area of personal privacy is involved. The court held that the commission had acted beyond its authority in discharging Norton. Before dismissing an employee for immorality, the CSC must show that the acts in question "have some ascertainable deleterious effect on the efficiency of the service" (1165). In this case, to the contrary, Norton's supervisor had testified that his work was not affected, and he was reluctant to dismiss him, agreeing to do so only when told it was customary agency policy and public scandal could result if the behavior were repeated. Bazelon concluded that to fire a protected employee such as Norton based on a potential threat of embarrassment was arbitrary and capricious and violated due process.

Norton represents the leading opinion in establishing the rights of gay federal employees, establishing that the government is required to show a relationship between "immoral" conduct and job performance before discharging an employee.

Several years later, the courts further refined the rights of gays in federal employment, specifically, the provision in the *Federal Personnel Manual Supplement* that "persons about whom there is evidence that they have engaged in or solicited others to engage in homosexual or sexually perverted acts with them, without evidence of rehabilitation, are not suitable for federal employment" (*Society for Individual Rights, Inc. v. Hampton* 1973, 399).

In *Hampton*, Donald Hickerson, an employee of the Department of Agriculture, filed suit when he was discharged from his position as supply clerk in the department's Consumer and Marketing Service after it was learned that he was gay. Citing *Norton*, district court judge Zirpoli ruled that the discharge was improper. Although society may disapprove of the plaintiff's activities, he said, the commission cannot simply fire him without showing that his conduct affects his job performance. The government's claim that embarrassment and contempt might result from the knowledge that it employed homosexuals does not meet this standard. The judge granted summary judgment for the plaintiff and ordered him reinstated with back pay.[14] Another significant event furthering the rights of gay federal employees (or aspiring employees) was the 1973 revision of the CSC *Personnel Manual*. It now instructed supervisors that they were barred from "find[ing] a person unsuitable for Federal employment merely because that person is a homosexual or has engaged in homosexual acts, nor may such exclusion be based on a conclusion that a homosexual person might bring the public service into public contempt . . . [unless] the evidence establishes that such person's homosexual conduct affects job fitness—excluding from such consideration, however, unsubstantiated conclusions concerning possible embarrassment to the Federal service" (quoted in *Singer v. United States Civil Service Commission* 1976, 255 n14).

Further revisions to the manual were made in 1975, removing "immorality" as grounds for discharging a civil service employee. Citing recent judicial rulings, the new Suitability Guidelines for Federal Employment stated that an applicant or employee may not be considered "unsuitable for Federal employment solely because that person is a homosexual or has engaged in homosexual acts . . . [unless] the evidence establishes that such person's sexual conduct affects job fitness" (quoted in *Singer* 1976, 255 n15).

In retrospect, *Norton* and *Hampton* were easy cases. There was no indication that either plaintiff's sexual orientation was related to his job performance or even known to his supervisors. They were fired on the basis of vague charges stemming from standards that required dismissal of employees who engaged in "criminal, infamous, dishonest, immoral, or notoriously disgraceful conduct."[15] In *Singer* (1976), however, the court confronted the situation of an employee who was open about his homosexuality and vocal in his protests about the policies governing his public and private life.

John Singer was hired on a one-year probationary period by the Equal Employment Opportunity Commission's (EEOC) Seattle office as a clerk typist in 1971. He informed the director at the time that he was gay. Less than a year later, he was told that an investigation revealed that he was openly gay and that he "received wide-spread publicity in this respect in at least two states" (249). The complaints against him included being a member of the Seattle Gay Alliance Board of Directors, appearing on a talk radio show, and being quoted in newspaper stories; in all these venues, he identified himself as an EEOC employee. After a series of letters and affidavits went back and forth between Singer and the commission, he received a letter from the Investigations Division informing him that "by reason of his 'immoral and notoriously disgraceful conduct,'" he was being separated from the federal civil service (250).[16]

In his internal appeal, Singer was told that despite his satisfactory job performance, his behavior detracted from the efficiency of the service, and his dismissal would be upheld. His suit against the CSC on First and Fifth Amendment grounds was dismissed by the trial court, and he appealed.

In his opinion for the Ninth Circuit, district court judge Jameson, sitting by designation, reviewed the parties' claims. Singer contended his discharge violated his right to due process and freedom of expression. The commission denied that he was fired because he was a homosexual; it claimed instead that its determination that he would potentially embarrass the agency and destroy the public's confidence in it was rationally based on his openly unconventional lifestyle.

The court held that although government employees are subject to greater regulation in their speech, they retain their constitutional right not to be discharged in an arbitrary and capricious manner. The key issue, therefore, was to evaluate the principles governing the discharge of homosexuals from the federal civil service. Citing *Norton* as the leading case, Jameson emphasized that it required the commission to link the employee's job performance to his homosexuality. Unlike Norton, however, Jameson said, Singer was not discharged "because of his status as a homosexual or because of any private acts of sexual preference." Rather, the commission had adhered to the dictates of *Norton* and *Hampton* and listed Singer's offenses in sufficient detail for the court to be able to reasonably find that his behavior had affected the "efficiency of the service."[17] Finally, the judge rejected Singer's First Amendment claim, holding that the commission could properly decide that its interests in efficiency outweighed his First Amendment right of "publicly flaunting and broadcasting his homosexual activities" (*Singer* 1976, 255–6).[18]

FEDERAL LAW ENFORCEMENT AGENTS

The special needs of federal law enforcement agencies, primarily the FBI, further tested the court's willingness to limit the executive branch's discretion in discharging or refusing to hire gays and lesbians.

One of the first cases to challenge the FBI's employment policy arose when Donald Ashton, an FBI file clerk, was dismissed from his position without a hearing. The District of Columbia trial court granted the bureau summary judgment, and Ashton appealed. After oral argument, the FBI filed a memorandum with the appellate court stating that it "has always had an absolute policy of dismissing proven or admitted homosexuals from its employ" (*Ashton v. Civiletti* 1979, 927). A few months later, FBI director William Webster was asked on national television whether there is "any real challenge to the national security, or the integrity of FBI operations, by having homosexual file clerks pushing mail carts through the J. Edgar Hoover building" (927).

Webster responded by saying that as in state and local law enforcement agencies, "there is a potential for compromise for those who engage in such conduct which is generally not approved by society, and in some places, illegal. Now," he continued, "we treat it [homosexuality] as a factor, and I must say in candor, it's a significant factor. It's a troublesome thing; I hope that . . . at some point we will have a better understanding of the problem and the policy that should be addressed to it" (927). He emphasized that the agency's only concern was with actions, not status or beliefs.

With McGowan writing the opinion for the circuit panel, the court held that Ashton had a reasonable expectation that he could be terminated only for cause related to his job performance and that he was entitled to a hearing prior to termination. Reversing the lower court, McGowan remanded the case to allow the lower court to determine whether the bureau's actions were justified under the *Norton* and *Hampton* standards.

A later FBI case, *Padula v. Webster* (1987), revolved around Margaret Padula's claim that the FBI's refusal to hire her because of her homosexuality violated both agency policy and the equal protection guarantee of the federal constitution. The first case adjudicated in an appellate court after *Bowers*, *Padula* demonstrates its pervasive effect on lower courts (Andersen 1998, 311).

Padula had applied for a position as special agent in 1982 and scored sufficiently high in the qualifying exam to proceed to the next stage of the hiring process. A background check revealed that she was gay, a fact she readily confirmed in her personal interview. Several months later she was rejected for the position, ostensibly because of the intense competition for the job. She subsequently filed suit, claiming a violation of bureau policy as well as equal protection, due process, and privacy.

She presented evidence that included correspondence between the FBI's legal counsel and several law school deans who were concerned that FBI campus recruiters were discriminating on the basis of sexual orientation. The counsel ambiguously replied that the FBI does not discriminate on the basis of sexual orientation, but that homosexual conduct may be a factor in hiring; he added that the bureau carefully evaluates each applicant's record to determine if there is conduct that might compromise job performance. One letter candidly stated that the writer could "offer no specific encouragement that a homosexual applicant will be found who satisfies all of the requirements" (*Padula* 1987, 98).[19]

The District of Columbia trial court granted summary judgment to the government, ruling in part that the FBI had not established an official policy on discrimination and was free to assess candidates individually. With respect to the constitutional claims, the court ruled that the FBI policy had met the required minimal level of rationality.

Speaking for the three-judge panel of the District of Columbia circuit court, Silberman noted that Padula had not raised the due process and privacy claims on appeal, leaving only the equal protection issue.[20] Addressing her argument that the agency had committed itself to a nondiscriminatory hiring policy, making an employee's sexual orientation irrelevant, he found that the bureau had merely promised "not to improperly discriminate against any applicant" and to "focus in personnel matters . . . on conduct rather than status or preference." Moreover, Silberman continued, the bureau had never relinquished its right to determine whether there was a relationship between sexual orientation and conduct that might compromise the employee's ability to perform the job. Indeed, he added, there is "no indication that the FBI renounced homosexuality as a basis for reaching employment decisions" (101).

The court also rejected Padula's argument that homosexuals should be treated as a suspect or semisuspect class, thus meriting a higher form of scrutiny. Silberman noted that the criteria used to categorize a class as suspect, a history of discrimination and political powerlessness, were inapplicable to gays. Invoking *Bowers* to negate the inference that the FBI policy can be characterized as invidious, he added that "it would be quite anomolous [sic], on its face, to declare status defined by conduct that states may constitutionally criminalize as deserving of strict scrutiny under the equal protection clause." He added that "if the Court was unwilling to object to state laws that criminalize the behavior that defines the class, it is hardly open to a lower court to conclude that state sponsored discrimination against the class is invidious. After all, there can hardly be more palpable discrimination against a class than making the conduct that defines the class criminal" (*Padula* 1987, 103).

Applying minimal scrutiny, the court held that the bureau's policy was justified on two grounds: First, its credibility would be threatened if its agents engaged in conduct for which they could be arrested in many states; and second, society's condemnation of homosexuals as well as the possibility of arrest would subject such individuals to the risk of exposure and constitute a threat to national security.

NATIONAL SECURITY

Although the risk of jeopardizing national security did not play a central role in *Padula*, the court believed the bureau could reasonably believe that gay employees would threaten the nation's safety. Concern over national security, omnipresent in the 1950s, was widely shared by the courts throughout the next several decades and played a significant role in undermining the employment prospects of gays and lesbians—both as civilian government workers and employees of private contractors on government projects.[21]

When Eisenhower's Executive Order No. 10450 was successfully challenged in *Greene v. McElroy* (1959), it was replaced by Executive Order No. 10865 in February 1960. The revised policy required the secretary of defense to promulgate regulations to protect classified information within industry as well as provide procedural guarantees.[22] However, the new executive order also "gave rise to the catchall phrase which haunts every decision denying security clearance to homosexuals—that the granting of such clearance would not be 'clearly consistent with the national interest'" (M. Lewis 1990, 140).

One of the earlier cases raising the linkage between homosexuality and national security was *Adams v. Laird* (1969). Here, a defense contractor's employee sued when his security clearance was revoked after he admitted during questioning to homosexual conduct. The lower court granted summary judgment to the government, and the plaintiff appealed. McGowan, for the District of Columbia circuit panel, rejected his claim of due process violations, noting that the court must defer to presidential authority in determining standards for security clearances. Decisions to grant or withhold security clearances are committed to the executive, McGowan said. It is inappropriate for the court to "secondguess that choice unless the Constitution commands us to do so," he said (239). The decision to deny Adams his security clearance was reasonable.[23]

A few years later, in *Wentworth v. Laird* (1972), the plaintiff sued when his security clearance was withdrawn. Judge Pratt of the District of Columbia district court emphasized that the security clearance decision is committed to the executive branch, and the court's "sole function is to determine whether or not the administrative process [is] accorded a fair hearing in accordance with procedural due process" (1155). Yet despite its deferential approach, the court ruled that because the government had prejudged all homosexuals as security risks and failed to prove a nexus between the plaintiff's homosexuality and his inability to keep government secrets, he was not given a fair hearing.

The Supreme Court's ruling in *Department of the Navy v. Egan* (1988), although not a gay rights case, is considered "the seminal case on judicial review of security clearances" (Maravilla 2001, 786).[24] It played an important role in circumscribing the courts' oversight of the government's decision making in national security policy. Indeed, it has been interpreted by some to preclude judicial review of security clearance decisions entirely (see W. Miller 2004; Maravilla 2001).

Thomas Egan was hired as a civilian laborer by the Department of the Navy pending receipt of his security clearance for access to "secret or confidential information." Approximately one year later, his security clearance was denied after investigation revealed information about his past felony arrests and convictions as well as treatment in an alcohol rehabilitation program. He was subsequently removed from his position by the navy for cause because he lacked a security clearance.

Following an internal appeal, at which he initially prevailed, his removal was subsequently upheld by the Merit Systems Protection Board (MSPB), and he appealed to the Court of Appeals for the Federal Circuit. Speaking for a divided panel, Judge Newman rejected the board's determination that it had no authority to review the navy's reasons behind its decision. The appeals court remanded the case, holding that the MSPB should have addressed the merits of the decision to revoke his security clearance (*Egan v. Department of the Navy* 1986).

The board appealed to the Supreme Court, and in a 5–3 decision, the Court reversed the lower court (*Department of the Navy v. Egan* 1988). With Blackmun announcing the opinion, the high court ruled that although the Civil Service Reform Act of 1978 provides that employees removed for cause may appeal to the MSPB, employees who are dismissed because they lack the security clearances required for a job are not entitled to a hearing.[25] Blackmun believed the dissenting lower court judge had it right. The navy possesses the necessary expertise to judge suitability for security clearances and has broad discretionary authority to determine access to classified information; neither the courts nor the MSPB has sufficient expertise to oversee this important decision.

The government argued that its compelling interest in safeguarding national security justified limitations on judicial review of the merits of the navy's decision to deny Egan's security clearance. Avoiding the merits of his case, the Court restricted itself to reviewing the procedure and held that Egan was not denied due process. He was given adequate notice of the reasons behind the decision to deny his security clearance, and he had sufficient opportunity to respond to the evidence against him and appeal to the board for review.

The next year, in *Carlucci v. Doe* (1988), the Supreme Court ruled on the National Security Agency's (NSA) authority to deny a security clearance to one of its civilian employees. The case arose in 1982, when "John Doe," a sixteen-year veteran of the NSA, an agency within the DoD, revealed he had engaged in homosexual relations with a number of other individuals, likely foreign nationals. The NSA required its employees to have a Top Secret security clearance because of their access to sensitive information. After investigation, NSA officials concluded that his access to such information was "'clearly inconsistent with national security'" (*Doe v. Weinberger* 1987, 1277). When the DoD denied him a hearing, he sued, claiming that he was entitled to a hearing and that the government's action was "capricious and arbitrary," thereby violating the Administrative Procedure Act (APA).[26]

The district court awarded the government summary judgment. In her opinion for the District of Columbia circuit court, chief judge Wald held that the Civil Service Reform Act, 5 U.S.C. §7532, controls NSA employee discharges and Doe was entitled to a pretermination hearing.[27]

The secretary of defense and the NSA director sought Supreme Court review, and White delivered the opinion for a unanimous Court, reversing the appellate court. Citing *Egan*, White found that the appellate court had incorrectly decided that §7532 was the exclusive means of removing an employee on national security grounds.[28] Instead, the NSA may act under the authority of the 1959 National Security Agency Act, which does not require it to provide employees with preremoval hearings.[29] The Court declined to reach the constitutional question of whether the decision to deny a security clearance on grounds of homosexuality is immune from review by the courts.

The Court addressed this issue in *Webster v. Doe* (1988), one of the most frequently cited cases involving judicial review of national security policy. It was clear that the court's traditional deference to the executive branch in military and national security policy would be heightened when litigants challenged adverse employment decisions of the CIA, an agency immune from many employment laws.[30]

The case against the CIA arose in 1982, when "John Doe," a covert CIA agent with an excellent record who worked as an electronics technician, voluntarily disclosed his homosexuality to a security officer.[31] Following an investigation, his counsel was told that "homosexuality was not a *per se* ground for dismissal but that it was a security concern which would be evaluated on a case-by-case basis" (*Doe v. Casey* 1985, 583, emphasis in the original). Shortly thereafter, without explanation, Doe was informed that his homosexuality created a "security threat," and he was asked to resign; when he refused, he was fired. He was also told he must inform the CIA whenever he applied for a job requiring a security clearance so that all potential employers could be told the CIA considered him a security risk because of his homosexuality.

Doe filed suit in the District of Columbia district court, claiming the agency violated its own regulations as well as the APA and the National Security Act of 1947.[32] He contended that he was denied due process because he did not have adequate notice, was not told of the reason for the decision, had no opportunity to respond to the charges, and was denied a hearing. Moreover, he claimed, the overriding national security concerns that justified his termination were never identified.

Evaluating Doe's due process claim, district court judge Parker compared Doe's case to Matlovich's, emphasizing the absence of explanation in both situations, a fact that had led the court to conclude that the air force's decision to discharge Matlovich was arbitrary and capricious (*Doe v. Casey* 1985).

The CIA argued that the National Security Act of 1947 gives the Director of Central Intelligence (DCI) the unfettered authority to fire an employee without providing a reason, a decision that is not subject to judicial review. Parker disagreed, declaring that the courts cannot be precluded from reviewing a decision involving a claim of abuse of discretion. Unless there is convincing evidence that Congress did not intend it, agency actions are presumed reviewable under the APA. He concluded by saying he understood the concern about sensitive issues within the CIA, but that there was nothing in the record to "suggest that overriding national security concerns are at stake or that affording the plaintiff Doe the relief he seeks, might disclose matters that would place at risk such concerns and interests" (589–90). He ordered Doe reinstated to administrative leave status pending a proper hearing.

Speaking for a divided appellate panel, Judge Edwards rejected the CIA's contention that employee discharges under §403(c) are immune from judicial review, noting that there is a strong presumption of judicial review under the APA and that exceptions must be narrowly construed (*Doe v. Casey* 1986).[33] Appraising the legislative history of the 1947 act, the court held that although Congress granted the CIA more discretion than most other agencies, it had not intended to preclude review of employee discharges entirely.

Edwards stressed that the law "leaves the decision to terminate CIA employment largely to the expertise and judgment of the Director" (1521). And the role of the court, he explained, will be generally limited to ensuring that agency directors do not exceed constitutional or other limits in exercising their discretion. However, he emphasized that the court's review must be highly deferential and accord the DCI a great deal of leeway to protect the nation's security.

Because of the sensitive nature of the agency's work and the risk that merely asking the director to explain the reasons for the discharge may endanger national security, there must be a presumption that the director is acting lawfully. Therefore, before the court will review an employee's claim of a wrongful discharge, there must be specific evidence that the director has acted improperly under §403(c). The circuit court concluded by affirming the lower court's holding that agency actions are subject to judicial review but reversed its order to reinstate Doe because it "had erred by showing insufficient deference to the judgment of the Director" (1524).[34]

On appeal, the high court affirmed the lower court's ruling in part and reversed in part (*Webster v. Doe* 1988). Speaking for a 6–2 majority, Rehnquist declared that the 1947 National Security Act generally, and

§403(c)(2) specifically, bars judicial review of the DCI's decision to terminate an employee.[35] The law clearly indicates that Congress intended the DCI to exercise discretion over employee discharges without oversight by the courts by establishing a "standard [that] fairly exudes deference to the Director." Such as standard, he said, "appears to us to foreclose the application of any meaningful judicial standard of review [and] short of permitting cross-examination of the Director concerning his views of the Nation's security and whether the discharged employee was inimical to those interests, we see no basis on which a reviewing court could properly assess an Agency termination decision" under §403(c) (600).

Thus, the high court reversed the appellate court's ruling that discharges made pursuant to §403(c) are subject to judicial review. But the controversy did not end there, for in addition to his charge that the agency violated §403(c), Doe had raised a number of constitutional claims in an amended complaint, contending that the APA required judicial review of these allegations. The government maintained that §403(c) precluded judicial review of the constitutional claims as well, but the Court disagreed, saying that if Congress intends such a result, it must do so very clearly. Although the decision to discharge an employee is entirely within the director's discretion under §403(c), there is no indication, Rehnquist said, that "Congress meant to preclude consideration of colorable constitutional claims arising out of the actions of the Director" (603).[36] The Court did not determine whether Doe had presented such as claim; it merely held that the district court had jurisdiction to make this determination and remanded the case to the lower court to resolve the matter.

On remand, district court judge Robinson denied Doe's equal protection claim. Applying minimal scrutiny, he found that the CIA's policy of discharging homosexuals rationally related to its interest in ensuring the nation's security. He based this on his view that "homosexuals engaging in homosexual conduct pose a greater security risk than heterosexuals." He believed that "Doe may be particularly susceptible to blackmail and coercion by hostile intelligence agents to protect himself or his partners even if he has admitted his homosexuality to friends and family. The fact is," he continued, "that homosexual conduct is a characteristic that hostile intelligence services are likely to target, and at least some homosexuals may be coerced or manipulated" (Doe v. Webster 1991, 3).

In ruling on Doe's due process claim, Robinson held that when Doe was fired, he was told only that he was "a security threat [but] he was not given the reasons for this determination nor did he have an opportunity to respond," adding that "at a minimum, Doe is entitled to notice and a hearing so that he may rebut the allegations" (5). He denied the agency's motion for summary judgment. On appeal, the appellate court reversed the district court's holding on the due process claim (*Doe v. Gates* 1993).[37]

A Ninth Circuit ruling following shortly after *Webster* was *Dubbs v. Central Intelligence Agency* (1989). In this case, Julie Dubbs, a senior technical illustrator at a nonprofit research institute, was denied a security clearance to certain classified information by the CIA in part because "certain hostile intelligence services regard homosexual behavior as a vulnerability which can be used to their advantage" (1119).[38] Moreover, according to the agency, her failure to disclose this information during the initial investigation of her security clearance indicated her willingness to deceive to protect her own and possibly her partner's status.

Dubbs filed suit in 1985, charging that the CIA violated the APA by acting arbitrarily and capriciously and also infringed on her constitutional rights. The lower court granted the government's motion for summary judgment, concluding that the CIA did not have a blanket policy of refusing to grant all homosexuals security clearances, and it was constitutional for the CIA to weigh homosexual conduct in an individualized consideration to grant security clearances. Moreover, the court absolved the CIA from having to explain its reasons for granting or denying security clearances.

Her appeal to the Ninth Circuit was put on hold pending the Supreme Court's decision in *Webster v. Doe*.[39] Once *Webster* was decided, the circuit court handed down its opinion. Speaking for the Ninth Circuit panel, Norris explained that, despite its denial, the CIA's own documents suggest it has an across-the-board policy of denying security clearances to homosexuals, and therefore, summary judgment was improper because "a fair-minded trier of fact could reasonably infer from the evidence that the CIA considers all persons who engage in homosexual activity to be unacceptable security risks" (1119). Although he offered no opinion on whether such a policy would be constitutional, Norris indicated in a footnote that a "blanket policy of security clearance denials to all persons who engage in homosexual conduct would give rise to a colorable equal protection claim" (1119 n8).[40]

The appeals court also reversed the trial court's conclusion that the CIA does not discriminate against homosexuals by treating them differently from heterosexuals in making security clearance determinations. Such a charge of disparate treatment raises a "colorable" constitutional claim that, according to *Webster*, merits judicial review.[41] The circuit court remanded the case to allow the district court to consider Dubbs's claim that the CIA unconstitutionally discriminated against homosexuals in its security clearance determinations.

Although *Webster* is widely cited for its role in opening the courthouse door to gay employees to litigate discriminatory employment practices, subsequent rulings indicate that it may have been a pyrrhic victory. The plaintiff in *Webster* prevailed because the Court acceded to his argument that district courts have the authority to adjudicate constitutional challenges of employee discharges; however, he was ultimately denied relief by the lower courts that considered his constitutional claims. Similarly, Julie Dubbs was told that her constitutional challenge to the CIA's denial of her security clearance was reviewable by the courts, yet five years later, her case was still pending.

Shortly after the first district court ruling in *Dubbs*, another California district court decided *High Tech Gays* (1987), a nationwide class action suit challenging the government's disparate treatment in investigating lesbian and gay applicants for Secret and Top Secret security clearances.[42] Under DoD policy guidelines, gays are subjected to different procedures, undergoing more intensive investigation, before they are allowed access to classified documents.[43] The justification for the policy as stated in the manual governing these investigations is reminiscent of the "sexual McCarthyism" of the 1950s; it characterizes "homosexuality as 'sexual misconduct' and 'aberrant sexual behavior' and states that participation in such 'deviant sexual activities' may tend to 'cast doubt on the individual's morality, emotional or mental stability and may raise questions as to his or her susceptibility to coercion or blackmail'" (1364).

On behalf of the class, the three named plaintiffs, Timothy Dooling, Joel Crawford, and Robert Weston, all of whom had applied for industrial security clearances in the early 1980s, claimed the policy deprived them of their right to equal protection as well as their speech and associational rights under the First Amendment. Addressing their equal protection claim, Judge Henderson held that because classifications based on sexual orientation are analogous to classifications based on gender, courts should apply the same level of scrutiny, that is, heightened scrutiny, to laws affecting gays. He thought that like gender, classifications based on sexual orientation bear no relationship to ability, derive from stereotypes, and are aimed at a politically powerless group. In a sweeping denunciation of society's prejudice against gays, he decried the fact that

> wholly unfounded, degrading stereotypes about lesbians and gay men
> abound in American society. Examples of such stereotypes include that

gay people desire and attempt to molest young children, that gay people attempt to recruit and convert other people, and that gay people inevitably engage in promiscuous sexual activity. Many people erroneously believe that the sexual experience of lesbians and gay men represents the gratification of purely prurient interests, not the expression of mutual affection and love. They fail to recognize that gay people seek and engage in stable, monogamous relationships. Instead, to many, the very existence of lesbians and gay men is inimical to the family. For years, many people have branded gay people as abominations to nature and considered lesbians and gay men mentally ill and psychologically unstable. (1369)

Henderson believed that strict scrutiny was warranted because the DoD regulations infringe on the fundamental right of lesbians and gays to engage in homosexual activity. But the level of scrutiny was irrelevant, he said; because the policy arises from bias against gays, it cannot even withstand minimal scrutiny. There is no reasonable basis, he declared, for treating gays differently from other applicants. Concluding the equal protection analysis, Henderson quickly dismissed the government's justification for the policy, declaring it derived from outmoded thinking and stereotypical views of homosexuals and failed to survive even the lowest level of scrutiny. He seemed to take special issue with the government's contention that its actions are justified because gays are more susceptible to blackmail and coercion and constitute a greater security risk.

Henderson granted the government summary judgment on the plaintiff's due process claim, but indicated that he found merit in their First Amendment theory, explaining that their right to associate prevents the government from justifying its policy on the basis of their membership in gay organizations.

On appeal, the Ninth Circuit panel rejected the district court's use of strict scrutiny, citing opinions in the Seventh Circuit (*benShalom* 1989b), the Federal Circuit (*Woodward* 1989), and the District of Columbia Circuit (*Padula* 1987). Speaking for the panel, Judge Brunetti also refused to accept the lower court's characterization of homosexuality as a fundamental right, citing *Bowers.* "Because homosexual conduct can thus be criminalized," he said, "homosexuals cannot constitute a suspect or quasi-suspect class entitled to greater than rational basis review" (*High Tech Gays v. Defense Industry Security Clearance Office* 1990a, 571).

Brunetti acknowledged that the Ninth Circuit had applied a higher level of scrutiny to the government's policy in *Beller* (1980) and *Hatheway* (1981) but emphasized that because those rulings were decided before *Bowers*, they were no longer valid. *Dubbs* (1989) and *Watkins* (1989) were also irrelevant, he said, as the courts in those cases had not reached the constitutional question of discrimination on the basis of the plaintiffs' sexual orientations.

Noting that the high court has never held that homosexuals constituted a suspect or semisuspect class, Brunetti reiterated the well-known criteria for inclusion in this category: having "a history of discrimination," "with immutable" traits of "a discrete group," and being "politically powerless" or demonstrating that the law burdens a "fundamental right."[44] Although he conceded that homosexuals satisfy the first, he declared that they failed to meet the other two. "Homosexuality," he said, "is not an immutable characteristic; it is behavioral and hence is fundamentally different from traits such as race, gender, or alienage, which define already existing suspect and quasi suspect classes" (*High Tech Gays v. Defense Industry Security Clearance Office* 1990a, 573). Last, he pointed to the passage of state and local antidiscrimination ordinances as evidence that gays do not lack political power.

Applying minimal scrutiny, the court held that the plaintiffs failed to show that the government lacks a rational basis for its policy. It is not required to prove that gays are more susceptible to blackmail; it merely has to show "that its investigatory policies and procedures for homosexuals are rationally related to permissible ends, and that the plaintiffs have failed to submit affirmative evidence to negate DoD's evidence" (576). He concluded that the DoD's policy of heightened investigations of gays was reasonably related to its interest in protecting national security. With hostile intelligence agencies singling gays out, it is reasonable for the government to proceed more cautiously to determine if they are likely to succumb to blackmail or coercion. Citing *Egan*, the court stressed that the judiciary must be especially deferential to executive branch agencies when reviewing decisions affecting national security.

The circuit court denied the plaintiff's petition for a rehearing en banc (*High Tech Gays* 1990b). A sharp dissent from the denial by Canby, joined by Norris, charged that the panel's "decision is wrong, and it will have tragic results" (376). He took issue with its indifferent attitude toward discrimination against gays, warning that "this history of discrimination makes it far more likely that differential treatment is simply a resort to old prejudices" (376–7).

Canby also objected to the majority's discussion of immutability. First, he said, immutability was not an essential requirement for a suspect class. But in any event, he argued, homosexuality should be considered "an immutable characteristic for equal protection purposes" (377). He rejected the majority's simplistic dichotomy between behavior and identification and argued that the court should properly focus on the cause of the behavior. Because sexual identity does not arise from "conscious or controllable choice" and "from everything we now know . . . they cannot change it without immense difficulty," it must be considered "an immutable characteristic" (377).

He challenged the majority's interpretation that gays are not politically powerless because they are protected by antidiscrimination ordinances in some states and cities. African Americans, the quintessential suspect class, he pointed out, are protected by three constitutional amendments and myriad federal and state civil rights laws. Indeed, gays are even less powerful than other minority groups that are accorded suspect status for at least two reasons: first, because they constitute only about 10 percent in the population; and second, with many hiding their identity to avoid discrimination, political mobilization is more difficult.

In Canby's view, gays should be considered a suspect class, and laws affecting them should be reviewed with strict scrutiny. And he was not persuaded, as the panel had been, that *Bowers* foreclosed this status. The panel had conflated equal protection and due process analysis, he said, and the Court's rejection of a fundamental right status for homosexuality was unrelated to the question of strict scrutiny.

Finally, he criticized the panel for declaring the policy rational, arguing the government had not produced sufficient evidence to support this finding. The government had relied heavily on old Soviet intelligence documents from the KGB to support its position. Among other things, Canby complained, the panel did not question whether the KGB's assessment of the vulnerability of gays to blackmail and coercion was itself rational. In his view, it was not; the KGB's program of targeting gays was simply offered by the government as a belated attempt to justify its policy. The real reason behind the policy was the government's biased view of gays as a class. The goal of protecting the nation's security is of paramount importance, he agreed, but citing an ACLU amicus brief that contained a reference to the World War II Japanese exclusion policy, he charged that "the last time we upheld class discrimination in the interest of national security, it took 42 years to remedy that wrong in the law of the circuit" (382).

The effect of *Egan* (and the limited reach of *Webster*) was also evident in another extensively litigated case decided in the 1990s. The case arose when Jan Krc, a "limited" Foreign Service appointee, admitted he engaged in homosexual conduct with two Yugoslav citizens as well as two other Foreign Service officers while posted in Yugoslavia in the 1980s, violating the United States Information Agency's (USIA) strict "no fraternization" policy.[45] Based on this information, the Director of USIA Security indicated he would not approve any additional foreign service postings for Krc because of the "strong security risk involved," adding that his "homosexuality would make him extremely vulnerable to hostile intelligence approaches" (393).

His appointment to the Foreign Service was terminated by the USIA, but he was appointed to a position in the domestic service, and his security clearance was not revoked. Following an appeal to the Foreign Service Grievance Board (FSGB), he was ordered reinstated.

Based on *Egan* (1988), the District of Columbia district court had held that the FSGB lacked the authority to review the USIA's decision and, in a second ruling, dismissed Krc's due process and statutory claims as well. The appellate court agreed that, despite some factual distinctions, *Egan* controlled. It held that the FSGB, like the MSPB, lacked the expertise to review the agency's determination of proper security clearance and affirmed the lower court's refusal to implement the board's reinstatement order (*United States Information Agency v. Krc* 1990).

To succeed on his APA claim, Krc had to prove that the USIA's actions were beyond its discretion. Speaking for the circuit panel, Wald noted that the Foreign Service Act places few limitations on the secretary of state's decision to terminate a "limited" foreign service appointee such as Krc. And the secretary may even reject a FSGB recommendation when national security is involved. "We are left with little doubt therefore that the Act 'fairly exudes deference' to the Secretary when Foreign Service personnel decisions implicate national security" (396). Because the agency acted within its discretion in terminating Krc, the court ruled against him on his APA claim.

The court agreed that the lower court properly dismissed Krc's claims that he was unconstitutionally deprived of his liberty and property interest in the job. But because the trial court had not ruled on his equal protection claim, the appellate court remanded to allow it to consider it. Wald exhorted the trial judge to carefully consider his remaining constitutional claim because, given the agency's discretion in terminating limited appointees such as Krc and its ability to withstand review of its national security determinations, "those constitutional claims may be the *only* check on agency actions that determine a person's career fortunes" (400) (emphasis in the original).

Wald appended a "separate statement" saying that although she thought the result consistent with the statute, she found "highly disconcerting the notion that government agencies can terminate outstanding civil servants without any substantive review simply by invoking 'national security.'" She went on, warning that "the possibility of unreviewable agency 'security officers' giving effect to homophobic or other biases is all too apparent" (400). In his own "separate statement, " Mivka echoed her sentiments, adding, "No one can be comfortable with the process that has been afforded the federal employee in this case, even though it may be all the process that is due under the statute" (400).

On remand, district court judge Richey rejected Krc's equal protection claim, granting summary judgment to the government. He was persuaded that Krc was dismissed because of his conduct, not because of a general policy toward homosexuals (*United States Information Agency v. Krc* 1991).

The appeals court affirmed, with Ginsburg announcing the opinion and Wald dissenting in part (*United States Information Agency v. Krc* 1993a). Ginsburg agreed with the lower court that by failing to demonstrate that he had been treated unfairly on the basis of his sexual orientation, that is, that his homosexuality was the reason for his discharge, Krc had not proved his equal protection claim. The government had defeated his claim by establishing that it would have made the same decision to discharge him had he not been homosexual and presenting evidence of at least four other cases in which heterosexuals were disciplined for engaging in sexual misconduct with foreign nationals; it also provided examples of sexual indiscretions by homosexuals who were not punished.

Wald's dissent argued that summary judgment was inappropriate because it robbed Krc of the opportunity to show that his homosexuality had been a significant factor in the USIA's decision to terminate his employment. She believed Krc proved that the USIA had inquired into the details of his sexual conduct after his revelation about his sexual orientation. In her view, Krc's situation was comparable to Woodward's because the investigations in both cases followed their admissions of homosexuality. She summed up, saying the majority had insufficient evidence to conclude, as the USIA claimed, that his dismissal was based on legitimate factors and was unrelated to his homosexuality.

With its finding that the agency's decision was not linked to Krc's homosexuality, the appeals court did not reach the merits of his equal protection claim, thus avoiding having to decide whether there was a rational basis for the government's action or whether it arose from bias against gays or a stereotypical view of them as greater national security risks. Although the outcome of the case might have been the same, had the court addressed his equal protection argument, at least the court would have confronted the issue head-on as the Ninth and Federal Circuits had done (Swisher 1994).

When the appellate court rejected Krc's petition to rehear the case en banc, Wald again dissented. She was troubled by the appeals court's decision in a case where the government had openly admitted it had "an exclusionary policy toward homosexuals." It is "hard to see," she said, "how a homosexual plaintiff will ever obtain a trial on the issue of whether he was fired or demoted because of sexual orientation" (*United States Information Agency v. Krc* 1993b, 1041).[46]

Buttino v. Federal Bureau of Investigation (1992a) represents one of the latest district court opinions on homosexuality and security clearances.[47] In it, Judge Armstrong of the California federal district court discussed the continuing problem of security clearances for gays. The case began like so many others. Special Agent Frank Buttino, a decorated twenty-year veteran with the FBI, was fired in 1990 following the bureau's receipt of an anonymous letter stating he had engaged in homosexual activity; a note, signed "Frank," discussing such activities, was included. Following an investigation in which Buttino denied writing the note, his Top Secret security clearance, required of all FBI agents, was revoked, and he was dismissed from the bureau.

Most of the facts are in dispute after this. The bureau claimed that he was terminated because of repeated lies and deceptions; Buttino admitted he lied about the note at first but owned up to it soon after and was truthful about everything else. He contended that "lack of candor" was merely a pretext, that he was fired because he was gay, a victim of the bureau's "traditional anti-gay policy"; he maintained he was treated more harshly than nongay employees in his situation (300).

Despite precedent to the contrary, the FBI argued that a decision to revoke a security clearance is not reviewable by a court. Although Armstrong agreed the court must defer to the experts in such decisions, she was not persuaded that judicial review was precluded whenever national security was at issue. "To be comfortable with such a rule," she warned, "is to be blind to the historical reality that 'national security' has frequently been asserted as the ostensible justification for sweeping deprivations of equal protection which, with hindsight, are nearly universally condemned and readily regarded as, at best, grossly disproportionate to the national security concerns at one time asserted as justifications" (302).

The bureau moved for summary judgment, which, under the federal rules of civil procedure, should be granted unless "a reasonable jury" would have to conclude that "his security clearance would have been revoked even if he were heterosexual" (303). The FBI argued that Buttino had presented no evidence that it acted on the basis of his homosexuality, but Armstrong disagreed, citing evidence of the bureau's intense interest in his personal life after it learned he was gay and its efforts to have him disclose the names of other gay agents. Additionally, she doubted whether the FBI would have questioned his security clearance if he were being charged with heterosexual sexual activity, especially because the FBI's own records showed he was treated more harshly than others for the offense of "lack of candor."

Finally, she pointed out, cases such as *Ashton* and *Padula*, as well as the declarations of former and current gay bureau employees, revealed ample evidence of the FBI's antigay bias in its employment policies. In discussing the appropriate level of scrutiny, Armstrong hinted that the Ninth Circuit's "active rational basis review" was preferable to mere rationality review, given the prejudice reflected in the bureau's policy. In any event, without specifying the appropriate level of scrutiny, she said she doubted whether the FBI policy was rational.

Armstrong also denied the FBI's motion on Buttino's equal protection claim, ruling that the bureau had failed to show it had not discriminated against him, or that the discrimination was rational. Shortly thereafter, in *Buttino v. Federal Bureau of Investigation* (1992b), the court certified a class "comprised of all past and present employees and all applicants of the FBI, who are gay, or who engage in homosexual conduct with consenting adults in private" (at 5).[48]

THE EMPLOYMENT NONDISCRIMINATION ACT

In May 1974, Congresswoman Bella Abzug, Democrat from New York, was the first federal official to sponsor legislation barring discrimination in employment on the basis of sexual orientation; her wide-ranging bill, entitled the Equality Act of 1974, would have banned discrimination on the basis of sex, marital status, and sexual orientation by private employers, state governments, and educational institutions. Considered beyond the pale, no one paid much attention to it, and it never cleared the House Judiciary Committee to which it was committed.[49]

A year later, Abzug and several others introduced the National Lesbian and Gay Civil Rights Bill in the 94th Congress. Limited to gay rights provisions, the bill would have added the category of "affectional or sexual preference" to categories of discrimination in Title VII of the 1964 Civil Rights Act.[50] When Abzug lost her seat in 1976, a version of the bill was introduced by Ed Koch, another Democrat from New York (and soon to become its mayor), and hearings were eventually held in the House. Starting with about two dozen cosponsors when Abzug first brought it to the floor, the bill was reintroduced in subsequent legislative sessions, usually with an increased number of cosponsors. But although support for it grew over the next few years, none of these bills ever came to the floor for debate or a vote (Endean 2006, Feldblum 2000; see Button, Rienzo, and Wald 1997; Haider-Markel 1999).[51]

The election of Bill Clinton with the strong support of the gay community restored energy to efforts to pass a civil rights bill. However, as Feldblum (2000) writes, the first gay rights issue of the new administration was military service, a matter affecting far fewer numbers than a civil rights bill would have. Work finally began on drafting a stand-alone gay civil rights bill that covered employment, housing, federally funded programs, and public facilities, borrowing from Title VII and the public accommodations provision of the ADA.[52] Because of its supporters' perceptions that a multifaceted bill would have been doomed upon introduction, they stripped it of all but the employment discrimination provisions, thus focusing on the area with the broadest public support. Toward this end, they also excluded discrimination on the basis of gender identity, a decision that became the subject of much controversy in the gay and transgender communities (see Frye 2003).

During the second session of the 103d Congress, Studds and Frank introduced H.R. 4636, the Employment Nondiscrimination Act (ENDA) of 1994, with a bipartisan group of 105 cosponsors. That same day, June 23, 1994, its counterpart, S. 2238, was introduced in the Senate by Kennedy and John Chafee, Republican from Rhode Island, with 30 cosponsors. Kennedy called the bill "another significant step on freedom's journey—another milestone in the civil rights march of our time . . . parallel[ing] protections against job discrimination already provided under title VII of the Civil Rights Act" (*Congressional Record* 1994, S7581). It was referred to Kennedy's Labor and Human Resources Committee, which held hearings, with testimony from members of the gay community and civil rights and labor leaders, but no further action was taken on it that year.

On June 15, 1995, Senator Jim Jeffords, Republican from Vermont, reintroduced ENDA as S. 932 with thirty cosponsors. He explained that the law would add sexual orientation to the list of prohibited categories of discrimination, saying, "The time has come to extend this type of protection to the only group—millions of Americans—still subjected to legal discrimination on the job." He added, "the principles of equality and opportunity must apply to all Americans. Success at work should be directly related to one's ability to do the job, period. People who work hard and perform well should not be kept from leading productive and responsible lives—from paying their taxes, meeting their mortgage payments and otherwise contributing to the economic life of the nation—because of irrational, non-work-related prejudice" (*Congressional Record* 1995, S8502).

Riddled with exceptions and qualifiers, the heart of bill was the section prohibiting employers with fifteen or more employees from discriminating on the basis of sexual orientation.[53] It exempted religious organization (except in their for-profit activities) and the military, disallowed quotas or preferential treatment, declared that it does not apply to employee benefits for same-sex partners, and barred disparate impact claims. As with Title VII, ENDA was to be enforced by the EEOC, the attorney general, and the federal courts; it precluded state immunity and made both federal and state governments liable under the act to the same extent that they were under Title VII.[54] Aside from its status as the first federal gay rights bill, ENDA would have eliminated the problem of inconsistency in state and local employment regulations around the nation and prevented employers from hiding behind a worker's sexual orientation to evade the ADA's ban on discrimination against workers with HIV or AIDS.

The bill was again referred to the Senate Labor and Human Resources Committee but went no further. It was again introduced in the House as H.R. 1863 by Studds, with 142 cosponsors, and referred to several committees, including the Subcommittee on the Constitution of the House Judiciary Committee, but no action was reported on it either.

A year later, on September 5, 1996, ENDA was reintroduced in the Senate as S. 2056 during the second session of the 104th Congress by Kennedy, Jeffords, and Joseph Lieberman, Democrat from Connecticut, with 28 cosponsors. Kennedy explained that the bill "prohibits employers from using sexual orientation as a basis for hiring, firing, promotion, or compensation. It's predicated upon the American ideal of equal opportunity. It gives gays and lesbians a fair chance in the workplace" (*Congressional Record* 1996, S9986).

Speaking in opposition to the bill, Nancy Kassebaum summarized her Republican colleagues' objections to it. She noted that, as in Title VII, the EEOC might rely on statistics to prove discrimination, forcing employers to document the "sexual preferences" of their employees.[55] "This is an example," she said, "of the unintended consequences that may flow from this bill."

Additionally, she pointed out, there was concern that exemptions given to the military and religious organizations might be construed to apply to other private employers. Finally, she said, "my own principal objection to this bill [is that] I do not believe that relying on more lawsuits and litigation, as this bill will do, will promote greater tolerance in the workplace. I believe," she continued, "prejudice and discrimination can be fought in other ways and I hope that it would be done—leading by way of example." In her view, she added, the law "will only lead to more division in the workplace, not less" (*Congressional Record* 1996, S10130–1).

Orrin Hatch, Republican from Utah, echoed her concerns, calling the bill "a litigation bonanza." He characterized it as "a massive increase in Federal power," predicting that "the Federal bureaucracy will have a field day with this bill." He quoted from letters from parents and school officials expressing concern that the law would make it impossible for them to discharge or refuse to hire gay teachers who do not provide "the role models" they want for their children; the letters warned of dire consequences for their children if the law were passed (*Congressional Record* 1996, S10132).

Ironically, opponents of ENDA typically offered two contradictory arguments against it. One side claimed, as Hatch did, that it would lead to a massive onslaught of litigation, flooding the courts; there was an implicit threat that the law would detract from the courts' ability to deal with more important matters. The other side contended that discrimination on the basis of sexual orientation is so rare that a federal law was not needed (Rubenstein 1998).

THE SENATE VOTES ON ENDA

Speaking in support of the bill, Senator Chuck Robb, Democrat from Virginia, stressed that the decision to end discrimination should not be a difficult one. He urged his colleagues to remember that "each American worker—whether they build houses, pave roads, serve meals in country diners, or manage corporations—deserves to be judged by their dedication to their job and the quality of their work. It is indefensible," he added, "that in a great country like ours men and women can lose their jobs, be passed over for promotions, or suffer harassment because they have—or are perceived to have—a different sexual orientation than the rest of us" (*Congressional Record* 1996, S10131).

After Kennedy threatened to introduce ENDA as an amendment to DOMA, he reached an agreement with Senate majority leader Lott to vote on each bill separately, with no amendments permitted on either. DOMA was voted on first, winning by an overwhelming majority of 85–14. ENDA sponsors had hoped that pairing it with DOMA would help pass ENDA because it would allow senators to take the popular election-year position against same-sex marriage and then demonstrate their fairness with a positive vote on ENDA immediately after. Jeffords, who voted for both bills, said, "People don't want to go too far on changing marriage and traditional relationships. But the feeling is when someone wants to work someplace, they ought to be able to get a job" (*New York Times* September 11, 1996). The strategy almost succeeded as thirty-five senators who voted for DOMA also voted for ENDA. But, in the end, although the victory would have been pleasant, it would not have mattered a great deal, for whatever the outcome in the Senate, the House was very unlikely to put ENDA to a vote that year (*Congressional Quarterly* September 13, 1996, 2597).

After a two-day Senate debate, a vote was taken on September 10, 1996. Vice President Al Gore was ready to interrupt his campaign schedule to cast the deciding vote in case of a tie, but the vote was 50–49 against the bill. David Pryor, Democrat from Arkansas, who had indicated he "probably" would support the bill, was not present to cast the tie vote; he was in Little Rock for his son's cancer surgery (*Congressional Quarterly* September 13, 1996, 2597). Forty-one Democrats and eight Republicans voted in favor; five Democrats and forty-five Republicans voted no.

Elizabeth Birch, executive director of HRC, commenting on the vote, delivered an upbeat message: "We came within a breath of victory today [and] we'll hit the ground running in the 105th Congress," she said (*New York Times* September 11, 1996). More generally, she declared, "we have witnessed gay civil rights in the 1990s completely embraced by the civil rights community in general [and] have firmly established that it is no longer a question of whether Congress will pass the employment non-discrimination act for gay Americans. It's a question of when" (*Congressional Quarterly* September 13, 1996, 2597).

Birch's optimism seemed misplaced. ENDA was introduced again in the House in June 1997 (the first session of the 105th Congress) as H.R. 1858 by Christopher Shays, Republican from Connecticut. Again, although the number of sponsors had increased to 160 and it was referred to several committees, no further action followed. In the Senate, Jeffords sponsored the Senate version, S. 869, and it was sent to the Senate Labor and Human Resources Committee, where hearings were held, but again no action resulted.

Over the next several years, versions of ENDA were introduced in both the Senate and House, but although the law gained support over the years—

in part because it was moderated to please conservatives—it never again received a vote on the floor of either house of Congress.[56] Perhaps with the new majority party in Congress as a result of the 2006 election, a new version of ENDA might be introduced again (see Wood 2003).

THE PRESIDENT ACTS

Two years after the "gays in the military" debacle ended, Clinton addressed the issue of gay rights by signing an executive order to clarify access to classified information. Signed on August 2, 1995, Executive Order No. 12968 prohibits the government from discriminating on the basis of sexual orientation in determining an individual's eligibility for receiving classified information (Clinton 1995a).[57]

Clinton (1995b) also came out in support of ENDA in 1995, sending a letter of endorsement to Kennedy on October 19, 1995. "Those who face this kind of job discrimination have no legal recourse, in either state or Federal courts," Mr. Clinton wrote. "This is wrong." He also sent his aide, George Stephanopoulos, to announce his support for it in a speech at a meeting of the National Association of Gay and Lesbian Journalists (see *Boston Globe* October 20, 1995; *Washington Post* October 20, 1995; *New York Times* October 20, 1995).

When asked about ENDA a year later during the second presidential debate shortly after the vote was taken in the Senate, Clinton simply said, "I'm for it. That's my policy. I'm for it. I believe that any law-abiding, tax-paying citizen who shows up in the morning and doesn't break the law and doesn't interfere with his or her neighbors ought to have the ability to work in our country and shouldn't be subject to unfair discrimination. I'm for it" (Clinton 1996). He continued making statements in support of ENDA, urging its passage again in 1997, saying it "is about the right of each individual in America to be judged on their merits and abilities and to be allowed to contribute to society without facing unfair discrimination on account of sexual orientation. It is about our ongoing fight against bigotry and intolerance, in our country and in our hearts" (Clinton 1997).

With congressional action on ENDA stalled, on May 28, 1998, Clinton issued an executive order banning discrimination in the federal workforce. Including sexual orientation within the prohibited areas of discrimination by the federal government, Clinton said that Executive Order No. 13087 "provides for a uniform policy for the Federal Government to prohibit discrimination based on sexual orientation in the Federal civilian workforce and states that policy for the first time in an Executive order of the President" (Clinton 1998a).[58] Although some members of the House attempted to undermine Clinton's executive order, they were unsuccessful (see Clinton 1998b).

THE PUBLIC'S VIEW

The inability to attract enough support for ENDA is somewhat surprising given the fact that the public strongly supports such a law. A Harris Interactive/Witeck-Combs Communications (2001) poll posed the question in a June 2001 survey "In mid-June, a federal law called the Employment Non-Discrimination Act will be considered that will prohibit job discrimination on the basis of sexual orientation. A law of this type currently does not exist. Do you favor or oppose this law?" By more than a 2–1 majority (58–27 percent), heterosexual respondents said they favor it.

The survey also asked, "Would you favor or oppose a federal law to prohibit job discrimination on the basis of sexual orientation?" Fifty-nine percent of heterosexual respondents said they would favor it, and only 21 percent were opposed. When the question was worded slightly differently— "In most jurisdictions in the United States, a person can be fired from their job for being gay or lesbian. Would you favor or oppose a federal law to prohibit discrimination on the grounds of sexual orientation?"—the percent of heterosexuals saying they would favor such a law was 57 percent, with 31 percent opposing. Ironically, almost half (42 percent) of all adults thought that a law banning job discrimination on the grounds of sexual orientation already existed.

In a study of workplace attitudes toward gays and lesbians from 2002 to 2004, Harris Interactive/Witeck-Combs Communications (2004) reported that when heterosexual adults were asked about job benefits for gay couples, each year slightly over three in five respondents "strongly" or "somewhat agreed" with the statement "Regardless of their sexual orientation, all employees are entitled to equal benefits on the job, such as health insurance for their partners or spouses."

The survey also found that the job climate was becoming less chilly for gays and lesbians. In 2002 when heterosexual adults were asked to respond to the statement "I would be uncomfortable if my boss were openly gay, lesbian, bisexual or transgender," 43 percent either "strongly" or "somewhat disagree[d]." A year later, 47 percent either "strongly" or "somewhat disagree[d]" with the statement, and in 2004, 49 percent "strongly" or "somewhat disagree[d]" that they would be "uncomfortable" with an "openly gay" boss. Moreover, when they were asked to react to the statement "I would be uncomfortable if any of my co-workers were openly gay, lesbian, bisexual or transgender," in 2002, 50 percent of the heterosexual respondents either "strongly" or "somewhat disagree[d]." In 2003 and 2004, the percent "strongly" or "somewhat disagree[ing]" had risen to 54 percent. Thus, by 2004, the majority of workers seemed to believe that sexual orientation was not a workplace concern.

Similarly, comparing the responses over time to the statement "How an employee does his or her job should be the standard for judging an employee, not their sexual orientation," in 2002, 77 percent of heterosexual respondents either "strongly" or "somewhat agree[d]." In 2003 and 2004, as many as 80 percent either "strongly" or "somewhat agree[d]" with the view that employees should not be judged on the bases of their sexual orientation.

Data from a Gallup (2005b) poll also show that by 2005, there was considerable agreement that "homosexuals should have equal rights in terms of job opportunities." In 1977, a slight majority (56 percent) of the respondents agreed gays should have equal rights; however, over the next two decades, based on the same question, a May 2005 survey found that support for equal rights had risen to 87 percent. When questioned about whether homosexuals should be hired for specific jobs, support was weakest for hiring gays as elementary school teachers (54 percent) and the clergy (49 percent). But substantial majorities agreed they should be doctors, high school teachers, salespeople, members of the armed forces, and even serve on the president's cabinet.

NOTES

1. Witeck-Combs Communications is a public relations and marketing firm that specializes in the GLBT market.

2. See Eskridge (1999, appendix B2) for local jurisdictions prohibiting discrimination on the basis of sexual orientation in public or private employment.

3. In 1975, Minneapolis became the first jurisdiction to adopt an ordinance against transgender discrimination. By 2006, according to the Transgender Law and Policy Institute (2006), seven states and a total of eighty-seven cities and counties had enacted laws prohibiting discrimination on the basis of gender identity (see Ekeberg and Tumber 2004).

4. See Fisk (1998) for the effect of the federal Employee Retirement Income Security Act (ERISA) on domestic partner benefits.

5. Michael Bowers, Georgia's attorney general, offered Robin Sharar a job in his office and withdrew it after learning of her same-sex "marriage" ceremony. The dis-

trict court dismissed her suit, and a panel of the Eleventh Circuit reversed, ordering Bowers to show he had a compelling interest to justify his action because her First Amendment right was involved.

On a rehearing en banc, over the dissent of four judges who accused the majority of ignoring the high court's reasoning in *Romer*, the circuit court agreed that her wedding would have affected her "credibility" and "interfered with the Department's ability to handle certain kinds of controversial matters" respecting gay people as well as "creat[ing] other difficulties within the Department which would be likely to harm the public perception of the Department" (*Sharar* 1997, 1105). The court found that the attorney general's interest in hiring an assistant attorney general in whom he had "trust" outweighed her First Amendment right to express herself in a same-sex marriage ceremony. The dissent argued that Bowers's actions arose from animus, which the Court had held in *Romer* was unacceptable.

6. States with laws prohibiting discrimination on the basis of sexual orientation are California, Connecticut, Hawaii, Illinois, Maine, Maryland, Massachusetts, Minnesota, Nevada, New Hampshire, New Jersey, New Mexico, New York, Rhode Island, Vermont, Washington, and Wisconsin as well as the District of Columbia (Human Rights Campaign 2006a).

7. This view is widely shared by all respondents; although Democrats and Independents were 85 percent in favor, 82 percent of Republicans also agreed (PollingReport.com 2006b).

8. The Court held in *Hopkins* (1989) that after a Title VII plaintiff proved that gender was a "motivating" factor in an employment decision, an employer must show that it would have made the same adverse decision even if it had not considered the employee's gender (244).

9. It makes matter worse that courts often confuse "sex" and "gender." Sex refers to biological or physical characteristics, gender to social roles, commonly identified as "masculine" and "feminine" behavior.

10. The ruling does not indicate whether Oncale is gay as the Court held that Title VII encompasses same-sex harassment.

11. The Supreme Court denied certiorari in *MGM Grand Hotel, Inc. v. Rene* (2003).

12. After the Supreme Court granted certiorari in *Dew* (1964a), the government reinstated him, thereby mooting the case (Cain 2000, 106–7). The Court dismissed the writ in *Dew* (1964b).

13. The appellate court ordered that Scott be considered an eligible applicant for a civil service position unless there was further evidence against him. The pattern essentially repeated itself when, in a subsequent interview, he again explained the circumstances of the arrests and addressed other evidence against him but refused to respond to a question about whether he had ever engaged in homosexual acts. He was again disqualified, this time presumably for his failure to answer questions, and he filed suit. The district court upheld the agency. With Judge McGowan now writing the majority opinion, the appellate court again reversed the lower court (*Scott* 1968).

14. The Society for Individual Rights (SIR) and the plaintiff had also sought to have the lawsuit certified as a class action consisting of all federal employees in his position. The judge refused to certify the class on the grounds that it was too broad. He did not feel that the civil service should be absolutely barred from terminating homosexuals if their job performances were affected, but he agreed to certify a narrower class of individuals who were terminated on the grounds that they might cause potential embarrassment for the agency. The Ninth Circuit upheld the denial of class relief (*Hampton* 1975).

15. The standards of unsuitability in 5 C.F.R. Part 73 have been revised over time; the word *immoral* was initially dropped in 1975, and the current definition of *unsuitability* in 5 C.F.R. §731.202(b)(2) is "criminal or dishonest conduct."

16. The letter specified that he was being dismissed because he had "flaunted and broadcast" his homosexuality. It also stated that the commission considered the

> potential disruption of service efficiency because of the possible revulsion of other employees to homosexual conduct and/or their apprehension of sexual advances and solicitations; the hazard that the prestige and authority of a Government position will be used to foster homosexual activity, particularly among the youth; the possible use of Government funds and authority in furtherance of conduct offensive to the mores and law of our society; and the possible embarrassment to, and loss of public confidence in your agency and the Federal civil service." (*Singer* 1976, 250 n3)

17. The court applied the rules in place when he had been fired, although suggesting that the outcome would be the same under the new rules. Singer appealed to the Supreme Court, which granted certiorari (*Singer* 1977) and vacated the lower court judgment, remanding the case to the Ninth Circuit for reconsideration in light of the new policy as stated by the solicitor general in his brief to the high court (see Eskridge 1999).

18. The court considered its decision consistent with *Pickering v. Board of Education of Township High School District 205* (1968, 568), in which the United States Supreme Court held that "the State has interests as an employer in regulating the speech of its employees that differ significantly from those it possesses in connection with regulation of the speech of the citizenry in general. The problem in any case is to arrive at a balance between the interests of the teacher, as a citizen, in commenting upon matters of public concern and the interest of the State, as an employer, in promoting the efficiency of the public services it performs through its employees."

19. Law schools were also involved in challenging the military's policy toward gays in *Rumsfeld v. Forum for Academic and Institutional Rights, Inc.* (2006), discussed in the previous chapter.

20. Because *Bowers* likely foreclosed winning on privacy and due process grounds, she did not raise these claims on appeal (Cain 2000, 186–7).

21. In 1990, about four million (of a total federal workforce of eight million) workers held government security clearances; one and a half million of these worked for federal contractors (M. Lewis 1990, 142).

22. In *Greene*, a case revolving around a security clearance of an alleged communist sympathizer, the Court held that, absent authorization from Congress or the president to the contrary, the security clearance procedure must incorporate an opportunity for the applicant to examine evidence and confront witnesses.

23. The Supreme Court denied certiorari in *Adams* (1970).

24. William Miller (2004) discusses the process of acquiring security clearances.

25. Under §7532(a) of the Civil Service Reform Act of 1978, an employee may not appeal the denial of a security clearance; §7513(d) of the act allows an employee to seek review from the MSPB following a termination for cause. Egan argued he was entitled to a MSPB hearing because the government had proceeded against him under §7513.

26. The Administrative Procedure Act, 5 U.S.C. §706(2)(A), requires courts to "hold unlawful and set aside agency action, findings, and conclusions found to be arbitrary, capricious, an abuse of discretion, or otherwise not in accordance with law."

27. 5 U.S.C. §7532(a), originally passed in 1950 and codified in 1966, applies to the Departments of State, Commerce, Justice, Defense; the Coast Guard; the Atomic Energy Commission; the National Aeronautics and Space Administration; and other agencies designated by the president; it provides that "the head of an agency may suspend without pay an employee of his agency when he considers that action necessary in the interests of national security." Under §7532(b), the head of an agency may "remove" the suspended employee if it is determined that "that removal is necessary or advisable in the interests of national security." Section 7532(c) specifies the proper procedures for the agency to follow, including a preremoval hearing.

28. The NSA Personnel Security Procedure Act of 1964, 50 U.S.C. §§831–833, allows the secretary of defense to discharge employees on national security grounds. The NSA did not rely on this statute in removing Doe.

29. The secretary of defense delegated appointment power to the NSA director as permitted by the 1959 act. The Court ruled that the power to remove is inherent in the power to appoint.

30. The CIA is not subject to the Civil Service Reform Act, the Veterans Preference Act, or the Administrative Procedure Act (Maravilla 2001, 785).

31. As the circuit court explained, the pseudonym was used because of the plaintiff's covert position, not because of his desire to hide his sexual orientation (*Doe v. Casey* 1986, 1512 n2).

32. The National Security Act of 1947, 50 U.S.C. §§401–406, established the National Security Council and the Central Intelligence Agency. Section 403(c) provides that

"the Director of Central Intelligence may, in his discretion, terminate the employment of any officer or employee of the Agency whenever he shall deem such termination necessary or advisable in the interests of the United States."

33. There are two statutory exceptions to judicial review under the APA: 5 U.S.C.
§701(a) provides that agency actions are subject to judicial review "except to the
extent that—(1) statutes preclude judicial review; or (2) agency action is committed to agency discretion by law."

34. Because the DCI's reasons for firing Doe were unclear, the court remanded
the case to the lower court.

35. O'Connor concurred in the first part of the opinion but wrote separately to
disagree with the last part. In her view, Congress intended to foreclose the courts
from interfering with the director's authority over discharges even when constitutional claims have been raised. Scalia dissented, expressing the same view. Kennedy
took no part in the decision.

36. In *Doe v. Schachter* (1992, 58), California district court judge Patel held that
the federal courts also have power to review constitutional challenges to national
security decisions made under delegated authority from the president.

37. The Supreme Court denied certiorari in *Doe v. Woolsey* (1993).

38. Her job required her to obtain a Top Secret clearance as well as Sensitive
Compartment Information clearance (SCI), the latter from the CIA. The DoD
granted her security clearance, but the CIA denied her the SCI clearance.

39. The lower court ruling had preceded *Webster*.

40. In *Dorfmont v. Brown* (1990, 1404), not a gay rights case, the Ninth Circuit
held that the plaintiff did not have a "colorable constitutional claim" that she was
denied due process when her security clearance was revoked by the Department of
Defense.

41. On remand, the district court denied the government's motion to dismiss
Dubbs's amended complaint. He ordered the parties to conference and suggested a
separate trial on whether the CIA has a policy of rejecting all gays for security clearances (*Dubbs* 1990).

42. The suit was by filed by an organization of gays working in defense industry
jobs.

43. In this lawsuit, the plaintiffs did not claim that the DoD unfairly denies gays
and lesbians the requested security clearances.

44. Goldman (2005) argues that *Lawrence* requires the Ninth Circuit to declare
gays a suspect class.

45. He was told only of the Foreign Service's "no fraternization" policy, which was
much more relaxed than the USIA's.

46. Since the court affirmed the summary judgment in the government's favor,
there was no trial on the merits. The Supreme Court denied certiorari in *Krc v.
United States Information Agency* (1994).

47. The lower court decision in *Krc* preceded the lower court ruling in *Buttino*.

48. Despite extensive searching for cases citing *Hi Tech Gays*, *Webster*, *Dubbs*, *Krc*, and *Buttino*, no later opinions regarding gays and security clearances were turned up after *Krc*. There were a number of cases related to the military's policy toward gays, but the issue of security clearances, which had been the subject of significant litigation in the 1980s and early 1990s, was no longer in the courts. Clinton's 1995 executive order barring the government from discriminating on the basis of sexual orientation in access to classified information appears to have obviated the need for litigation.

49. Abzug's bill would have made it illegal to discriminate on the basis of sexual orientation or marital status in private employment or education. It also proposed to extend civil rights protection to women by making it illegal to discriminate on the basis of sex or marital status in public accommodations, federally assisted programs, or public facilities (Feldblum 2000). There is still no federal law banning discrimination in public accommodations on the basis of sex or marital status.

50. There were also attempts to amend the Fair Housing Act to include discrimination on the basis of sexual orientation.

51. The bill was first introduced in the Senate in 1979, the first session of the 96th Congress (Endean 2006).

52. Feldblum (2000) notes that the civil rights community would not have supported an amendment to existing civil rights legislation because of the danger it would pose to those laws. Jasiunas (2000) argues that passing the antidiscrimination law as a stand-alone statute, rather than as an amendment to Title VII, made it a less potent weapon in the fight against discrimination.

53. Section 4 provided that "a covered entity, in connection with employment or employment opportunities, shall not—
   (1) subject an individual to a different standard or different treatment on the basis of sexual orientation;
   (2) discriminate against an individual based on the sexual orientation of a person with whom such individual is believed to associate or to have associated; or
   (3) otherwise discriminate against an individual on the basis of sexual orientation."

54. Suits for injunctive relief and money damages were permitted, but unlike Title VII, claims for disparate impact, that is, claims that challenge a neutral employment practice with a disproportionate impact on homosexual or bisexual individuals, were barred.

55. Section 11 of the bill gave the EEOC the same power to enforce and administer Title VII; under Title VII, the EEOC collects statistics on race and gender. The bill was silent on the subject, but the concern was that the EEOC might undertake to collect statistics on sexual orientation.

56. Later versions prohibited the EEOC from gathering statistics or ordering covered entities to collect statistics and exempted organizations such as the Boy Scouts from its reach.

57. Part 3, §3.1(c) specifies that "the United States Government does not discriminate on the basis of race, color, religion, sex, national origin, disability, or sexual orientation in granting access to classified information." Section 3.1(d) states that "no inference concerning the standards in this section may be raised solely on the basis of the sexual orientation of the employee."

58. Clinton's new order amended the existing Executive Order No. 11478.

CHAPTER 6

Conclusion

THROUGHOUT the 1970s and 1980s, the gay community mobilized as a civil rights movement, emulating many of the strategies and tactics of earlier social movements by devoting significant resources to advancing their goals though litigation. Taken together, their legal challenges to the laws and policies that restricted their rights and choices asked the courts to ensure that they were given the opportunity to conduct their lives with the same degree of dignity, equality, and privacy expected by the heterosexual world. Most of the litigation sought to apply federal constitutional guarantees of equal protection, due process, free expression, and privacy; in some cases, primarily challenges to marriage restrictions, litigants requested that the courts enforce state constitutional protections.

In turning to the courts, the gay community has asked the state and federal judiciary, primarily the latter, to strike state sodomy and obscenity laws that stigmatized them and treated their desires and interests as outside the range of acceptable behavior; to enforce laws against discrimination in employment, housing, and public accommodations; to permit them to share the benefits and responsibilities of civil marriage that other citizens take for granted; to allow them to serve in the military without additional restrictions; to avoid blanket condemnation as national security risks; and to guarantee their right to participate as equal members of private organizations and groups. In their efforts to achieve these goals, they needed to convince the courts to approach laws discriminating on the basis of sexual orientation as they do laws discriminating on the basis of sex and race, or failing that, to convince the courts that laws distinguishing among persons on the basis of sexual orientation are based on stereotypes and bias and thus are irrational. As the cases indicate, however, with few exceptions, the courts consistently refused to equate discrimination against gays with discrimination against racial minorities or women.

SUPREME COURT LITIGATION

One of the earliest incidents of litigation activity in the United States Supreme Court to secure gay rights began in the 1950s with a challenge to the actions of the United States Postal Service in confiscating the magazine *One*. Although it eventually ended well for the magazine, this case and others like it reflected society's distaste for material considered deviant and abnormal—out the mainstream. In keeping with the general expansion of First Amendment principles during the Warren Court era, the justices of the United States Supreme Court gradually grew tired of their role as the nation's censors and eased restrictions on obscenity regulations, including regulations on literature aimed at a gay audience. However, although the litigation benefited the gay community, the Court did not focus on the harm done them; nor did it spend a great deal of time dwelling on the fact that the majority was imposing its view of appropriate reading material on members of a minority group. Rather the decision in *One* and others like it evolved from the Court's desire to constrain the government's authority to censor the films and books available to the general population.

The next focus of litigation activity was on state sodomy laws. During the nation's history, most states criminalized sodomy; some laws were neutral as to sexual orientation, some were specifically aimed at homosexual conduct. Gradually, most states began to abolish these laws. In any event, even with the laws on the books, they were rarely enforced: Arrests were few and prosecutions even fewer. Nevertheless, the existence of sodomy laws played an important role in subjugating the gay community. Among other things, they justified the harassment and arrest of gays for generic crimes such as disturbing the peace and loitering and led to police records that were used against them in employment and family law disputes.

In the latter part of the 1980s, the arrest of a Georgia man for violating the state sodomy law prompted the gay community to challenge its constitutionality in the United States Supreme Court. The Court's ruling in *Bowers* rejected the litigants' argument that the right of privacy extends to same-sex sodomy, thereby upholding the state's authority to enforce its vision of morality. Although the Georgia law applied to sodomy without regard to the sex of the participants, by framing the issue in this way, the Court was able to avoid the broader question of whether to interpret the Fourteenth

Amendment to protect the individual's right to make choices in private relations. As it turned out, both the reasoning and the outcome of the case
demonstrated the error of the litigation strategy. Ironically, a little more than
a decade later, the Georgia Supreme Court struck the sodomy law on the
basis of the state constitution's privacy clause.

A decade later, the *Romer* Court came closest to acting in a countermajoritarian manner by overturning a policy supported by state lawmakers and
a majority of the voters. The antigay message that resonated with the majority of Colorado's voters was that Amendment 2 was necessary to eliminate
the "special rights" that gays had achieved through their undue influence on
local governments. Despite the fact that Amendment 2 represented an
expression of voter preference, the Court struck it, rejecting the concept of
"special rights," and finding the policy most likely motivated by "animosity"
toward members of the gay community. Nevertheless, the Court moved cautiously in *Romer*. Although it disapproved of the "special rights rhetoric" and
struck Amendment 2 despite its popular support, it declined to extend
heightened scrutiny to laws affecting sexual orientation. In applying minimal scrutiny to the Colorado policy, the Court refused to include gays and
lesbians within the category of oppressed minority groups that require special protection from the courts.

In allowing laws affecting gays to be justified with the lowest level of
scrutiny, the Court exercised judicial restraint. *Romer* demonstrated that the
Court was willing to advance gay rights but wanted to stop short of protecting gays from less blatantly discriminatory policies than Colorado's.
Overall, despite their victory over the antigay forces in Colorado, gay rights
litigants were not accorded the same degree of protection from the majority as the Court has accorded other minority groups.

Whether *Romer* should be classified as countermajoritarian is uncertain, for although Amendment 2 was supported by a majority of Colorado
voters, a national survey conducted a few years after the decision showed
that the belief that there were too many laws protecting gays and lesbians
represented a minority view. Thus, in striking a policy supported by a local
majority, *Romer* appeared consistent with public opinion on a national level.

Almost twenty years after *Bowers*, with much of the personnel on the
Court new since 1986, the Court revisited the issue it had decided in *Bowers*.
Lawrence required the Court to reaffirm *Bowers* or acknowledge it as a bad
decision and overturn it. In choosing the latter course, the Court upheld the
rights of gays and lesbians to conduct their intimate affairs in private, to the
same degree as heterosexuals. In conflating due process and equal protection

analysis, however, the Court avoided revisiting its decision in *Romer* that laws implicating sexual orientation are not entitled to a higher form of scrutiny. The Court was also careful to limit the decision to the facts of the case and clearly spell out other areas of intimate association to which the ruling did not apply.

Nevertheless, at the time, *Lawrence* was a great victory for the gay community, vindicating the litigants' decision to urge the Court to reassess its decision in *Bowers*. Did it fuel the flames about the Court's countermajoritarianism? Although overriding the policy decisions of Texas lawmakers, national public opinion polls showed that the ruling was consistent with the majority's position on the right of privacy at the time. *Lawrence* also confounds the definition of judicial activism. Overturning state law and substituting the Court's view for the state legislature's suggest activism, but in reflecting national public opinion, the Court did not override the views of the people, one of the criteria of activist decision making.

These three Supreme Court cases in which the high court adjudicated the constitutionality of the Georgia, Texas, and Colorado laws illustrate the complexity in determining whether litigation is an effective tool for achieving social policy reform and whether the Court rightfully deserves being depicted as a countermajoritarian institution. Overall, the litigation proved effective in two of the three cases, and, in those two cases, the decisions reflected general agreement with the mood of the nation. These cases also indicate that countermajoritarianism is not unidimensional. Although the Court overturned state laws and thus negated the decisions of the subnational policymakers and in one case, the sentiments of a majority of the state's citizens, it did so in concert with the views of majority public opinion in the nation. Taken together, these cases suggest that a litigation strategy can be effective but also indicate that the Court is unwilling to take bold steps to advance the cause of equal rights for gays.

LITIGATION IN THE LOWER FEDERAL COURTS

Although discussions of countermajoritarianism usually focus on Supreme Court cases, the lower federal courts, and more recently, the state courts, have also been labeled as judicial activists and portrayed as running roughshod over coordinate policymakers and the views of the public. Given the paucity of cases decided by the Supreme Court over the last fifty years, the inquiry into judicial activism and efficacy must expand to include the state and lower federal courts as well.

Many gays and lesbians experience employment discrimination at some time in their working lives, especially in the fields of education and law enforcement. Overall, however, it appears that attempts to diminish discrimination on the job have been fairly successful over time. Over the last several decades, numerous state and local governments have added discrimination on the basis of sexual orientation to their list of prohibited behaviors. Indeed, a few localities have taken the lead in creating domestic partner benefits and, in at least one city, mandating that city contractors provide such benefits as well. Thus, despite some incidents of backlash, the gay community has been generally successful in establishing a norm of fair employment practices in the nation, an accomplishment that speaks to the efficacy of local mobilizing efforts to secure equal rights.

Laws banning employment discrimination at the state and local level did not, however, translate into equal opportunity for federal workers. For the most part, litigation was necessary to achieve this goal. The federal lawsuits challenging discriminatory practices in federal employment have had mixed success. For the most part, federal judges have been unwilling to read Title VII's prohibition on sex discrimination broadly enough to apply it to discrimination on the basis of sexual orientation. Moreover, at least in the early cases, the courts were reluctant to contravene the judgment of the federal Civil Service Commission that homosexual workers were detrimental to the efficiency of the service. Gradually, however, a number of judges began to require proof of these assertions and demand evidence of the effect of homosexuality on job performance. Finding the commission unable to back up its stereotypical views of gays, the courts brought about a change in the discriminatory employment practices to which federal civilian employees had been subjected.

In reforming the federal civil service, however, the courts often drew the line at interfering with employment decisions that implicated national security concerns. Not dismissing their claims outright, the courts adjudicated plaintiffs' constitutional challenges to policies that they claimed were discriminatory, but chiefly limited their review to ensuring procedural fairness. Most courts hesitated to override the determinations by national security and federal law enforcement agencies that homosexuals constituted security risks. Although some lower court judges believed that this classification on the basis of sexual orientation merited a higher form of scrutiny and that blanket characterization of gays as security risks was discriminatory, they were constrained by precedent to uphold the policies. In deferring to agency judgments to grant or deny security clearances because they believed they lacked the expertise to assess the merits of the decision, the courts often helped perpetuate the stereotypical view of gays as immoral, untrustworthy, and vulnerable to blackmail.

With the exception of cases related to national security issues, the courts' rulings in employment cases were generally consistent with the actions of coordinate policymakers at the state and federal level. Although Congress never matched the acts of the subnational governments in prohibiting employment discrimination, it came within only one vote of enacting ENDA, a national antidiscrimination policy. Additionally, President Clinton, elected with the votes of a majority of the gay electorate, promulgated two executive orders, one banning consideration of sexual orientation in the federal workforce and the other removing it as a factor in national security decision making. Moreover, surveys show that the public as a whole is much opposed to allowing sexual orientation to play a role in employment decisions.

In sum, for the most part, litigation proved effective in helping to achieve the goal of equal opportunity in employment, but in striking discriminatory employment policies, judicial decision making was consistent with the views of the public and the actions of other policymaking institutions. Thus, the litigation strategy was a good one, but so was the strategy of pursuing other types of political activity, including lobbying and public education. Far from countermajoritarian, for the most part, the courts' rulings reflect the broad societal consensus that it is inappropriate to allow sexual orientation to be factored into employment decisions.

The successful litigation in the area of employment has not been reflected in the federal court decisions involving the military's restrictions on gays. Here, despite strong public support for allowing gays and lesbians to serve openly in the military, the courts have been firmly opposed, exhibiting the greatest degree of judicial restraint of all the cases in this inquiry.

Following the lead of the Supreme Court, the lower courts expressed awareness of the obligation to adhere to precedent and principles of separation of powers and defer to the military's judgment and expertise. However, in acquiescing in the government's judgment that excluding gay military personnel would help maintain morale, good order, and discipline, the courts largely abdicated their constitutional duty.

In challenging the restrictions imposed by the military, both before and after the implementation of "Don't Ask, Don't Tell," litigants found that appeals to constitutional claims based on principles of equality, due process, privacy, and free expression were largely ineffective when viewed through the lens of judicial deference to the military. They argued that the courts must distinguish between homosexual conduct and homosexual orientation. In case after case, the plaintiffs urged the courts to apply heightened scrutiny to the government's policy, attempting to convince the judges that gays were an oppressed minority group deserving of special judicial protection, and rationality was an insufficient justification for polices that were motivated by bigotry. For the most part, they failed to do so as the courts accepted the government's judgment that homosexuality was a legitimate bar to military service.

A few judges, chiefly in the district courts, but also in the Ninth and District of Columbia Circuits, acknowledged their duty to defer to the military's expertise and judgment, yet supported the litigants' attempts to advance their constitutional rights. However, in the end the plaintiffs in these courts did not prevail because the judges' expansive interpretations of equal protection and due process were either in dissenting or concurring opinions or were overturned on appeal. No circuit accepted the argument that the military has breached the constitutional rights of gay service members.

By ruling that military policymaking should be left to the democratic process and refusing to interfere with the government's policy toward gays in the military, the courts have effectively removed themselves from the policy arena, making litigation in this area futile.

STATE COURT LITIGATION

Throughout the 1990s, the state courts plainly demonstrated their reluctance to interfere with the legislative prerogative to define marriage. Their concern that they would be labeled activists led them to reject the demands of gay rights advocates to strike restrictive marriage laws. The cost of their restraint was abnegation of their duty to adjudicate properly presented constitutional claims. Had the courts similarly deferred to legislative judgments in the social reform litigation campaigns of the 1950s, 1960s, and 1970s, the nation's progress in racial and gender relations would have been drastically slowed.

After their fleeting victories in Hawaii and Alaska, the first real success for gay rights advocates in the legal battle against same-sex marriage laws occurred in Vermont. Perhaps because the court did not mandate the legalization of same-sex marriage, the reactions by opponents were somewhat subdued. The decision in Massachusetts that shook the nation in 2003 precipitated a range of reactions from hope that other state courts would follow the lead of that state's supreme court to fear that they would.

Assessing three decades of litigation against state marriage policies shows that the judiciary's support for same-sex marriage has been mixed, with most judges anxious to avoid accusations of judicial overreaching and interference with the legislative domain. Given their willingness to defer to the legislature's judgments, the wisdom of pursuing a rights-based litigation strategy might appear questionable. However, as this study indicates, based on the actions of a few state courts, advocates of same-sex marriage have generally fared better among the state judiciary than in other policymaking venues—at the state or federal level. When given an opportunity, the other branches of government have been almost uniformly antagonistic to same-sex marriage, endeavoring to block implementation of judicial rulings and ensure that restrictions on it remain firmly in place. And in their efforts to maintain the status quo, these lawmakers have often sought and obtained support from the public.

Opinion polls indicate that although the public appears to have become more accepting of same-sex marriage, it is still largely unwilling to accept it. And although most do not view a constitutional amendment at the federal level as a necessary weapon to combat it, most voters have indicated over and over again at the polls that they are unwilling to sanction same-sex marriage within their borders.

Despite the rhetoric suggesting that activist judges are waiting to overturn state marriage policies, the reality is quite different. Most courts have been unwilling to interpose themselves in the policy debate by contravening the decisions of the coordinate policymakers or frustrating the will of the people that is evidenced in their strong support for constitutional amendments or statutory bans on same-sex marriage. But as the Massachusetts Supreme Judicial Court majority explained, the court's duty to interpret the state charter required it to declare the state's restrictions on same-sex marriage an unconstitutional infringement on the right of citizens to engage in a fundamental right. And, it believed, its obligation to protect the rights of the minority must be satisfied, regardless of the contrary wishes of a majority.

GAY RIGHTS IN COURT

Most Americans are opposed to discrimination in employment, are shocked by hate crimes, and are willing to allow same-sex couples to benefit from some sort of domestic partner arrangements. Yet gay rights advocates suffered significant losses in the public policy arena over the last several decades, as seen in the restrictions on gays in the military, the passage of the Defense of Marriage Act in 1996, Congress's failure to enact antidiscrimination legislation, and the ongoing struggle over same-sex marriage. These contradictions suggest that the nation has still not come to terms with its gay citizens, and the debate over homosexuality is, and will likely continue to be, a maelstrom in the U.S. political system in the near future.

This book has shown that the struggle for equality and ending discrimination on the basis of sexual orientation has met substantial resistance throughout the last five decades. Gay rights victories propelled antigay forces into gathering momentum to block new initiatives and reverse those already won. Increasingly, these battles came to resemble a morality play with conservative forces utilizing the progressive symbol of democracy—voter referenda—to create the impression of a battle of the forces of good against the forces of evil.

As the results of the litigation demonstrate, the efforts of gay rights advocates in court were often vitiated by principles of majoritarianism and judicial restraint. The extent to which courts felt obligated to defer to decisions made by the more representative branches of government explains a great deal about the victories and defeats of the gay rights movement in court.

What conclusions about the role of the courts in the struggle for gay rights can be drawn from the evidence presented here? The cases demonstrate that sizeable resources have been expended to pursue gay rights litigation. Was such a decision wise, and did the litigation help to further gay rights claims for equality, privacy, and tolerance?

The study has been guided by two overarching questions: First, it has asked whether and to what extent the courts were an effective instrument in bringing about the social policy reforms the litigators sought. Although the rights-based approach has had its share of critics, in emulating the strategy and tactics of earlier civil rights movements, gay rights activists have actively sought judicial intervention in their struggle for social reform, for the most part by challenging infringements on their right of privacy and equal protection guarantees. In examining the role of the courts in gay rights litigation over the last fifty years, this study has demonstrated that the courts have aided, although certainly not always consistently, in the fight against discrimination on the basis of sexual orientation.

In our system of federalism and separation of powers, it is unlikely that a single institution, especially if forced to operate under the constraints imposed on the judiciary by legal principles and case law, is likely to be fully effective in meeting the demands of a group seeking to change social policy.

Thus, rather than asking whether litigation represents an effective strategy in pursuing gay rights claims, the study has sought to determine whether litigation is a *more* effective means of pursuing policy change than appeals to representative institutions or direct voter action. A succinct answer to the question is a qualified "yes." It is "yes" because the adjudicatory role of the courts allowed them to satisfy the demands of the gay community in a great many instances; but the yes must be qualified because of the realization that the courts were often either unable to or unwilling to do so because of internal or external constraints imposed on them. Many judges clearly showed that they believed that discrimination on the basis of sexual orientation primarily stemmed from bias and a stereotypical view of the gay community. Had their views prevailed, the courts would have been a more effective force in the struggle for gay rights, and the litigation strategy would have been seen as even more efficacious. As it was, with a few exceptions, the courts were more receptive to gay rights claims than other policymakers.

The second question guiding this analysis asked whether and to what extent the courts acted as countermajoritarian institutions in deciding cases brought by the gay rights litigants. This question was answered by assessing the degree to which the courts were willing to negate the policymaking choices of the other branches of government at the state and federal level and the prevailing opinion of the public as reflected in survey data and voting behavior. The analysis showed that the two factors were inversely related. For the most part, when the courts issued countermajoritarian rulings, they were more effective in bringing about social reform changes. The extent to which the courts believed they must defer to the legislative and executive branches of government, as in the military and same-sex marriage cases, diminished their role as instruments of social change.

In sum, this study vindicates those who believe in the strategy of pursuing litigation; often the courts have been the best, if not the only, source of support for the gay community. However, given the constraints on the courts, imposed largely by principles of democracy and majority rule, when they deferred to the policy choices of the other branches of government at both the national and subnational levels, their support for reform diminished. In short, the portrayal of federal and state court judges as judicial activists has often been deserved and, in such cases, has been essential to advancing the interests of the gay community.

ᐅᔥ References

Adam, Barry, D. 1995. *The Rise of A Gay and Lesbian Movement*, rev. ed. Boston: Twayne Publishers.

Aguiar, William M. 1996. Recent Decisions of the United States Court of Appeals for the District of Columbia. *George Washington Law Review* 64: 1091–1102.

Alaska Judicial Appointment Process. 2006, www.state.ak.us/courts/ctinfo.htm#appointment.

Alexander, Sharon E. Debbage. 2002. *Romer v. Evans* and the Amendment 2 Controversy: The Rhetoric and Reality of Sexual Orientation Discrimination in America. *Texas Forum on Civil Liberties and Civil Rights* 6: 261–302.

American Bar Association Section Family Law Working Group on Same Sex Marriages and Non-Marital Unions. 2004. *A White Paper: An Analysis of the Law Regarding Same-Sex Marriage, Civil Unions, and Domestic Partnerships*. Chicago: American Bar Association, www.abanet.org/family/reports/whitepaperfullreport.pdf.

American National Election Studies. 2000. Center for Political Studies, University of Michigan, www.umich.edu/~nes.

———. 2004. Center for Political Studies, University of Michigan, www.umich.edu/~nes.

Andersen, Ellen Ann. 1998. The Stages of Sodomy Reform. *Thurgood Marshall Law Review* 23: 283–319.

———. 2005. *Out of the Closets and into the Courts: Legal Opportunity Structure and Gay Rights Litigation*. Ann Arbor: University of Michigan Press.

Andriote, John-Manual. 2000. The Ryan White Care Act: An Impressive, Dubious Accomplishment. In *Creating Change: Sexuality, Public Policy, and Civil Rights*, ed. John D'Emilio, William B. Turner, and Urvashi Vaid, 407–20. New York: St. Martin's Press.

Association of the Bar of the City of New York, Committee on Sex and Law. 1997. The Employment Non-Discrimination Act. *The Record* 52: 735–46.

Barnard, Thomas H., and Timothy J. Downing. 1999. Emerging Law on Sexual Orientation and Employment. *University of Memphis Law Review* 29: 555–76.

Barnett, James E. 1999. Updating *Romer v. Evans*: The Implications of the Supreme Court's Denial of Certiorari in *Equality Foundation of Greater Cincinnati v. City of Cincinnati*. *Case Western Reserve Law Review* 49: 645–70.

Barth, Jay, and Janine Parry. 2005. Arkansas: Still Swingin' in 2004. *American Review of Politics* 26: 133–54.

Bash, John. 2004. Abandoning Bedrock Principles?: The Musgrave Amendment and Federalism. *Harvard Journal of Law and Public Policy* 27: 985–1013.

Bawer, Bruce. 1994. *New Republic* 210 (June 13): 24–9.

Benecke, Michelle M., and Kirstin S. Dodge. 1996. Military Women: Casualties of the Armed Forces' War on Lesbians and Gay Men. In *Gay Rights, Military Wrongs: Political Perspectives on Lesbians and Gays in the Military*, ed. Craig A. Rimmerman, 71–108. New York: Garland Publishing.

Bernstein, Ryan M. 2004. The Supreme Court Strikes Down Sodomy Statute by Creating New Liberties and Invalidating Old Laws: *Lawrence v. Texas*, 539 U.S. 558 (2003). *North Dakota Law Review* 80: 323–54.

Bianco, David Ari. 1996. Echoes of Prejudice: The Debates over Race and Sexuality in the Armed Forces. In *Gay Rights, Military Wrongs: Political Perspectives on Lesbians and Gays in the Military*, ed. Craig A. Rimmerman, 47–70. New York: Garland Publishing.

Bickel, Alexander, M. 1962. *The Least Dangerous Branch: The Supreme Court at the Bar of Politics*. Indianapolis: Bobbs-Merrill.

Blasius, Mark. 1994. *Gay and Lesbian Politics: Sexuality and the Emergence of a New Ethic*. Philadelphia: Temple University Press.

Bodine, Margot R. 1986. Opening the Schoolhouse Door for Children with AIDS: The Education of All Handicapped Children Act. *Boston College Environmental Affairs Law Review* 13: 583–641.

Borchers, Patrick, J. 2005. The Essential Irrelevance of the Full Faith and Credit Clause to the Same-Sex Marriage Debate. *Creighton Law Review* 38: 353–63.

Bossin, Phyllis. 2005. Same Sex Unions: The New Civil Rights Struggle or an Assault on Traditional Marriage? *Tulsa Law Review* 40: 381–420.

Bowman, Cynthia Grant. 2004. Legal Treatment of Cohabitation in the United States. *Law & Policy* 26: 119–51.

Boykin, Keith. 2000. Where Rhetoric Meets Reality: The Roe of Black Lesbians and Gays in "Queer" Politics. In *The Politics of Gay Rights*, ed. Craig A. Rimmerman, Kenneth D. Wald, and Clyde Wilcox, 79–96. Chicago: University of Chicago Press.

Brennan, William J., Jr. 1986. The Bill of Rights and the States: The Revival of State Constitutions as Guardians of Individual Rights. *New York University Law Review* 61: 535–53.

Brewer, Sarah E., David Kaib, and Karen O'Connor. 2000. Sex and the Supreme Court: Gays, Lesbians, and Justice. In *The Politics of Gay Rights*, ed. Craig A. Rimmerman, Kenneth D. Wald, and Clyde Wilcox, 377–408. Chicago: University of Chicago Press.

Bruce, Teresa M. 1996. Neither Liberty nor Justice: Anti-Gay Initiatives, Political Participation and the Rule of Law. *Cornell Journal of Law and Public Policy* 5: 431–513.

Bush, George, W. 2004a. Address before a Joint Session of the Congress on the State of the Union. *Weekly Compilation of Presidential Documents* (January 20), http://frwais.access.gpo.gov[docid:pd26ja04_txt-10].

———. 2004b. Statement on the Decision of the Massachusetts Supreme Judicial Court on Same-Sex Marriage. *Weekly Compilation of Presidential Documents* (February 4), http://frwais.access.gpo.gov[docid:pd09fe04_txt-14].

———. 2004c. Remarks Calling for a Constitutional Amendment Defining and Protecting Marriage. *Weekly Compilation of Presidential Documents* (February 24), http://frwais.access.gpo.gov[docid:pd01mr04_txt-10].

———. 2004d. Statement Calling for a Constitutional Amendment Defining and Protecting Marriage. *Weekly Compilation of Presidential Documents* (May 17), http://frwais.access.gpo.gov[docid:pd24my04_txt-11].

———. 2006a. President's Radio Address, June 3, 2006, www.whitehouse.gov/news/releases/2006/06/20060603.html.

———. 2006b. Remarks by the President on the Marriage Protection Amendment, June 5, 2006, www.whitehouse.gov/news/releases/2006/06/20060605-2.html.

Button, James W., Barbara A. Rienzo, and Kenneth D. Wald. 1997. *Private Lives, Public Conflicts: Battles over Gay Rights in American Communities*. Washington, DC: Congressional Quarterly Press.

———. 2000. The Politics of Gay Rights at the Local and State Level. In *The Politics of Gay Rights*, ed. Craig A. Rimmerman, Kenneth D. Wald, and Clyde Wilcox, 269–89. Chicago: University of Chicago Press.

Cain, Patricia A. 1993. Litigating for Lesbian and Gay Rights: A Legal history. *Virginia Law Review*. 79: 1551–1641.

———. 2000. *Rainbow Rights: The Role of Lawyers and Courts in the Lesbian and Gay Civil Rights Movement*. Boulder, CO: Westview Press.

Callahan, Colin, and Amelia Kaufman. 2004. Constitutional Law Chapter: Equal Protection. *Georgetown Journal of Gender and the Law* 5: 17–62.

Campbell, Colin C., and Roger H. Davidson. 2000. Gay and Lesbian Issues in the Congressional Arena. In *The Politics of Gay Rights*, ed. Craig A. Rimmerman, Kenneth D. Wald, and Clyde Wilcox, 347–76. Chicago: University of Chicago Press.

Canon, Bradley C., and Charles A. Johnson. 1999. *Judicial Policies: Implementation and Impact*, 2d ed. Washington, DC: Congressional Quarterly Press.

Carter, David. 2004. *Stonewall: The Riots That Sparked the Gay Revolution*. New York: St. Martin's Press.

Casper, Jonathan D. 1976. The Supreme Court and National Policy Making. *American Political Science Review* 70: 50–63.

Cawley, Reuben H. 2004. Sleeping on the Couch: Government Booted from the Bedroom in *Lawrence v. Texas*. *Journal of Law and Family Studies* 6: 127–38.

Chermerinsky, Erwin. 2004. In Defense of Judicial Review: A Reply to Professor Kramer. *California Law Review* 92: 1013–25.

Chermerinsky, Erwin, and Catherine Fisk. 2001. Perspectives on Constitutional Exemptions to Civil Rights Laws: *Boy Scouts of America v. Dale*: The Expressive Interest of Associations. *William and Mary Bill of Rights Journal* 9: 595–617.

Clendinen, Dudley, and Adam Nagourney. 1999. *Out for Good: The Struggle to Build a Gay Rights Movement in America*. New York: Simon and Schuster.

Clinton, Bill. 1993a. Presidential Press Conference on the Military. *William J. Clinton Foundation* (January 29), www.clintonfoundation.org/legacy/012993-presidential-press-conference-on-military.htm.

———. 1993b. Memorandum for the Secretary of Defense on Ending Discrimination on the Basis of Sexual Orientation in the Armed Forces. *Weekly Compilation of Presidential Documents* (February 1), http://frwais.access.gpo.gov[docid:pd01fe93_txt-19].

———. 1993c. Remarks Announcing the New Policy on Gays and Lesbians in the Military. *Weekly Compilation of Presidential Documents* (July 26), http://frwais.access.gpo.gov[docid:pd26jy93_txt-6].

———. 1995a. Executive Order 12968—Access to Classified Information. *Weekly Compilation of Presidential Documents* (August 2), http://frwais.access.gpo.gov [docid:pd07au95_txt-20].

———. 1995b. Letter to Senator Edward M. Kennedy on the "Employment Non-Discrimination Act." *Weekly Compilation of Presidential Documents* (October 19), http://frwais.access.gpo.gov[docid:pd23oc95_txt-17].

———. 1996. Remarks by President at Second Presidential Debate, www.clintonfoundation.org/legacy/101696-remarks-by-president-at-second-presidential-debate.htm.

———. 1997. Remarks by President on Employment Non Discrimination Act (April 24), www.clintonfoundation.org/legacy/042497-remarks-by-president-on-employment-non-discrimination-act.htm.

———. 1998a. Statement on Signing Executive Order on Equal Employment Opportunity in the Federal Government. *Weekly Compilation of Presidential Documents* (May 28), http://frwais.access.gpo.gov[docid:pd01jn98_txt-17].

———. 1998b. Statement on House Action on the Hefley Amendment. *Weekly Compilation of Presidential Documents* (August 6), http://frwais.access.gpo.gov[docid:pd01au98_txt-20].

CNN. 2004a. Ballot Measures (November 3), www.cnn.com/ELECTION/2004/pages/results/ballot.measures/.

———. 2004b. U.S. President/National/Exit Poll (November 3), www.cnn.com/ELECTION/2004/pages/results/states/US/P/00/epolls.0.html.

———2006. Key Ballot Measures (November 8), www.cnn.com/election/2006/pages/results/ballot.measures/.

Coles, Matthew. 2005. Defining Marriage in the Twenty-First Century: *Lawrence v. Texas* and the Refinement of Substantive Due Process. *Stanford Law and Policy Review* 16: 23–56.

Collis, Gary Alan. 1997. *Romer v. Evans*: Gay Americans Find Shelter after Stormy Legal Odyssey. *Pepperdine Law Review* 24: 991–1037.

Congressional Record. 101st Cong., 2d sess., 1990. Vol. 136.

Congressional Record. 103d Cong., 2d sess., 1994. Vol. 140.

Congressional Record. 104th Cong., 1st sess., 1995. Vol. 141.

Congressional Record. 104th Cong., 2d sess., 1996. Vol. 142.

Congressional Record. 109th Cong., 2d sess., 2006. Vol. 152.

Coolidge, David Orgon. 1998. Playing the *Loving* Card: Same-Sex Marriage and the Politics of Analogy. *Brigham Young University Journal of Public Law* 12: 201–38.

Craig, Larry. 1999. The Americans with Disabilities Act: Prologue, Promise, Product, and Performance. *Idaho Law Review* 35: 205–25.

Crane, Jonah M. A. 2003/2004. Legislative and Constitutional Responses to *Goodridge v. Department of Public Health*. *New York University Journal of Legislation and Public Policy* 7: 465–85.

Cruikshank, Margaret. 1992. *The Gay and Lesbian Liberation Movement.* New York: Routledge.

Culhane, John G., and Stacey L. Sobel. 2005. The Gay Marriage Backlash and Its Spillover Effects: Lessons from a (Slightly) "Blue State." *Tulsa Law Review* 40: 443–65.

Dahl, Robert, A. 1957. Decision-Making in a Democracy: The Supreme Court as a National Policy-Maker. *Journal of Public Law* 6: 279–95.

D'Amico, Francine. 2000. Sex/uality and Military Service. In *The Politics of Gay Rights*, ed. Craig A. Rimmerman, Kenneth D. Wald, and Clyde Wilcox, 249–65. Chicago: University of Chicago Press.

Delchin, Steven A. 1996. Scalia 18:22: Thou Shall Not Lie with the Academic and Law School Elite; It Is an Abomination—*Romer v. Evans* and America's Culture War. *Case Western Reserve Law Review* 47: 207–52.

D'Emilio, John. 1983. *Sexual Politics, Sexual Communities.* Chicago: University of Chicago Press.

———. 1992. *Making Trouble.* New York: Routledge.

———. 2000. Cycles of Change, Questions of Strategy: The Gay and Lesbian Movement after Fifty Years. In *The Politics of Gay Rights*, ed. Craig A. Rimmerman, Kenneth D. Wald, and Clyde Wilcox, 31–53. Chicago: University of Chicago Press.

Dodson, Robert. 1999. Homosexual Discrimination and Gender: Was *Romer v. Evans* Really a Victory for Gay Rights? *California Western Law Review* 35: 271–312.

Dodson, Scott. 2004. The Peculiar Federal Marriage Amendment. *Arizona State Law Journal* 36: 783–804.

Dole, Bob. 1996. *Debating Our Destiny.* "1996: Careful What You Say." (October 16), www.pbs.org/newshour/debatingourdestiny/dod/1996-broadcast.html.

Donovan, Todd, Jim Wenzel, and Shawn Bowler. 2000. Direct Democracy and Gay Rights: Initiatives after *Romer.* In *The Politics of Gay Rights*, ed. Craig A. Rimmerman, Kenneth D. Wald, and Clyde Wilcox, 161–90. Chicago: University of Chicago Press.

Duberman, Martin. 1993. *Stonewall.* New York: Dutton.

Dubnoff, Caren G. 1997. *Romer v. Evans*: A Legal and Political Analysis. *Law and Inequality Journal* 15: 275–322.

Duncan, Dwight G. 1996. Parading the First Amendment through the Streets of Boston. *New England Law Review* 30: 663–94.

Duncan, William C. 2004. The Litigation to Redefine Marriage: Equality and Social Meaning. *Brigham Young University Journal of Public Law* 18: 623–63.

———. 2005. The Role of Litigation in Gay Rights: The Marriage Experience. *St. Louis University Law Review* 24: 113–27.

Duong, Phong. 2003/2004. A Survey of Gay Rights Culminating in *Lawrence v. Texas*. *Gonzaga Law Review* 39: 539–73.

Dyer, Kate, ed. 1990. *Gays in Uniform: The Pentagon's Secret Reports*. Boston: Alyson Publications.

Egan, Patrick, Nathaniel Persily, and Kevin Wallsten. 2006. Gay Marriage, Public Opinion and the Courts. Prepared for Delivery at the 2006 Annual Meeting of the Midwest Political Science Association, April 20–April 23, 2006, Chicago.

Ekeberg, Erin, and Ramona Tumber. 2004. Sexuality and Transgender Identity Issues in Employment. *Georgetown Journal of Gender and the Law* 5: 387–406.

Endean, Steve. 2006. *Bringing Lesbian and Gay Rights into the Mainstream: Twenty Years of Progress*. Ed. Vicki Eaklor. New York: Harrington Park Press.

Epstein, Lee, Andrew Martin, Lisa Baldez, and Tasina Nitzschke Nihiser. 2004. Constitutional Sex Discrimination. *Tennessee Journal of Law and Policy* 1: 11–68.

Eskridge, William N., Jr. 1999. *Gaylaw: Challenging the Apartheid of the Closet*. Cambridge, MA: Harvard University Press.

———. 2002. *Equality Practice: Civil Unions and the Future of Gay Rights*. New York: Routledge.

Evans, Carrie. 2004. *Equality from State to State: Gay, Lesbian, Bisexual and Transgender Americans and State Legislation*. Washington, DC: Human Rights Campaign Foundation.

Faderman, Lillian. 1991. *Odd Girls and Twilight Lovers: A History of Lesbian Life in Twentieth-Century America*. New York: Columbia University Press.

Feather, Nancy J. 1997. Defense of Marriage Acts: An Analysis under State Constitutional Law. *Temple Law Review* 70: 1017–35.

Feldblum, Chai, R. 1997. The Moral Rhetoric of Legislation. *New York University Law Review* 72: 992–1008.

———. 2000. The Federal Gay Rights Bill: From Bella to ENDA. In *Creating Change: Sexuality, Public Policy, and Civil Rights*, ed. John D'Emilio, William B. Turner, and Urvashi Vaid, 149–87. New York: St. Martin's Press.

Fisk, Catherine L. 1998. Emerging Issues in Sexual Orientation Law: ERISA Preemption of State and Local Laws on Domestic Partnership and Sexual Orientation Discrimination in Employment. *UCLA Law Review* 8: 267–312.

Fitzpatrick, Robert K. 2004. Neither Icarus Nor Ostrich: State Constitutions as an Independent Source of Individual Rights. *New York University Law Review* 79: 1833–72.

Fotopoulos, Spiro F. 1994. The Beginning of the End for the Military's Traditional Policy on Homosexuals: *Steffan v. Aspin*. *Wake Forest Law Review* 29: 611–45.

Friedman, Barry. 1998. The History of the Countermajoritarian Difficulty, Part One: The Road to Judicial Supremacy. *New York University Law Review* 73: 333–433.

Frye, Phyllis Randolph. 2003. Transgenders Must Be Brave While Forging This New Front on Equality. *Georgetown Journal of Gender and the Law* 4: 767–79.

Fuller, Elisa. 1985. *Hardwick v. Bowers*: An Attempt to Pull the Meaning of *Doe v. Commonwealth's Attorney* Out of the Closet. *University of Miami Law Review* 39: 973–95.

Gallup Poll. 2002. New York Times Policy Focuses Attention on Homosexual Civil Unions. Princeton, NJ: The Gallup Organization (August 22), http://brain.gallup.com/content/default.aspx?ci=6655 (available only by subscription).

———. 2003a. Six in 10 Americans Agree That Gay Sex Should be Legal. Princeton, NJ: The Gallup Organization (June 27), www.gallup.com/poll/content/print.aspx?ci=8722 (available only by subscription).

———. 2003b. U.S. Next Down the Aisle toward Gay Marriage. Princeton, NJ: The Gallup Organization (July 22), www.gallup.com/poll/content/print.aspx?ci=8881 (available only by subscription).

———. 2003c. Public OK with Gays, Women in the Military. Princeton, NJ: The Gallup Organization (December 23), www.gallup.com/poll/content/print.aspx?ci=10240 (available only by subscription).

———. 2004a. Support for Gay Marriage/Civil Unions Edges Upward. Princeton, NJ: The Gallup Organization (May 17), www.gallup.com/poll/content/print.aspx?ci=11689 (available only by subscription).

———. 2004b. Gays in the Military: Public Says Go Ahead and Tell. Princeton, NJ: The Gallup Organization (December 21), www.gallup.com/poll/content/print.aspx?ci=14419 (available only by subscription).

———. 2005a. Americans Turn More Negative toward Same-Sex Marriage. Princeton, NJ: The Gallup Organization (April 19), www.gallup.com/poll/content/print.aspx?ci=15889 (available only by subscription).

———. 2005b. Homosexual Relations. Princeton, NJ: The Gallup Organization (May), www.gallup.com/poll/content/print.aspx?ci=1651 (available only by subscription).

———. 2005c. Gay Rights Attitudes a Mixed Bag. Princeton, NJ: The Gallup Organization (May 20), www.gallup.com/poll/content/print.aspx?ci=16402 (available only by subscription).

———. 2006a. Homosexual Relations. Princeton, NJ: The Gallup Organization, http://poll.gallup.com/content/default.aspx?ci=1651&pg=1 (available only by subscription).

———. 2006b. Homosexual Relations. Princeton, NJ: The Gallup Organization, http://poll.gallup.com/content/default.aspx?ci=1651&pg=2 (available only by subscription).

Gartner, Nadine A. 2004. Restructuring the Marital Bedroom: The Role of the Privacy Doctrine in Advocating the Legalization of Same Sex Marriage. *Michigan Journal of Law Reform* 11: 1–26.

Gavin, Meghan M. 2004. The Domestic Partners Rights and Responsibilities Act of 2003: California Extends Significant Protections to Registered Domestic Partners and Their Families. *McGeorge Law Review* 35: 482–95.

Gehman, Andrea, and Veronica D. Gray. 2005. Sexuality and Transgender Issues in Employment. *Georgetown Journal of Gender and the Law* 6: 575–96.

Gerstmann, Evan. 2003. *The Constitutional Underclass: Gays, Lesbians, and the Failure of Class-Based Equal Protection*. Chicago: University of Chicago Press.

Glidden, Melissa A. 2004. Recent Development: Federal Marriage Amendment. *Harvard Journal on Legislation* 41: 483–99.

Goldman, Jeffrey M. 2005. Protecting Gays from the Government's Crosshairs: A Reevaluation of the Ninth Circuit's Treatment of Gays Under the Federal Constitution's Equal Protection Clause Following *Lawrence v. Texas*. *University of San Francisco Law Review* 39: 617–40.

Goldstein, Anne. 1988. History, Homosexuality, and Political Values: Searching for the Hidden Determinants of *Bowers v. Hardwick*. *Yale Law Journal* 97: 1073–1103.

Green, John C. 2000. Antigay: Varieties of Opposition to Gay Rights. In *The Politics of Gay Rights*, ed. Craig A. Rimmerman, Kenneth D. Wald, and Clyde Wilcox, 121–38. Chicago: University of Chicago Press.

Greenberg, Julie A. 2002. What Do Scalia and Thomas Really Think about Sex? Title VII and Gender Nonconformity Discrimination: Protection for Transsexuals, Intersexuals, Gays, and Lesbians. *Thomas Jefferson Law Review* 24: 149–59.

Greyerbiehl, Brian P. 1996. Marching toward Equality: The Positive Implications of *Hurley v. Irish-American Gay, Lesbian and Bisexual Group of Boston* for the Gay Rights Movement. *Wayne Law Review* 43: 233–56.

Griffin, Pat, and Bobbie Harro. 1997. Heterosexism Curriculum Design. In *Teaching for Diversity and Social Justice: A Sourcebook*, ed. Maurianne Adams, Lee Ann Bell, and Pat Griffin, 141–69. New York: Routledge.

Guillerman, Diane M. 1997. The Defense of Marriage Act: The Latest Maneuver in the Continuing Battle to Legalize Same-Sex Marriage. *Houston Law Review* 34: 425–75.

Gunther, Gerald. 1972. The Supreme Court, 1971 Term—Foreword: In Search of Evolving Doctrine on a Changing Court: A Model for a Newer Equal Protection. *Harvard Law Review* 86: 1–48 (internal quotations omitted).

Haeberle, Steven H. 1999. Gay and Lesbian Rights: Emerging Trends in Public Opinion and Voting Behavior. In *Gays and Lesbians in the Democratic Process: Public Policy, Public Opinion, and Political Representation*, ed. Ellen D. B. Riggle and Barry L. Tadlock, 146–69. New York: Columbia University Press.

Haggerty, Timothy. 2003. History Repeating Itself: A Historical Overview of Gay Men and Lesbians in the Military before "Don't Ask, Don't Tell." In *Don't Ask Don't Tell: Debating the Gay Ban in the Military*, ed. Aaron Belkin and Geoffrey Bateman, 9–49. Boulder, CO: Lynne Rienner.

Haider-Markel, Donald P. 1999. Crediting Change—Holding the Line: Agenda Setting on Lesbian and Gay Issues at the National Level. In *Gays and Lesbians in the Democratic Process: Public Policy, Public Opinion, and Political Representation*, ed. Ellen D. B. Riggle and Barry L. Tadlock, 242–68. New York: Columbia University Press.

Halley, Janet E. 1993. Reasoning about Sodomy: Act and Identity in and after *Bowers v. Hardwick*. *Virginia Law Review* 79: 1721–79.

Harris Interactive. 1998. Modest 52% to 41% Majority Favor Laws to Make It Illegal to Discriminate against Gays and Lesbians. New York: Harris Interactive (August 19), www.harrisinteractive.com/harris_poll/index.asp?PID=166.

———. 2000. Attitudes to Gays and Lesbians Have Become More Accepting, but Most People Still Disapprove of Single-Sex Marriages and Adoption by Same Sex Couples. New York: Harris Interactive (February 9), www.harrisinteractive.com/harris _poll/index.asp?PID=1.

———. 2001. By More Than 2-to-1 Most Americans Favor Legislation to Prohibit Job Discrimination against Gays and Lesbians. New York: Harris Interactive (June 13), www.harrisinteractive.com/harris_poll/index.asp?PID=236.

———. 2002. Gays and Lesbians Face Persistent Workplace Discrimination and Hostility Despite Improved Policies and Attitudes in Corporate America. New York: Harris Interactive (September 12), www.harrisinteractive.com/news/allnewsbydate.asp? NewsID=503.

———. 2003. 6 of 10 Heterosexuals Say Benefits for Married Heterosexual Employees Should Be Equally Available for Employees in Same-Sex Couples. New York: Harris Interactive (October 1), www.harrisinteractive.com/news/allnewsbydate.asp? NewsID=678.

———. 2004. Majorities of Heterosexuals Agree Same-Sex Partners Deserve Same Adoption Benefits and Leave Rights Offered by Employers as Married Co-Workers' Spouses Receive. New York: Harris Interactive (September 28), www.harrisinteractive.com/ news/allnewsbydate.asp?NewsID=849.

Hawaii State Judiciary. 2006, www.courts.state.hi.us/page_server/Courts/Supreme/ Judges/5FCA912B84259E92EBD80CFEF5.html.

Herek, Gregory M. 1996. Social Science, Sexual Orientation. In *Out in Force*, ed. Gregory M. Herek, Jared B. Jobe, and Ralph M. Carney, 3–14. Chicago: University of Chicago Press.

Hertzog, Mark. 1996. *The Lavender Vote: Lesbians, Gay Men, and Bisexuals in American Electoral Politics*. New York: New York University Press.

Hillygus, D. Sunshine, and Todd G. Shields. 2005. Moral Issues and Voter Decision Making in the 2004 Presidential Election. *PS: Political Science and Politics* 38: 201–9.

Hogue, L. Lynn. 1998. State Common-Law Choice-of-Law Doctrine and Same Sex Marriage: How Will States Enforce the Public Policy Exception? *Creighton Law Review* 32: 29–43.

Holland, Maurice J. 1998. The Modest Usefulness of DOMA Section 2. *Creighton Law Review* 32: 395–408.

Human Rights Campaign. 2005a. *Equality from State to State*, http://anon.newmediamill .speedera.net/anon.newmediamill/stateleg/2005_equality_in_the_states.pdf.

———. 2005b. *Proposed State Constitutional Amendments Limiting Marriage And/Or Other Forms of Relationship Recognition in 2005*, www.hrc.org/Template.cfm?

Section=About_HRC&Template=/ContentManagement/ContentDisplay.cfm&Cont entID=25259.

———. 2005c. *Relationship Recognition in the U.S.*, www.hrc.org/Template.cfm?Section= Your_Community&Template=/ContentManagement/ContentDisplay.cfm&Content ID=16305.

———. 2005d. *Statewide Marriage Laws*, www.hrc.org/Template.cfm?Section=Your_ Community&Template=/ContentManagement/ContentDisplay.cfm&ContentID= 19449.

———. 2006a. *Non-Discrimination Laws: State by State*, http://hrc.org/Template .cfm?Section=Get_Informed2&Template=/TaggedPage/TaggedPageDisplay.cfm& TPLID=66&ContentID=20650.

———. 2006b. *Washington State Bans Discrimination against Gay, Lesbian, Bisexual and Transgender Citizens*, http://hrc.org/Template.cfm?Section=Non-Discrimination_ Policies&CONTENTID=30798&TEMPLATE=/ContentManagement/ContentDisplay .cfm.

Hutchinson, Darren Lenard. 2005. The Majoritarian Difficulty: Affirmative Action, Sodomy, and Supreme Court Politics. *Law and Inequality* 23: 1–93.

Introduction: Stonewall at 25. 1994. *Harvard Civil Rights–Civil Liberties Law Review* 29: 277–82.

Irons, Peter. 1990. *The Courage of Their Convictions*. New York: Penguin Books.

Jacobs, Andrew M. 1993. The Rhetorical Construction of Rights: The Case of the Gay Rights Movement. *Nebraska Law Review*. 72: 723–58.

Jacobson, Peter D. 1996. Sexual Orientation and the Military: Some Legal Considerations. In *Out in Force*, ed. Gregory M. Herek, Jared B. Jobe, and Ralph M. Carney, 39–61. Chicago: University of Chicago Press.

Jasiunas, J. Banning. 2000. Is ENDA the Answer? Can a "Separate but Equal" Federal Statute Adequately Protect Gays and Lesbians from Employment Discrimination? *Ohio State Law Journal* 61: 1529–57.

Kameny, Franklin E. 2000. Government v. Gays: Two Sad Stories with Two Happy Endings, Civil Services Employment and Security Clearances. In *Creating Change: Sexuality, Public Policy, and Civil Rights*, ed. John D'Emilio, William B. Turner, and Urvashi Vaid, 188–208. New York: St. Martin's Press.

Keen, Lisa, and Suzanne B. Goldberg. 2003. *Strangers to the Law: Gay People on Trial*. Ann Arbor: University of Michigan Press.

Kelly, Scott. 2002. Scouts' (Dis)Honor: The Supreme Court Allows the Boy Scouts of America to Discriminate against Homosexuals in *Boy Scouts of America v. Dale*. *Houston Law Review* 39: 243–74.

Kersch, Ken. 1997. Full Faith and Credit for Same-Sex Marriages? *Political Science Quarterly* 112: 117–36.

Kimball, Andrea M. 1996. *Romer v. Evans* and Colorado's Amendment 2: The Gay Rights Movement's Symbolic Victory in the Battle for Civil Rights. *Toledo Law Review* 28: 219–45.

Kimpel, Jason D. 1999. Distinctions without a Difference: How the Sixth Circuit Misread *Romer v. Evans*. *Indiana Law Journal* 74: 991–1017.

King, Tiffany L. 2002. Working Out: Conflicting Title VII Approaches to Sex Discrimination and Sexual Orientation. *University of California Davis Law Review* 35: 1005–44.

Klarman, Michael J. 1996. Rethinking the Civil Rights and Civil Liberties Revolutions. *Virginia Law Review* 82: 1–67.

———. 2005. *Brown and Lawrence (and Goodridge)*. *Michigan Law Review* 104: 431–89.

Kmiec, Keenan D. 2004. The Origin and Current Meanings of "Judicial Activism." *California Law Review* 92: 1441–77.

Knauer, Nancy J. 2004. *Lawrence v. Texas*: When "Profound and Deep Convictions" Collide with Liberty Interests. *Cardozo Women's Law Journal* 10: 325–36.

Koppelman, Andrew. 1988. The Miscegenation Analogy: Sodomy Law as Sex Discrimination. *Yale Law Journal* 98: 145–64.

———. 1996. Same Sex Marriage and Public Policy: The Miscegenation Precedents. *Quinninipiac Law Review* 16: 105–34.

———. 2002a. *The Gay Rights Question in Contemporary American Law*. Chicago: University of Chicago Press.

———. 2002b. Signs of the Times: *Dale v. Boy Scouts of America* and the Changing Meaning of Nondiscrimination. *Cardozo Law Review* 23: 1819–38.

Kramer, Larry D. 2004. Popular Constitutionalism, circa 2004. *California Law Review* 92: 959–1011.

Kubasek, Nancy, K., Alex Frondorf, and Kevin J. Minnick. 2004. Civil Union Statutes: A Shortcut to Legal Equality for Same-Sex Partners in a Landscape Littered with Defense of Marriage Acts. *Florida Journal of Law and Public Policy* 25: 229–59.

Lehring, Gary, L. 2003. *Officially Gay*. Philadelphia: Temple University Press.

Leonard, Arthur S. 2000. From *Bowers v. Hardwick* to *Romer v. Evans*: Lesbian and Gay Rights in the U.S. Supreme Court. In *Creating Change: Sexuality, Public Policy, and Civil Rights*, ed. John D'Emilio, William B. Turner, and Urvashi Vaid, 57–77. New York: St. Martin's Press.

———. 2004/2005. Sexual Minority Rights in the Workplace. *Brandeis Law Journal* 43: 145–64.

Leslie, Christopher R. 2005. The Importance of *Lawrence* in the Context of the Supreme Court's Historical Treatment of Gay Litigants. *Widener Law Review* 11: 189–220.

Lewis, Gregory B., and Jonathan Edelson. 2000. DOMA and ENDA: Congress Votes on Gay Rights. In *The Politics of Gay Rights*, ed. Craig A. Rimmerman, Kenneth D. Wald, and Clyde Wilcox, 193–216. Chicago: University of Chicago Press.

Lewis, Gregory L. 2005. Same Sex Marriage and the 2004 Presidential Election. *PS: Political Science and Politics* 38: 195–9.

Lewis, Marion Halliday. 1990. Unacceptable Risk or Unacceptable Rhetoric? An Argument for a Quasi-Suspect Classification for Gays Based on Current Government Security Clearance Procedures. *Journal of Law and Politics* 7: 133–76.

Loughery, John. 1998. *The Other Side of Silence: Men's Lives and Gay Identities*. New York: H. Holt.

MacCoun, Robert J. 1996. Sexual Orientation and Military Cohesion: A Critical Review of the Evidence. In *Out in Force*, ed. Gregory M. Herek, Jared B. Jobe, and Ralph M. Carney, 157–76. Chicago: University of Chicago Press.

MacKinnon, Catharine A. 2003. *Sex Equality*. New York: Foundation Press.

Maravilla, Christopher Scott. 2001. Judicial Review of Security Clearances for Homosexuals Post–*U.S. Department of the Navy v. Egan*. *St. Thomas Law Review* 13: 785–801.

Marcosson, Samuel A. 1995. A Price Too High: Enforcing the Ban on Gays in the Military and the Inevitability of Intrusiveness. *University of Missouri at Kansas City Law Review* 64: 59–98.

Marcus, Eric. 2002. *Making Gay History: The Half-Century Fight for Lesbian and Gay Equal Rights*. New York: HarperCollins.

Marotta, Toby. 1981. *The Politics of Homosexuality*. Boston: Houghton Mifflin.

Massachusetts Court System. 2006, www.mass.gov/courts/courtsandjudges/courts/supremejudicialcourt/about.html.

Mazur, Diane H. 1999. The Unknown Soldier: A Critique of "Gays in the Military" Scholarship and Litigation. *University of California Davis Law Review* 29: 223–81.

———. 2004. Is "Don't Ask Don't Tell" Unconstitutional After *Lawrence v. Texas*? What It Will Take to Overturn the Policy. *Florida Journal of Law and Public Policy* 15: 423–41.

McCann, Michael W. 1994. *Rights at Work: Pay Equity and the Politics of Legal Mobilization*. Chicago: University of Chicago Press.

McFeeley, Tim. 2000. Getting It Straight: A Review of the "Gays in the Military" Debate. In *Creating Change: Sexuality, Public Policy, and Civil Rights*, ed. John D'Emilio, William B. Turner, and Urvashi Vaid, 236–50. New York: St. Martin's Press.

Menand, Louis. 2004. Permanent Fatal Errors: Did the Voters Send a Message? *New Yorker*, December 6.

Meyer, David D. 2004. Domesticating *Lawrence*. *University of Chicago Legal Forum* 2004: 453–93.

Mezey, Susan Gluck. 2003. *Elusive Equality: Women's Rights, Public Policy, and the Law*. Boulder, CO: Lynne Rienner.

———. 2005. *Disabling Interpretations: Judicial Implementation of the Americans with Disabilities Act*. Pittsburgh: University of Pittsburgh Press.

Miller, Diane Helene. 1998. *Freedom to Differ: The Shaping of the Gay and Lesbian Struggle for Civil Rights*. New York: New York University Press.

Miller, Kenneth, P. 2005. Anatomy of a Backlash: The Response to *Goodridge v. Dept. of Public Health*. Prepared for delivery at the 2005 Annual Meeting of the American Political Science Association, September 1–September 4, 2005, Washington, DC.

Miller, William H. 2004. Position of Trust: Security Clearance Decisions after September 11, 2001. *George Mason University Civil Rights Law Journal* 14: 229–54.

Mishler, William, and Reginald S. Sheehan. 1993. The Supreme Court as a Counterma-joritarian Institution? The Impact of Public Opinion on Supreme Court Decisions. *American Political Science Review* 87: 87–101.

Murdoch, Joyce, and Deb Price. 2001. *Courting Justice: Gay Men and Lesbians v. the Supreme Court.* New York: Basic Books.

Neal, Odeana R. 1996. The Limits of Legal Discourse: Learning from the Civil Rights Movement in the Quest for Gay and Lesbian Civil Rights. *New York Law School Law Review* 40: 679–718.

Nguyen, Huong Thien. 2001. Irrational Prejudice: The Military's Exclusion of Gay, Lesbian, and Bisexual Service Members after *Romer v. Evans. Hastings Constitutional Law Quarterly* 28: 461–504.

Niemczyk, Brian N. 2005. *Baker v. Nelson* Revisited: Is Same-Sex Marriage Coming to Minnesota? *Hamline Law Review* 28: 425–64.

Nolan, Laurence C. 1998. The Meaning of *Loving*: Marriage, Due Process and Equal Protection (1967–1990) as Equality and Marriage, from *Loving* to *Zablocki. Howard Law Journal* 41: 245–70.

Note. 1993. Constitutional Limits on Anti-Gay-Rights Initiatives. *Harvard Law Review* 106: 1905–25.

Note. 2005. Unfixing Lawrence. *Harvard Law Review* 118: 2858–81.

Osburn, C. Dixie. 1995. A Policy in Desperate Search of a Rational: The Military's Policy on Lesbians, Gays and Bisexuals. *University of Missouri at Kansas City Law Review* 64: 199–236.

Osburn, C. Dixie, and Michelle M. Benecke. 1996. Conduct Unbecoming Continues: The First Year Under "Don't Ask, Don't Tell, Don't Pursue." In *Gay Rights, Military Wrongs: Political Perspectives on Lesbians and Gays in the Military*, ed. Craig A. Rimmerman, 249–93. New York: Garland Publishing.

Pacelle, Richard. 1996. Seeking Another Forum: The Courts and Lesbian and Gay Rights. In *Gay Rights, Military Wrongs: Political Perspectives on Lesbians and Gays in the Military*, ed. Craig A. Rimmerman, 195–226. New York: Garland Publishing.

Paige, Rebecca S. Wagging the Dog—If the State of Hawaii Accepts Same-Sex Marriage Will Other States Have To?: An Examination of Conflict of Laws and Escape Devices. *American University Law Review* 47: 165–85.

Papadopoulos, Mark E. 1997. Inkblot Jurisprudence: *Romer v. Evans* as a Great Defeat for the Gay Rights Movement. *Cornell Journal of Law and Public Policy* 7: 165–202.

Paris, Bob. 1998. *Generation Queer: A Gay Man's Quest for Hope, Love, and Justice.* New York: Warner Books.

Parshall, Lisa K. 2005. Redefining Due Process Analysis: Justice Anthony M. Kennedy and the Concept of Emergent Rights. *Albany Law Review* 69: 237–98.

Peterson, Kavan. 2004. 50-State Rundown on Gay Marriage Laws. *Stateline.org* (November 4), www.stateline.org/live/ViewPage.action?siteNodeId=137&languageId=1&contentId=15576.

———. 2005a. 50-State Rundown on Gay Marriage Laws. *Stateline.org* (February 4), updated February 9, 2005, www.stateline.org/live/ViewPage.action?siteNodeId =136&languageId=1&contentId=15966.

———. 2005b. Same-Sex Unions—A Constitutional Race. *Stateline.org* (March 29), updated September 8, 2005, www.stateline.org/live/ViewPage.action?siteNodeId =137&languageId=1&contentId=20695.

Pew Research Center. 2006. Less Opposition to Gay Marriage, Adoption and Military Service. Washington, DC: Pew Research Center for the People and the Press (March 22), http://pewtrusts.org/pdf/PRC_GayMarriage_0306.pdf.

Pierceson, Jason. 2005. *Courts, Liberalism, and Rights: Gay Law and Politics in the United States and Canada*. Philadelphia: Temple University Press.

Pinello, Daniel R. 2006. *America's Struggle for Same-Sex Marriage*. Cambridge: Cambridge University Press.

Pizzutillo, Amy E. 1997. A Perry, Perry Poor Policy Promoting Prejudice Rebuked by the Reality of the *Romer* Ruling: *Thomasson v. Perry. Villanova Law Review* 42: 1293–1341.

PollingReport.com. 2006a. *Law/Civil Rights*, www.pollingreport.com/civil.htm.

———. 2006b. *Law/Civil Rights* (2), www.pollingreport.com/civil2.htm.

———. 2006c. *Values*, http://pollingreport.com/values.htm.

Putignano, Pat P. 1997. Why DOMA and Not ENDA? A Review of Recent Federal Hostility to Expand Employment Rights and Protection Beyond Traditional Notions. *Hofstra Labor Law Journal* 15: 177–206.

Rayside, David A. 1996. The Perils of Congressional Politics. In *Gay Rights, Military Wrongs Political Perspectives on Lesbians and Gays in the Military*, ed. Craig A. Rimmerman, 147–93. New York: Garland Publishing.

Rimmerman, Craig A. 1996. Promise Unfulfilled: Clinton's Failure to Overturn the Military Ban on Lesbians and Gays. In *Gay Rights, Military Wrongs: Political Perspectives on Lesbians and Gays in the Military*, ed. Craig A. Rimmerman, 111–26. New York: Garland Publishing.

———. 2000. Beyond Political Mainstreaming: Reflections on Lesbian and Gay Organizations and the Grassroots. In *The Politics of Gay Rights*, ed. Craig A. Rimmerman, Kenneth D. Wald, and Clyde Wilcox, 54–78. Chicago: University of Chicago Press.

———. 2002. *From Identity to Politics: The Lesbian and Gay Movements in the United States*. Philadelphia: Temple University Press.

Rom, Mark Carl. 2000. Gays and AIDS: Democratizing Disease? In *The Politics of Gay Rights*, ed. Craig A. Rimmerman, Kenneth D. Wald, and Clyde Wilcox, 217–48. Chicago: University of Chicago Press.

Rosenberg, Gerald N. 1991. *The Hollow Hope: Can Courts Bring About Social Change?* Chicago: University of Chicago Press.

Rubenstein, William B. 1998. Do Gay Rights Laws Matter?: An Empirical Assessment. *Southern California Law Review* 75: 65–119.

Rubin, Peter J. 1998. Equal Rights, Special Rights, and the Nature of Antidiscrimination Law. *Michigan Law Review* 97: 564–98.

Schacter, Jane S. 1994. The Gay Civil Rights Debate in the States: Decoding the Discourse of Equivalents. *Harvard Civil Rights–Civil Liberties Law Review* 29: 283–317.

Schroedel, Jean Reith, and Pamela Fiber. 2000. Lesbian and Gay Policy Priorities: Commonality and Difference. In *The Politics of Gay Rights*, ed. Craig A. Rimmerman, Kenneth D. Wald, and Clyde Wilcox, 97–118. Chicago: University of Chicago Press.

Schultz, David A., ed. 1998. *Leveraging the Law: Using the Courts to Achieve Social Change.* New York: Peter Lang.

Schwartz, Martin A. 2004. *Lawrence v. Texas*: The Decision and Its Implications for the Future. *Touro Law Review* 20: 221–49.

Seamon, Aaron A. 1999. The Flawed Compromise of 10 U.S.C. 654: An Assessment of the Military's "Don't Ask, Don't Tell" Policy. *University of Dayton Law Review* 24: 319–47.

Servicemembers Legal Defense Network. 2004. *Ten Years of Don't Ask, Don't Tell. A Disservice to the Nation*, www.sldn.org/binary-data/SLDN_ARTICLES/pdf_file/1453.pdf.

———. 2005. *Annual "Don't Ask, Don't Tell" Dismissals* (April 12), www.sldn.org/binary-data/SLDN_ARTICLES/pdf_file/1455.pdf.

Shilts, Randy. 1982. *The Mayor of Castro Street: The Life and Times of Harvey Milk.* New York: St. Martin's Press.

———. 1993. *Conduct Unbecoming: Gays and Lesbians in the U.S. Military.* New York: St. Martin's Press.

Smith, Jeremy B. 2005. The Flaws of Rational Basis with Bite: Why the Supreme Court Should Acknowledge Its Application of Heightened Scrutiny to Classifications Based on Sexual Orientation. *Fordham Law Review* 73: 2769–814.

Smith, Raymond A., and Donald P. Haider-Markel. 2002. *Gay and Lesbian Americans and Political Participation.* Santa Barbara, CA: ABC-Clio.

Stoddard, Tom. 1997. Bleeding Heart: Reflections on Using the Law to Make Social Change. *New York University Law Review* 72: 967–91.

Sunstein, Cass, R. 1988. Sexual Orientation and the Constitution: A Note on the Relationship between Due Process and Equal Protection. *University of Chicago Law Review* 55: 1161–79.

Swisher, Anthony. 1994. Nobody's Hero: On Equal Protection, Homosexuality, and National Security. *George Washington Law Review* 62: 827–54.

Thornton, Joseph Robert. 1987. *Bowers v. Hardwick*: An Incomplete Constitutional Analysis. *North Carolina Law Review* 65: 1100–23.

Transgender Law and Policy Institute. 2006. *US Jurisdictions with Transgender Inclusive Non-Discrimination Laws*, www.transgenderlaw.org/ndlaws/index.htm.

Tribe, Laurence. 1988. *American Constitutional Law*, 2d ed. Mineola, NY: Foundation Press.

Trosino, James. 1993. American Wedding: Same-Sex Marriage and the Miscegenation Analogy. *Boston University Law Review* 73: 93–120.

Troum, Neal. 2002. Expressive Association and the Right to Exclude: Reading between the Lines in *Boy Scouts of America v. Dale*. *Creighton Law Review* 35: 641–91.

Turner, William B. 2000. Mirror Images: Lesbian/Gay Civil Rights in the Carter and Reagan Administrations. In *Creating Change: Sexuality, Public Policy, and Civil Rights*, ed. John D'Emilio, William B. Turner, and Urvashi Vaid, 3–28. New York: St. Martin's Press.

Tushnet, Mark. 1999. *Taking the Constitution Away from the Courts*. Princeton, NJ: Princeton University Press.

United States General Accounting Office. 1992. *Defense Force Management: DOD's Policy on Homosexuality*, http://archive.gao.gov/d33t10/146980.pdf.

———. 2005. *Military Personnel: Financial Costs and Loss of Critical Skills Due to DOD's Homosexual Conduct Policy Cannot Be Completely Estimated*, www.gao.gov/new.items/d05299.pdf.

United States House Committee on the Judiciary. H.Rep. No. 104–664. 1996. *Defense of Marriage Act*, 104th Cong., 2d sess.

———. H.Rep. No. 108–614. 2004. *Marriage Protection Act*, 108th Cong., 2d sess.

United States House of Representatives. 2004. *Final Vote Results for Roll Call 410* (July 22), http://clerk.house.gov/evs/2004/roll410.xml.

Vaid, Urvashi. 1995. *Virtual Equality: The Mainstreaming of Gay and Lesbian Liberation*. New York: Anchor Books.

Valdes, Francisco. 1994. Sexual Minorities in the Military: Charting the Constitutional Frontiers of Status and Conduct. *Creighton Law Review* 27: 384–475.

Van Ness, Gretchen. 1996. Parades and Prejudice: The Incredible True Story of Boston's St. Patrick's Day Parade and the United States Supreme Court. *New England Law Review* 30: 625–62.

Vermont Statutes Online. 2006. *Constitution of the State of Vermont*, www.leg.state.vt.us/statutes/const2.htm.

Wald, Kenneth D. 2002. The Context of Gay Politics. In *The Politics of Gay Rights*, ed. Craig A. Rimmerman, Kenneth D. Wald, and Clyde Wilcox, 1–28. Chicago: University of Chicago Press.

Walzer, Lee. 2002. *Gay Rights on Trial*. Indianapolis: Hackett Publishing Co.

Wardle, Lynn D. 1998. *Loving v. Virginia* and the Constitutional Right to Marry. *Howard Law Journal* 41: 289–347.

Wells-Petry, Melissa. 1995. Sneaking a Wink at Homosexuals? Three Case Studies on Policies Concerning Homosexuality in the United States Armed Forces. *University of Missouri at Kansas City Law Review* 64: 3–55.

Wilcox, Clyde, and Robin Wolpert. 1996. President Clinton, Public Opinion, and Gays in the Military. In *Gay Rights, Military Wrongs: Political Perspectives on Lesbians and Gays in the Military*, ed. Craig A. Rimmerman, 127–45. New York: Garland Publishing.

———. 2000. Gay Rights in the Public Sphere: Public Opinion on Gay and Lesbian Equality. In *The Politics of Gay Rights*, ed. Craig A. Rimmerman, Kenneth D. Wald, and Clyde Wilcox, 409–32. Chicago: University of Chicago Press.

Wilson, William M. 1997. *Romer v. Evans*: "Terminal Silliness" or Enlightened Jurisprudence? *North Carolina Law Review* 75: 1891–1941.

Wood, Michael A. 2003. The Propriety of Local Government Protections of Gays and Lesbians from Discriminatory Employment Practices. *Emory Law Journal* 52: 515–54.

Woodruff, William A. 1995. Homosexuality and Military Service: Legislation, Implementation, and Litigation. *University of Missouri at Kansas City Law Review* 64: 121–78.

Yackle, Larry W. 1993, Parading Ourselves: Freedom of Speech at the Feast of St. Patrick. *Boston University Law Review* 73: 791–871.

Yang, Alan S. 1997. Trends: Attitudes toward Homosexuality. *Public Opinion Quarterly* 61: 477–507.

Zaleskas, Kristine M. 1996. Pride, Prejudice or Political Correctness? An Analysis of Hurley v. Irish-American Gay, Lesbian & Bisexual Group of Boston. *Columbia Journal of Law and Social Problems* 29: 507–49.

⁓ General Index

Adam, Barry, D., 15
AIDS/HIV, 28, 33–40, 43–4nn32–6, 59, 85n52, 155, 156, 162; and Americans with Disabilities Act, 39–40, 44nn35–6, 85n52, 217; and Congress, 35–40, 217; and Education of All Handicapped Children Act, 43n32; and Ryan White Care Act, 36–8
American Civil Liberties Union, 6, 12n7, 49, 81n13, 112; Lesbian and Gay Rights Project of, 6; Women's Rights Project of, 5
Andersen, Ellen Ann, 5, 46, 82n19

Bawer, Bruce, 27
Bickel, Alexander M., 6
Black, Hugo, L., 22, 24
Blackmun, Harry, A., 52, 53, 74, 82nn22–3, 89, 203
Blasius, Mark, 34
Bodine, Margot R., 43n32
Bowman, Cynthia Grant, 133n54
Boykin, Keith, 11
Brennan, William J., Jr., 23, 24, 52, 53, 89, 129n28
Breyer, Stephen, G., 62, 70, 73
Bryant, Anita, 31–2, 43nn28–30
Burger, Warren E., 50, 52, 53, 75, 89, 196
Bush, George Herbert Walker, 38
Bush, George, W., 41, 80, 113–5, 126, 131n43

Bush (George W.) administration, 41
Button, James W., 12n1, 30

Cain, Patricia A., 7, 27, 81n13
Chermerinsky, Erwin, 13n12
civil rights movement, 1, 2, 4, 5, 11, 12n4, 26, 27
civil unions, 102–4, 106, 107, 109, 116, 117, 119, 121–3, 124–5, 132n50, 133nn55–6
Clark, Tom, C. 23, 24, 46
Clinton, Bill, 30, 40, 100–1, 158–62, 163, 184–5n51, 185n57, 216, 220–1, 228n58
Clinton administration, 186n68
Coles, Matthew, 80, 86n60
Congress, 7, 30; and AIDS/HIV, 35–40, 44n35; and "Don't Ask, Don't Tell," 158–62, 163, 169, 173–4, 175–6, 178, 185nn53–4, 186nn62–4, 186n66; and employment discrimination, 192–3, 215–20, 227nn49–56, 234; and Ryan White Care Act, 36–8; and same-sex marriage, 98–100, 113–6, 127n1, 131n39
Congressional Black Caucus, 4, 12n3
countermajoritarianism, 7–8, 12n9, 229, 231, 232–4, 238
Cruikshank, Margaret, 34
Culhane, John G., 43n28

Dahl, Robert, A., 7, 8
D'Amico, Francine, 187n84

257

⟨𝒶⟩ Index of Cases

About the Author

Susan Gluck Mezey is a professor of political science at Loyola University Chicago. She is the author of six books, including *Disabling Interpretations: Judicial Implementation of the Americans with Disabilities Act* (2005) and *Elusive Equality: Women's Rights, Public Policy, and the Law* (2003).